Human–Computer Interaction Series

The Human–Computer Interaction Series, launched in 2004, publishes books that advance the science and technology of developing systems which are effective and satisfying for people in a wide variety of contexts. Titles focus on theoretical perspectives (such as formal approaches drawn from a variety of behavioural sciences), practical approaches (such as techniques for effectively integrating user needs in system development), and social issues (such as the determinants of utility, usability and acceptability).

HCI is a multidisciplinary field and focuses on the human aspects in the development of computer technology. As technology becomes increasingly more pervasive the need to take a human-centred approach in the design and development of computer-based systems becomes ever more important.

Titles published within the Human–Computer Interaction Series are included in Thomson Reuters' Book Citation Index, The DBLP Computer Science Bibliography and The HCI Bibliography.

More information about this series at http://www.springer.com/series/6033

Nelson Zagalo

Engagement Design

Designing for Interaction Motivations

Springer

Nelson Zagalo
Department of Communication and Art
University of Aveiro
Aveiro, Portugal

ISSN 1571-5035 ISSN 2524-4477 (electronic)
Human–Computer Interaction Series
ISBN 978-3-030-37084-8 ISBN 978-3-030-37085-5 (eBook)
https://doi.org/10.1007/978-3-030-37085-5

This Springer imprint is published by the registered company Springer Nature Switzerland AG
The registered company address is: Gewerbestrasse 11, 6330 Cham, Switzerland

Dedicated to

Diana and Pedro

Foreword

Imagine yourself as a skilled skier, having come off the lift, now advancing to the beginning of the slope. You scan the slope ahead, knowing that in moments you will be speeding across the snow. Your body dodging and weaving, maintaining speed and posture, and your spirit soaring. You are both freed from your everyday existence yet tied to the world through the textures of the snow, some powdery, some packed and slick, as your feet glide over and through them, their familiar sounds and vibrations guiding you almost unawares.

People often say that such moments are among the best of their lives. Whether we participate in sports, play games, visit museums or take our families to the park or the beach, we go to great lengths to craft engaging experiences for ourselves. And designers of interactive technologies have heard the message.

For the past two decades, fields such as HCI, interaction design, video game design, digital media production and more have increasingly focused on designing engaging experiences. Recognizing that usability is not enough, and that good interaction is grounded in purpose, meaning and value—not features—developers of interactive communications have pushed for better experiences.

Yet, good experiences are not easy to design. They are ephemeral and intangible. They are difficult to define, let alone model—at least in a way that captures what really matters about them. Speaking as a professor of experience design, a designer and a consumer, great experiences all too often seem to slip out of my grasp, and design efforts too often come up short.

Academic efforts to understand *experience* have unfolded throughout the disciplinary spectrum. Engaging experiences have been variously framed as a scientific endeavor, an aesthetic practice and an outcome of art and design, and theorized in psychology, philosophy, media studies, cybernetics, design, literary criticism, anthropology, video games, information science, semiotics and more.

The result has been a bewildering proliferation of theoretical vocabularies, frameworks, systems, theories, methodologies and practices. Often apparently contradicting or incommensurate with one another, and lacking clear entry points and design implications, this body of interdisciplinary theory can be difficult to use for the practitioner.

Nelson Zagalo's *Engagement Design: Designing for Interaction Motivations* is a welcome and timely response to this challenge. It offers a readable yet authoritative synthesis of the art, science and design of engaging experiences. It offers both the foundations of engagement design across a range of disciplines and a highly original synthesis of them. The book demonstrates that despite their vast terminological and methodological differences, the various theorizations of engagement can be integrated.

And like the best of such integrations, Zagalo's final framework is easy to learn and apply, while having an extraordinary depth. Zagalo proposes that engagement can be understood in relation to three "streams": progression, expression and relation. Progression captures the purpose of interactions—the temporal unfoldings of competencies into actions into realized goals. Expression captures the creative, playful and enacted dimensions of engagement. Relation captures the ways that artifacts, contexts, the concrete, our minds and our emotions are composed in engaging experiences.

I have introduced the core contribution in a few sentences, and yet each gracefully unfolds into a resource of tremendous depth. The game Othello was long marketed as "minutes to learn but a lifetime to master". Zagalo's book might be similarly described as fast to get into, but complex to savor and reflect—perhaps not surprising, given its author's career as a game researcher and designer himself.

As such, *Engagement Design* belongs on the bookshelf of every UX practitioner, video game designer and media artist. It will serve as an outstanding textbook for both undergraduate and graduate courses in interaction design.

This is a book with both science and soul. It is at once erudite and practical. I have no doubt that like me, you will find it thoroughly engaging.

IN, USA
2019

Jeffrey Bardzell

Acknowledgements

This book is the result of a collective adventure, involving not only dozens of fellow researchers and scholars, but various institutions that have backed me throughout this whole project, a project that took too much time to finish, for which I can only blame myself.

Therefore, I need to start by thanking my former colleagues, Adérito Marcos and Pedro Branco, who I met at the Computer Graphics Center at the University of Minho, where together we founded the laboratory engageLab. Their work and multidisciplinary approach were instrumental in creating a space for intellectual growth. With the departure of Adérito Marcos to the Open University, an even more intense period of collaboration with Pedro Branco began, which would dictate a strengthening of the domain of Human–Computer Interaction and would become one of the main foundations of this book.

With so much knowledge and material, I needed a push to force me to reflect on it all. This eventually arose from the need to confront these ideas, prompted by the invitations to present keynotes at conferences. In this way, this book is also the result of the people who invited me, instigated and led me in selecting the multiple paths possible. I would like to thank Guilhermina Miranda (TicEduca), Ana Amélia Carvalho (EJML), Ernesto Filgueiras (UBIGames), Álvaro Barbosa de Sousa (ErgoTrip), Iris Pereira and Altina Ramos (DigiLitEY) and Pilar Lacasa and Félix Ortega (AE-IC VI).

My passage through Communication Sciences at the University of Minho offered me a set of perspectives that eventually dictated much of what this book has become. Similarly, the return to my Multimedia cradle, at the University of Aveiro, would eventually create the final climate needed to finish this work. Thanks to all of my former colleagues from the Department of Communication Sciences at UM and all my current colleagues from UA at the Department of Communication and Art and the DigiMedia—Digital Media and Interaction.

This list would not be complete without the many students—Ph.D., Masters and Bachelors—whom I've met over the years and with whom I have discussed and challenged my concepts. All were very important because some were enthusiastic and offered me examples that I ended up using here, others who were less surprised by my approaches eventually forced me to go further.

Engagement Design has gone through a blind peer-review process that has ensured relevant feedback, but also in its final phase it has benefited immensely from the revisions and discussions with David Callahan and Jeffrey Bardzell, which have helped to complete it. To all, colleagues and academics, my great thanks, in particular, to Jeffrey for the kindness of writing the Foreword.

Finally, a great thank you for the affability of Helen Desmond, the Springer editor, who turned out to be a key player in this whole process, from my first contact to publication.

Of course, none of this would have been possible without a deeply friendly woman by my side, Filipa, and two magnificent children, Pedro and Diana.

Contents

About the Author

Nelson Zagalo has a Ph.D. in Communication Technologies with a thesis on the convergence of cinema and virtual reality, for which he developed affective and interactive design experiments. When young, he studied in the areas of STEM and entered university to study engineering, because it was the best shot for future employment. But at the same time, and self-taught, he studied what he loved most: cinema and all its ramifications in philosophy and psychology. Eventually, he dropped out of engineering, seeking to follow cinema, but ultimately graduating with a Ph.D. about cinema and new technologies. He always believed that the ideal world rested in the fusion between art and technology, between science and humanities, but today he prefers to accept that there are different ways of being in life, and that if there is a fringe that loves to make these bridges, not everyone can, wants to or needs to do it.

In 2009, he created the engageLab Laboratory and the Portuguese Society of Videogame Sciences. In 2014 he invented the Bridging Book patent, and in 2018 he launched the open access *Journal of Digital Media & Interaction*. In between, he wrote two books—*Interactive Emotions* (2009) and *Videogames in Portugal* (2013); edited more than 20 books, proceedings and journal special issues; and published over a hundred peer-reviewed papers. He has always dedicated himself to multidisciplinary working, bringing together computing, design, communication, arts and psychology. He is Associate Professor at the University of Aveiro and Scientific Coordinator of DigiMedia—Digital Media and Interaction Research Centre.

List of Figures

Chapter 1
Introduction

It is a commonwealth in which work is play and play is life.
George Bernard Shaw (1904)

Abstract This chapter presents the reasoning, motivation, relevance of the research subject, in addition to the methodological approaches employed, along with the structure through which the book's theoretical, empirical concerns will be addressed.

Why do we insist on thinking that different people should experience reality equally? Why do we insist on expecting different people to reason the same way? Why do we insist on making different people alike? We are living with social advances that tend to equalize opportunities, where financial conditions or our birth family no longer dominate the decisions we make regarding our careers, our spouses, and our lives. They tell us to follow passion and personal taste, to be happy to do what we like best with whom we love the most. Consequently, we have gained the freedom to have particular and even eccentric cultural tastes, all of which are accepted because everything represents what each of us is in our most authentic individuality. On the other hand, we are also experiencing a time of great pressure against this set of principles. We are told that taking higher education in the arts and humanities is a waste of time and that there is no work, and that such training offers nothing useful or productive to society. We are told that salvation is in technology, in STEM. That we should all learn to code. That universities should close their humanities courses. That women should abandon psychology and devote themselves to engineering.

Looking at the products of culture, e.g. cinema or literature, never have so many works been created, with so many different themes, from so many different perspectives (some never previously widely discussed) in the most varied structural approaches. However, when we look at interactive media, in particular videogames, we notice a strong insistence on the same models of interaction, models that predominantly served a single profile of interactors—the teenagers who owned the first personal computers. There seems to exist in our more technology-related cultural production the same problem as identified in the relationship of society to the choice

N. Zagalo, *Engagement Design*, Human–Computer Interaction Series,
https://doi.org/10.1007/978-3-030-37085-5_1

of professions: a tendency for technology to push us all in the same direction. Maybe that's the way it is, because according to Kevin Kelly "technology has domesticated us. As fast as we remake our tools, we remake ourselves. We are coevolving with our technology" (2010, p. 37) and so being culturally conditioned There is probably an underlying character to the technology that contaminates everything, and eventually pushes and demands from us. However, if videogames have managed to broaden their demographics and extend their millionaire gains, they are still far from achieving the pervasive acceptance of literature and film, and so a question arises: **do we have a problem, a mismatch, between interactive media engagement and the differences between people?**

Over the past few years we have sought to understand how interactive experiences vary, not only in digital environments, but also in physical as well as hybrid environments, for which reason we founded the laboratory engageLab[1] in 2009. In this lab we have been able to launch several works, not only analyzing the resulting experiences with interactive media, but also designing and developing interactive applications focusing on affective, experiential and engagement aspects. As a result of all this work, the main questions that this book attempts to convey have emerged.

What motivations lead people to interact with interactive artefacts (e.g. videogames, among other interactive media)? Why do they play some types of games and not others? What motivates a player to prefer one type of interaction over another? And finally, are there any epistemologies underlying motivations for interaction?

1.1 Deepening the Problem

It has become immensely common, whenever one wants to talk about the opposition between the sciences and the humanities, or between the exact sciences and literature, to evoke CP Snow's *The Two Cultures* lecture of 1959. The text generated immense discussion at the time of its publication and continues to do so to the present day. However, on reading it in more detail for the writing of this book, we felt some disappointment. Much of what we had read supported by this text had served to support ideas far beyond those expressed by Snow. Recall what he told us.

> A good many times I have been present at gatherings of people who, by the standards of the traditional culture, are thought highly educated and who have with considerable gusto been expressing their incredulity at the illiteracy of scientists. Once or twice I have been provoked and have asked the company how many of them could describe the Second Law of Thermodynamics. The response was cold: it was also negative. Yet I was asking something which is the scientific equivalent of: Have you read a work of Shakespeare's? (Snow, 1959)

Snow's focus is on communication between scientists and literary people. He worries that they do not communicate, but does not try to understand what really separates them. Probably this was because Snow being a physicist and writer, the lack of relation just seemed awkward to him. In this sense, what Snow talks about in *The Two*

[1] The laboratory engageLab (https://www.engagelab.org) was founded in 2009 at the University of Minho, where I remained as co-director until 2017, the year I moved to the University of Aveiro.

Cultures is not really what defines each group—goals, mindsets, working methods—but only the fact that these two groups don't like each other. And that's why John Brockman's response, in his book *The Third Culture*, only makes sense in response to Snow's findings. In it, Brockman points to a third culture, already proposed by Snow in the revision of his lecture (1963), which would result from what we today define as Science Communication (Gregory, 2015), the simplification of knowledge and the creation of bridges with society, creating new scientific discourse that is more open and accessible. Brockman speaks of names like Roger Penrose, Richard Dawkins, Stephen Jay Gould, Daniel C. Dennett, or Steven Pinker, who contributed immensely to the scientific literacy revolution of the twentieth century, bringing down many of the walls that prevented access to knowledge. Several authors, including Pinker, used this approach to deliver harsh, even violent, attacks on fellow academics in the humanities—notably Nietzsche, Foucault and Bauman (Pinker, 2018, Chaps. 22 and 23). It is true that these kind of answer-attacks have arisen in response to the immense attacks from the humanities against science, namely since Kuhn's book *The Structure of Scientific Revolutions* (1962), resulting in the infamous "Science Wars" of the 1990s (Ross, 1996), which have been highly re-energized during the last decade's explosion of social media and its meddling in politics, aided by the resurgence of populism. Pinker's last book (2018) is mainly directed at this resurgence, but also intends to tackle the new front of attacks on technology (e.g. Google, Facebook, Twitter), accusing the technology developers of being only "half-educated" (Naughton, 2017) and pointing to ethical and subjectivity training flaws in the domains of science (Bazzul, 2016). But deep down, all of this happens in the name of defining who owns the power and word within the Academy. Honestly, I don't see how anyone might want to reach consilience when they simply attack each other. It seems to us, that it remains relevant to work toward understanding and accepting the differences, not only in our proposed work but also in how each group approaches reality, because both cultures are relevant to what we are, although each side considers the other irrelevant.

On the other hand, there is really a third culture or knowledge track that does not fit on either side, which was identified by Nigel Cross as that of "Design" (1982). Long before, Alfred North Whitehead had also identified a third way, listing the following three cultures: "the way of literary culture, the way of scientific culture, the way of technical" (1917). That "technical", also referred to as "technological" by Whitehead, would be linked by Cross to "Design" (1982), and would later emerge in a text by Kelly (1998), in which he makes his interpretation of the third culture differently from Brockman, pointing rather to the communication technology revolution, to the new "inventors", icons like Bill Gates, recalling that Thomas "Edison would have been at home with computers and the Web" (1998). But we can go much further back to track this underrepresented third way, by remembering the man who can be seen as the mentor of it all, Leonardo Da Vinci, who wrote about the way he and his work were looked at by literary and scientific people (Da Vinci, 1540) as we will see next.

Therefore, we must start by understanding that this differentiation did not arise with Snow: it was already present in Plato's Agora. He himself tried to take the arts and literature out of the academy:

> And now we may fairly take the poet and place him by the side of the painter, for he is like him in two ways: first, inasmuch as his creations have an inferior degree of truth—in this, I say, he is like him; and he is also like him in being concerned with an inferior part of the soul; and therefore we shall be right in refusing to admit him into a well-ordered State, because he awakens and nourishes and strengthens the feelings and impairs the reason. (Plato, 380BC, Chap. X)

After that we had multiple discussions that somehow anticipated Snow's assertion, such as the separation between Rationalists and Empiricists (James, 1907). Even if endowed with different principles, when the details are analyzed we can find points of contact. Then, the rise of industry in the arms of science excavated the last ditch, namely when it became fully dominant in the socioeconomic landscape. Concern over the education system was one of the things that marked the Victorian period. Matthew Arnold in the nineteenth century spoke of two groups, those with "special aptitude for knowing men—the study of the humanities" and those with "special aptitude for knowing the world—the study of nature", for which he advocated a "bifurcation" in teaching, only from the age of 16, with the aim of creating a "circle of knowledge" for all (Dowling, 1961, p. 727). Also, in 1917 A.N. Whitehead was already discussing the two groups for their differences and shortcomings in the face of a third group, linked with the emergence of the technologies of the Industrial Revolution. In that lecture, Whitehead attests to enormous prescience, anticipating by 100 years the discussions on creativity and entrepreneurship in Europe, saying:

> The immediate need of the nation is a large supply of skilled efficient workmen, of men with inventive genius, and of employers alert in the development of new ideas" [and for that] "There is only one way to obtain these admirable results. It is by producing workmen, men of science, and employers who enjoy their work" [because] "inventive genius requires pleasurable mental activity as a condition for its vigorous exercise. (Whitehead, 1917)

Thus, Whitehead proposed dividing the curriculum into three domains—scientific, literary and technological—with the assurance that all should study all domains, but that there should be "one dominant emphasis" (1917, p. 24), with the individual following his "peculiar interest", "because, for some reason, he wants to know it" (1929, p. 11). If for Arnold the most important thing was to ensure that there was a "circle of knowledge" that was similar for everyone, Whitehead realized that times had changed and that with the extension of existing modern knowledge "it would not be possible for a single individual to know everything", opening the necessary door to "specialization" (Dowling, 1961, p. 728). Whitehead's proposal was twofold: on the one hand to ensure that the three areas were robust enough to be accepted as of equal value, and on the other to open the door to one's aptitude.

When Snow gave his talk, the literary people were placing themselves on a pedestal, calling themselves the only intellectual elite. Scientists and technologists were closeted in their labs, leaving the social arena free for literary rule. But with the increasing evolution of technology, its presence and relevance to society, as well as the emergence of an intellectual group of communicators on the science side, as Brockman points out, this dominion has been decreasing. By the beginning of this century, news could be read of the closure of entire humanities departments (Grove,

Table 1.1 A three cultures view of epistemology by Cross (1982)

	Science	Humanities	Design
Phenomenon	The natural world	Human experience	The man-made world
Methods	Controlled experiment, classification, analysis	Analogy, metaphor, criticism, evaluation	Modelling, pattern-formation, synthesis
Values	Objectivity, rationality, neutrality, and a concern for 'truth'	Subjectivity, imagination, commitment, and a concern for 'justice'	Practicality, ingenuity, empathy and a concern for 'appropriateness'

2015). That is, the power struggle is real and contaminates much of what defines disciplinary divisions, and consequently what is relevant to our work here is the focus on the groups of people and their profiles, and less on disciplines.

Cross (1982) in the discussion of the third culture of design presented a set of categories from which he framed the three pathways—phenomenon, methods and values—that we present in Table 1.1. While not fully agreeing with everything Cross lists in that table, it can already give us some pointers on these three profiles, notably with regard to cognitive needs, behaviours and methods, but also as to what distinguishes them in the way they look at reality, this last point being highly relevant for us (and which will be explored in more detail in Chap. 3).

Taking the division proposed by Cross as a starting point, let us look at how each of these views of knowledge affect the world and society, considering whether it really continues to make sense, and if so, whether they are separate or convergent.

1.2 The Relevance of Different Cultures

Of the three areas, the most easily recognized are the sciences and the humanities because of their long history of clashes and debates. The power of modern science has been most intensely felt since theorization gave place to application, creating and revolutionizing the whole economic structure of labour with industrialization, and in turn all other societal structures, from national politics to family homes. Science became the new guiding truth after the millennial religions started to crumble. Science is in the twenty-first century the undeniable supporting structure of society's well-being; from medicine to the entertainment industries, there exists no branch of human doing and living where science has not contributed value to optimize and make our lives better.

Strangely, all this support seems to be mistrusted by the society that most benefits from it. We see that distrust of scientific experts being spoken aloud—e.g. the denial of global warming. But this is not happening because society is liking scientists less, instead it happens because politics remains the main structure that organizes mass thought. At this point we are no stranger to the fact that politicians have been mostly trained in the humanities. This is not to say that the humanities are to blame for the state of current politics, or distrust of science, but rather to say that it still maintains all its relevance for politics. And the reason politics sticks to the humanities is precisely because of the human variable, and the ways it affects society's evolution. Notice how Everett defines human culture:

> Culture is an abstract network shaping and connecting social roles, hierarchically structured knowledge domains and ranked values. Culture is dynamic, shifting, reinterpreted moment by moment. The roles, knowledge and values of culture are only found in the bodies (the brain is part of the body) and behaviors of its members. (Everett, 2017, Chap. 4)

That is, culture is intrinsically dependent on the social, and this is all the more important if we follow the reasons for the evolution of our brain and intellectual abilities. Dunbar (1998) distrusts the hypothesis that brains evolved to support "ecological problem-solving tasks", and instead worked towards demonstrating the "social brain hypothesis", which states "large brains reflect the computational demands of the complex social systems that characterize the order" (1998, p. 178). Dunbar demonstrates why "bond relationships are cognitively so demanding" (2009), explaining the evolutionary need to evolve social skills and consequently impacting our brains and our intelligence. Previously, De Waal (1982) had used Machiavelli's political theories to describe primate social manoeuvring, saying that "the social organization of chimpanzees is almost too human to be true—entire passages of Machiavelli seem to be directly applicable to chimpanzee behaviour", launching the "Machiavellian intelligence hypothesis", which became the main support for Dunbar's "social brain hypothesis".

Consequently, science is fundamental in ensuring more and better quality of life, but the humanities are fundamental in the ability to take advantage of these improvements. One cannot exist without the other. We cannot think of having universities with only science and engineering courses, nor can we think of having only humanities politicians. We need to have both domains in dialogue with each other, knowing that they are different and that aim for difference, but which need to cooperate.

As for the third way, of Design and Technology, despite its enormous relevance it remains quite secondary in the knowledge landscape. In the early twenty-first century there was no shortage of appeals to design as the most important discipline of the century (Bangle, 2001; Isaacson, 2011; Pink, 2006), something that as we have seen above has been said for 100 years, since Whitehead. Nigel Cross says this happens because it "has been neglected, and has not been adequately named or articulated" (1982), and the same was said by Leonardo:

> Because writers have had no knowledge of the science of painting, they have not been able to describe its gradations and parts (…) since those who practised painting were for long ignorant as to how to explain its theory, it lacked advocates for a considerable time; because it does not speak itself, but reveals itself and ends in action, and poetry ends in words, which in its vainglory it employs for self-praise. (Da Vinci, 1519)

For Leonardo the fundamental was always in the experience, not in the books, as he said to the literary community:

> They will say that being unskilled in letters I cannot find true expression for the matters of which I desire to treat; they do not know that in my subjects experience is a truer guide than the words of others, for experience was the teacher of all great writers, and therefore I take her for guide, and I will cite her in all cases. (Da Vinci, 1519)

As to those related to the sciences:

> in regard to these mathematical matters, that they who merely study the masters and not the works of nature are the grandchildren, and not the children, of nature, the mistress of good masters. (Da Vinci, 1519)

This was completely defended by A.N. Whitehead regarding the technological curriculum:

> In estimating the importance of technical education we must rise above the exclusive association of learning with book learning. First-hand knowledge is the ultimate basis of intellectual life. To a large extent book learning conveys second-hand information, and as such can never rise to the importance of immediate practice. (Whitehead, 1917)

In essence, design and technology together have opened a whole new space of relevance in the twenty-first century as Kelly said:

> While science and art generate truth and beauty, technology generates opportunities: new things to explain; new ways of expression; new media of communications (...) In the third culture, the way to settle the question of how the mind works is to build a working mind (...) The status of the technologist is ascending because for now, and for the foreseeable future, we have more to learn from making new tools than we do from making new concepts or new measurements. (Kelly, 1998)

The importance of this Third Way has been strongly acknowledged by twenty-first century political agendas, notably in addressing Asia's vast manufacturing force, forcing the West increasingly to take refuge in inventive and creative areas. Politically this became more clear with all the pressure placed on the creative and cultural industries, with discourses loaded with buzzwords like creativity, innovation and entrepreneurship and the funding of millions from the European Commission for programe on building a so-called Creative Europe since 2007.[2]

The main point of all this discussion has to do with the need to understand that there are different ways of understanding reality, and essentially of acting on it. Recognizing the need to know a little of everything, the density of existing knowledge makes it difficult to develop a broad and wide education, but more importantly, there are natural questions related to one's aptitude and individual motivations. If we have to work increasingly in collaborative ways, it makes even less sense to think that everyone should know the same, or that certain areas of knowledge are more important than others. We need to accept that there is a difference and work to get the best out of it, using true multidisciplinarity in more robust collaborative ways.

Similarly, if we want to intensify people's experiences in their relationships with interactive artefacts, we must understand that the way they act, react and interact

[2] All information about the European programmes can be find online at https://eacea.ec.europa.eu/creative-europe_en and https://ec.europa.eu/programmes/creative-europe/node_en.

differs. This is not a mere cultural problem that we can simply wait to become equalized. There are tendencies, preferences, and motivations that lead people to act in one way and feel good, and other situations in which they feel great difficulties, often not understanding why. The difficulty presented by people in relation to artefacts is real, and it is not that some are better or worse, or that some have trained more or less, but instead that the ways of approaching and understanding the world are different. And one of the greatest proofs of this is found in videogames, in a somehow forgotten and little discussed design issue: that of difficulty regulators. These regulators, which will be discussed in detail in the final chapter, serve as an effective demonstration of what has been pointed out, of what differentiates and separates players and interactive media users, because, as we will see, these regulators are more than difficulty adjusters: they specifically respond to engagement needs, they respond to different ways of acting and reacting to reality.

1.3 Approach and Structure

As the title indicates, we are focused on engagement design and we are interested in understanding how we engage people, how we assure their interest, or grasp and maintain it throughout the interaction. As we will see in Chap. 2, in recent years the domain of HCI has gone through the revolution of experience, the need to design and create experiences, forgetting that this belongs to a very particular stronghold of each subject's intimacy, their subjectivity. Obviously, we have to talk about experience when we talk about how users feel and think, but moving from subjective worlds into sets of patterns for those experiences is unreasonable. What would literature and cinema be if by some transcendent capacity we could standardize the experiences of the receivers?

Therefore, we believe that the way we can contribute to the improvement of user experiences is by working on specific components of the experience, components that can somehow be worked to large standards that serve general groups of users. Hence the above discussion about epistemologies, the great trends of relationship with the real of the subjects. We understood that it was vital to find differences and similarities in that relationship. Because we understood that the way people choose to invest their sometimes very scarce time in one interactive work, and not with another, would give us relevant indicators to find these differences. Thus we wanted to explore the motivations for playing, and we wanted to deepen the psychological personalities of the subjects. On the other hand, the construction of the engagement is not something done merely through personality or taste, as we will discuss in the subsequent chapters. The engagement that is produced from the creation of meaning for the subjects also depends on the design of the artefact and on the context that involves the subject and the artefact. There can be no communication, meaning making and engagement without these three components.

Thus, if Chap. 2 is devoted to dismantling the relationship between experience and engagement, addressing the fundamental components that form the structure of engagement, Chaps. 3–5 are devoted to each of its components—subject profiles, epistemic contexts, and the artefacts. Then in the last chapter we present the synthesis of all components in a general analysis model, from which we extract the essential components of our proposed Engagement Design Model.

References

Bangle, C. (2001). How BMW turns art into profit. *Harvard Business Review*, (January), 47–56.

Bazzul, J. (2016). *Ethics and science education: How subjectivity matters*. https://doi.org/10.1007/978-3-319-39132-8.

Cross, N. (1982). Designerly ways of knowing. *Design Studies*, *3*(4), 221–227.

Da Vinci, L. (1519). *Thoughts on art and life* (M. Baring, ed.). Boston: Merrymount Press.

Da Vinci, L. (1540). *A treatise on painting (Codex Rurbinas Latinus)*. Roma: Vatican.

De Waal, F. (1982). *Chimpanzee politics: power and sex among apes*. London: Jonathan Cape

Dowling, H. M. (1961). Science and culture: A false antithesis. *New Scientist*, (253), 727–729. Retrieved from https://books.google.pt/books?id=ajFGeY0xuncC.

Dunbar, R. (1998). The social brain hypothesis. *Evolutionary Anthropology: Issues, News, and Reviews*, *6*(5), 178–190. https://doi.org/10.1002/(SICI)1520-6505(1998)6:5%3c178::AID-EVAN5%3e3.0.CO;2-8.

Dunbar, R. (2009). The social brain hypothesis and its implications for social evolution. *Annals of Human Biology*, *36*(5), 562–572. https://doi.org/10.1080/03014460902960289.

Everett, D. L. (2017). *How language Began: The story of Humanity's Greatest Invention*. New York: W. W. Norton Company.

Gregory, J. (2015). Science communication. In *International encyclopedia of the social & behavioral sciences* (pp. 219–224). https://doi.org/10.1016/B978-0-08-097086-8.95088-8.

Grove, J. (2015). Social sciences and humanities faculties "to close" in Japan after ministerial intervention. *Times Higher Education*. Retrieved from https://www.timeshighereducation.com/news/social-sciences-and-humanities-faculties-close-japan-after-ministerial-intervention.

Isaacson, W. (2011). *Steve Jobs*. New York: Simon & Schuster.

James, W. (1907). *Pragmatism. A new name for some old ways of thinking*. New York: Dover Publications.

Kelly, K. (1998). Essays on science and society. *Science*, *279*(5353), 992–993. https://doi.org/10.1126/science.279.5353.992.

Kelly, K. (2010). *What technology wants*. New York: Viking.

Kuhn, T. S. (1962). *The structure of scientific revolutions*. Chicago: University of Chicago Press.

Naughton, J. (2017, November 19). How a half-educated tech elite delivered us into chaos. *The Guardian*. Retrieved from https://www.theguardian.com/commentisfree/2017/nov/19/how-tech-leaders-delivered-us-into-evil-john-naughton.

Pink, D. (2006). *A whole new mind: why right-brainers will rule the future*. New York: Riverhead Books.

Pinker, S. (2018). *Enlightenment now: The case for reason, science, humanism, and progress*. New York: Penguin.

Plato. (380BC). *Republic* (B. Jowett, ed.). Public Domain.

Ross, A. (1996). *Science wars*. Durham: Duke University Press Books.

Shaw, G. B. (1904). *John Bull's other island*. London: Royal Court Theatre.

Snow, C. P. (1959). *The two cultures and the scientific revolution*. London: Cambridge University Press.

Snow, C. P. (1963). *The two cultures: And a second look*. London: Cambridge University Press.

Whitehead, A. N. (1917). Presidential address: Technical education and its relation to science and literature. *The Mathematical Gazette*, *9*(128), 20. https://doi.org/10.2307/3605222.

Whitehead, A. N. (1929). The aims of education. In *The aims of education & other essays* (pp. 1–14). New York: Macmillan.

Chapter 2
From Experience to Engagement

Abstract Interactive media artefacts are not just products; they work with messages and have specific needs beyond their design. However, the design impacts and transforms these messages. To improve the design of interaction of these media, we have approached experience as being studied in HCI. However, this demonstrated that it was not able to deliver the needs of design. We propose then to move the research on interactive media design from experience to engagement. In this chapter, we discuss how to make this move and present a pragmatic approach that will be followed to describe the model of engagement in the rest of the book.

The culture produced by the artistic media has been responsible for the creation of human experiences, which neither nature nor the direct relation between human beings could simulate or provide experience of in the course of a single life. Think of the minds of others we meet when we read a book, the worlds we admire when we sit in front of a screen, or the actions we make when playing a video game. These experiences are triggered by what we call artefacts, works generated by humans, which, although created as autonomous artworks, always aim at establishing a relationship between subjects—creators and recipients—without which the experience would not exist. Knowing the existence of the materiality of the artefacts, created by the creators, the experience can only exist in a recipient subject, as an effect of stimulus produced by the artworks. According to Dewey: "Art is quality of doing and of what is done (…) The product of art—temple, painting, statue, poem—is not the work of art. The work takes place when a human being cooperates with the product so that the outcome is an experience that is enjoyed because of its liberating and ordered properties" (1934, p. 222). This experience that Dewey refers to is defined by Hassenzahl as "an episode, a chunk of time that one went through—with sights and sounds, feelings and thoughts, motives and actions; they are closely knitted together, stored in memory, labelled, relived and communicated to others" (2010, p. 8). Accordingly, experience does not exist in space, in a vacuum, but emerges from the experiencing subject, empowered by the artefact, but intimately dependent on who the subject is, as well as on how the subject relates to the artwork. It is the relationship between the artefact and the recipient subject, as well as the "commutative interaction of an

N. Zagalo, *Engagement Design*, Human–Computer Interaction Series,
https://doi.org/10.1007/978-3-030-37085-5_2

organic self with the world" (Dewey, 1934, p. 229), that fosters the emergence of a "chunk of time" that can be individuated and identified.

2.1 Proustian Experience

> And soon, mechanically, dispirited after a dreary day with the prospect of a depressing morrow, I raised to my lips a spoonful of the tea in which I had soaked a morsel of the cake. No sooner had the warm liquid mixed with the crumbs touched my palate than a shiver ran through me and I stopped, intent upon the extraordinary thing that was happening to me. An exquisite pleasure had invaded my senses, something isolated, detached, with no suggestion of its origin. And at once the vicissitudes of life had become indifferent to me, its disasters innocuous, its brevity illusory—this new sensation having had the effect, which love has, of filling me with a precious essence; or rather this essence was not in me, it was me. I had ceased now to feel mediocre, contingent, mortal. Whence could it have come to me, this all-powerful joy? (Proust, 1913, p. 60)

This is one of the most famous reports of experience in literature and known simply as "the madeleine of Proust". The author was known for the ability to call upon memory and describe, in depth and detail, the feelings that accompanied each of his memories. Proust gives an account of what he feels, and wonders why he feels so intensely, which he answers with the following paragraph:

> And suddenly the memory revealed itself. The taste was that of the little piece of madeleine which on Sunday mornings at Combray (because on those mornings I did not go out before mass), when I went to say good morning to her in her bedroom, my aunt Léonie used to give me, dipping it first in her own cup of tea or tisane. The sight of the little madeleine had recalled nothing to my mind before I tasted it; perhaps because I had so often seen such things in the meantime, without tasting them, on the trays in pastry-cooks' windows, that their image had dissociated itself from those Combray days to take its place among others more recent; perhaps because, of those memories so long abandoned and put out of mind, nothing now survived, everything was scattered; the shapes of things, including that of the little scallop-shell of pastry, so richly sensual under its severe, religious folds, were either obliterated or had been so long dormant as to have lost the power of expansion which would have allowed them to resume their place in my consciousness. (Proust, 1913, p. 63)

In this deconstruction, Proust assumes the role of a researcher, in search of the reasons for such a strong sensorial impact. In fact, the whole description of Proust ends up being a sort of neuropsychological evaluation, as Lehrer points out in *Proust was a Neuroscientist* (2007). Realizing that the madeleine is the cause, the triggering object does not block his attention on the physical or chemical properties, but rather maintains the seeking of answers within himself. Proust assumes the object, the madeleine, as merely responsible for initiating a chain of reactions within himself, which are born of his memories, in his past. In this sense, he acts as a psychologist, trying to find clues and elements in his past that relate to the madeleine, allowing him to reconstitute a narrative, which according to him would have been the real reason for such intense experience. It is not a mere experience, because as Proust says, the initial sight of the cake did not call him particularly, perhaps because, as he says, he continued for many years to see these in the city. It was only when he tasted it with tea, and because he had not proved it since then, that the aroma was released in his palate and the reaction was triggered, provoking the intense experience. We can then say that it was at that moment that the cake and its properties became present to Proust, and gained a meaning.

Now, this is precisely the point that interests us, the meaning of the experience, without which we would have only the experience of all the remaining moments in which we are conscious, or as Hassenzahl put it "a continuous commentary on the current state of affairs" (2010, p. 1). Thus, the strong emotion described by Proust must be read not as a mere tasting effect of a cake, but as an experience developed from the tasting properties of the cake and its relation to its own nostalgia. We have a whole process of relationship between the artefact (cake) and the receiver (Proust): a set of design variables (what defines the artefact), cognitive (what defines the subject) and relational (what defines the context) (Fig. 2.1). Experiencing is then systemic (Bateson, 1972), which determines a need for a pragmatic approach (Dewey, 1934; Peirce, 1991) to its understanding. Proust begins by identifying the artefact as a simple cake, but is the context that emanates from the savouring that evokes the memories and provokes the experience, which we should say is a full communication process.

Analysing the experience as a communication process allows us to move forward with a discussion of the experience on all fronts related to the arts and media—from book to film, theatre, dance or music, going even, as we saw in the example, to the arts of gastronomy—but this is not our objective. It would be arrogant to think of a design model capable of accounting for all kinds of culturally mediated experiences, although much of what is discussed here is easily portable and applicable to other domains. Our interest is particular, and it focuses on artefacts created for media

Fig. 2.1 Pragmatic view of experience as a communication process. Artefact: the madeleine and its properties; Subject: Proust relating senses and cognition; Context: Combray, the past that links Proust's cognition to the properties of the madeleine, building the meaning of engagement. (Illustration by the author)

with possibilities of two-way communication—the interactive media: multimedia artworks, games and interactive movies.

Likewise, it is not our goal to account for the experience with interactive media in all its human extension, but rather to present a focused model of that experience capable of presenting the basic elements of design, offering emphasis on those who promote it and are susceptible, or accessible, to the performance of the designer. That is to say, knowing that a relevant part of the experience is on the recipient side, and that it bears heavily on subjectivity (in the case of Proust's madeleine, in its past experiences and living history, something that narrative design can use; see, for example, the use of nostalgia in the television series "Stranger Things" (Duffer & Duffer, 2016)), the implications for human experience go far beyond the engagement, not pertaining in a work of design, but belonging more to research in anthropology or philosophy (Keller, 1999; Russon, 2010; Steiner, 1996). So, the big question that drives all this work is: **how can we improve the communication process of experience in interactive media by design?**

2.1.1 Communication Is Meaning

> Every art communicates because it expresses. It enables us to share vividly and deeply in meanings to which we had been dumb, or for which we had but the ear that permits what is said to pass through in transit to overt action. For communication is not announcing things, even it they are said with the emphasis of great sonority. Communication is the process of creating participation, of making common what had been isolated and singular; and part of the miracle it achieves is that, in being communicated, the conveyance of meaning gives body and definiteness to the experience of the one who utters as well as to that of those who listen. (Dewey, 1934, p. 253)

Nowadays, speaking of communication implies talking about a huge area of scientific study that established itself internationally only in the second half of the twentieth century. Although being a recent area, its affirmation in the academy has not stopped growing, and it can even be said that it has begun to take a space that previously belonged to more fundamental disciplines, like social sciences and humanities, because of its multidisciplinary condition, which makes perfect sense since communication deals with the study of what generates, allows and maintains human relations, requiring a broad understanding of what constitutes the human being. And it is precisely for this reason that communication surfaces here, because it is through it that we can begin to define the surrounding variables of the whole equation that involves the needs of the design of experience. Thus, we will start by trying to understand the importance and scope of communication in the definition of the human variable, analysing the methods and models available for its comprehension, after which we will establish the connection with the artefact variables, so that we can start looking into the differences and needs of that relationship.

Communication sciences came about with computer science, but they have developed far beyond it. Initially, it was only a question of ensuring that the messages sent by different means and channels reached the recipient comprehensibly. This was the time when mathematicians and engineers began to transform the analog world into digital. Sending information through electrical impulses was counterproductive, because the signal deteriorated along the way. In turn, using bits, 0 and 1, the information that arrived was guaranteed to be the same as sent previously (Shannon, 1948) (see Fig. 2.2). However, this was only the dawn of concerns for communication. A message that exits as 0101 and arrives as 0101 assures me that it has arrived correctly with the addressee, but in terms of its meaning, this does not guarantee anything. That is, I need to know if anyone on the other side of the broadcast understands what I mean by my message. The major problem of communication thus lies in the significance of information. In a model like Shannon's, what the message has to say is irrelevant, only its form matters. Informing is a process of transmitting information, the process of communicating goes beyond that, implying the understanding of the information on both sides, because only then is the first goal of communication achieved—"putting in common" (Wolton, 2009). Therefore, in a process of interaction, the simple transmission of information is not enough: there must be a process of exchange and sharing that builds a communication, or as Tomasello put it, "for me to get your help, or to help you, or to share with you (…) is through communication, and so I decide to make mutually manifest to us (in our current joint attentional frame) a communicative act" (2008, p. 97). This is also where Winograd put the emphasis when defining Interaction Design, saying that "the computer, with its attendant peripherals and networks, is a machine that provides new ways for people to communicate with other people" (1997). The end goal for interaction becomes the creation of relationship, which is what happens regularly between two human beings during a conversation (Dubberly & Pangaro, 2015) (see Fig. 2.3).

This was the next step, which became known as cybernetics, a science created by Wiener (1948), a contemporary of Shannon, who sought to account for the ways in which dialogue was established between our actions and machine reactions, and generated a certain popular fascination for the future applicability to androids, and their relationship with us. Cybernetics studies the relationship between agents (in which one will be a nonhuman) as systems, and therefore focuses its full attention on

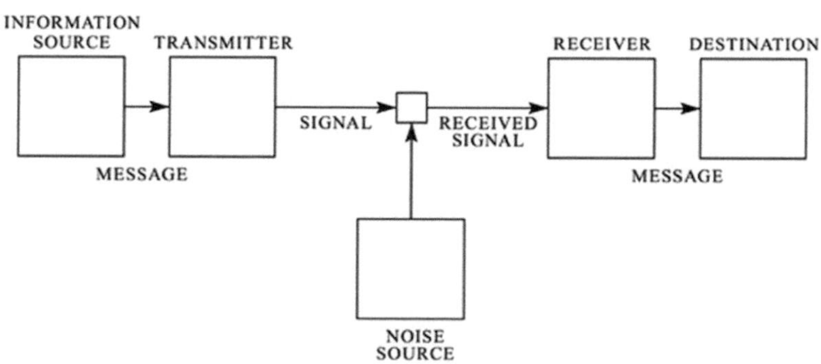

Fig. 2.2 Mathematic model of communication from Shannon (1948)

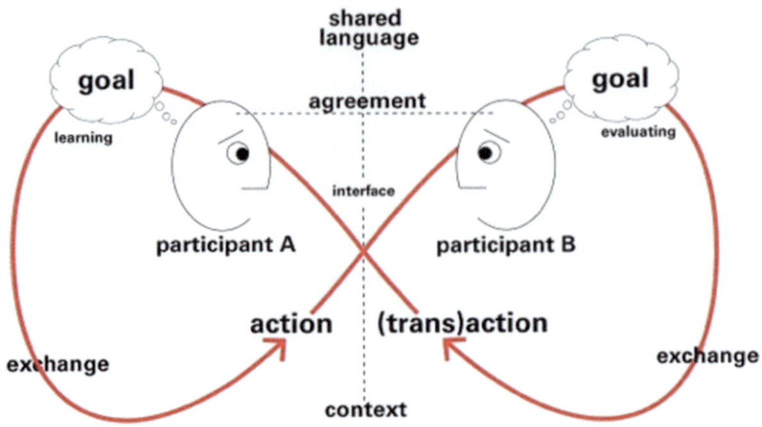

Fig. 2.3 Conversation framework for designing systems and services (Pangaro, 2009)

the modes of control of these systems. So, if the information sciences were focused on ensuring the technical information that comes out is the same as that which comes in, cybernetics was focused on how that information has sufficient meaning for the agents to stay engaged. The simplest example can be seen in the handling of a boat: our actions on the rudder have effects on the change of direction of this boat; taking into account that we want to reach a certain point in the lake, we will adjust the rudder to reach the destination. The interaction produced between our hand and the rudder produces a set of information that is evaluated moment by moment and actuated until reaching our goal. For us humans, this is something easy and natural—"the loop: acting, sensing, comparing to goal" (Pangaro, 2012)—it is how we understand the world and understand one another, through a continuous dialogue with the real (Maturana & Varela, 1984; Varela, Rosch, & Thompson, 1991). Problems arise when we want a machine, whether Siri or any video game, to behave in this way. Thus, if Shannon conceived the first model of communication, it was Wiener who truly understood the implications of this communication, which went beyond mere data transmission.

Then studies on communication had to define models capable of responding to the meaning of information. The main science for this effect came from the linguistic side, the semiotics of Peirce (1931) and the semiology of Saussure (1915), both sciences dedicated to the study of signs. A sign always represents something beyond itself, a referent, which in turn implies a subject capable of establishing the relation, through the information at its disposal. From here came the categories of syntax, the form of the signal and the semantics, the meaning of that signal. Thus, when Proust sees the madeleine, it is merely form, syntax. In the moment that he defines it as cake—object of sweet soft texture—it enters the area of semantics, the meaning. However, as we have seen before, it is not from the meaning, that is, from knowing it is a cake, that the surrounding experience emanate, which means that there is something else happening during the process of interaction between Proust and the madeleine. Bakhtin (1979) talks about a dialogical process of self-assessment of the interaction. The recollections of the place where the cake was eaten for the first time and the surroundings and people that the cake's flavour evokes are not part of the syntax or semantics: they form a third layer, which was defined by Morris (1946) as the pragmatics of communication, or "behavioural effects" (Watzlawick, Bavelas, & Jackson, 1967, p. 22). We can then say that an experience is a communication process in which pragmatics, as the main guarantor of relational meaning between the artefact and the subject, defines the engagement produced, or that **engagement occurs when we have a behavioural change in the receptor**.

2.1.2 Evaluation and Design

Communication processes, with their theories and methodologies, are very important in understanding what happens during the experiencing of an interactive artefact. However, our goal here goes beyond merely analysing or evaluating the experience (Hartson & Pyla, 2012). Of course, we need to understand the experience, but above all we want to understand how we can act upon it. A big share of the discussion in the user experience (Albert, Tullis, & Albert, 2008; Bernhaupt, 2009; Hodent, 2017; Sauro & Lewis, 2012) and even some experience design models (Shedroff, 2001) has followed a path that is still too close to usability studies, more concerned with metrics and quantifications of the experience created than with the real design of the experience. Of course, the analysis of the experience while being designed gives feedback to the designer and helps in refining it. However, the design has its own predicaments—insights, intuitions, challenges, models, patterns and synthesis—which are not done through mere methodologies of evaluation of users' behavioural changes. The design goals for creating cultural products are not the same as for creating task-oriented products. The main relevance of the experience emerges from the surprise of being involved by a novel idea, concept, theme, story or activity. For that, we need to create and build something to be expressed, which cannot be guessed by the receptors but needs to be fantasized and imagined.

Grounded in previous years of designing affective interactive experiences (Zagalo, Torres, & Branco, 2005, Zagalo & Torres, 2008, Zagalo, 2009, Figueiredo et al., 2013), we recently developed a UX model (Zagalo, 2017a) supported by the approach purposed by McCarthy and Wright in *Technology as Experience*, with its four "threads" ("compositional, sensual, emotional and spatio-temporal") and six "sense-making" elements ("anticipating, connecting, interpreting, reflecting, appropriating and recounting") (2004) (see Fig. 2.4). We defined for the first level the "Usability", focused on functionality, understanding and satisfaction, following the elementary heuristics (Nielsen, 1994). The satisfaction of the usability level opened the need to deepen the experience, therefore creating a second level of analysis, the "Sensorial", which analyses the emotional aspects, awareness, feelings and the awareness of feelings, creating the consciousness, following the theoretical model of emotion by Damasio (1999). The consciousness of the feelings opened the need to go even

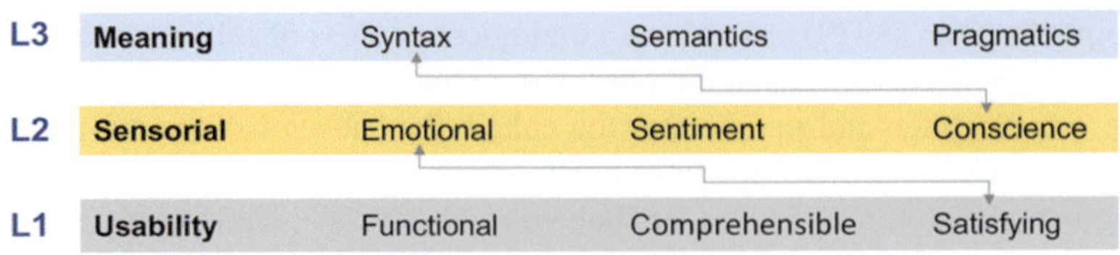

Fig. 2.4 Levels of evaluation of UX in interactive media

deeper in the experience analysis, creating the third level, "Meaning", for which we used the tripartite approach of the pragmatics of communication (Watzlawick et al., 1967).

What we've learned from building and applying this model is that the idea of meaning was not enough to achieve an understanding of the patterns of experience design. As McCarthy and Wright said "meaningful engagement depends on the event or action being felt, known, and valued in unique ways" (2004, p. 56), or as they say by the end of the presentation of their elements of meaning, "the sense-making processes must be understood in the context of the sensibilities to felt life" (2004, p. 128). This means that we are fully surrounded by subjectivity, and that all these elements served us only in describing the subject mind in each particular interaction, which could serve well in the optimization of design, but not very much in the inventive and creative processes of new design. In these models, there is little to guide the designers in the processes of ideation and invention. These components of evaluation let us know if the artefacts are producing the expected experiential results, and consequently drive the design towards optimization, but that's it.

We then believe we need to move from the overall idea of experience, the larger all-time conscience of reality; and move on from the idea of relational meaning to the emergent sense of the dialogical process. We need motivational patterns that engage humans, not meanings generated by users while engaged. Trying to unveil the meaning of engagement only serves the specificity, and designing is about common denominators. In support of this change, we can look at the UX game model presented by Hodent in which she had already proposed adding to the study of usability the dimension of engagement (2017), or the recently published paper "Human-engaged computing: the future of Human–Computer Interaction" (Ren, Silpasuwanchai, & Cahill, 2019), defending the move in HCI towards human engagement. Also, in the previous decade, we saw Yvonne Rogers arguing for a new agenda in UbiComp, proposing "technologies for engaging user experiences (…) to engage them [the users] more actively in what they currently do" (Rogers, 2006). We need then to deepen our knowledge of the most objective elements of the subject–artefact–context relationship, focusing on questioning: **what properties constitute engagement, and how can we design for it?**

2.1.3 Engagement

Engagement has been a topic of debate over the past decade in different domains, from Education (Antonetti & Garver, 2015; Butin & Seider, 2012; Moore, 2013) to Management (Rothmann, 2016; Saks, 2019; Seijts & Crim, 2006) and Marketing (Brodie, Hollebeek, Jurić, & Ilić, 2011; Harmeling, Moffett, Arnold, & Carlson, 2017), and particularly with the emergence of social media (Harrigan, Evers, Miles, & Daly, 2017; Hollebeek, Glynn, & Brodie, 2014; Voorveld, van Noort, Muntinga, & Bronner, 2018). There has been an interest in understanding how engagement occurs, not only in how it produces meaning but in how it affects behaviour and through which patterns. However, as we have already seen, an enormous barrier of subjectivity inhibits it. If we followed through communication pragmatics, focused on meaning-making, with Watzlawick (e.g. "axioms of communication"), we would be completely captive to subjectivity, context-dependent, with every case being a case, on its own and belonging to no general category. At the other end of the spectrum, we could follow with the recent cutting-edge digital tools of marketing, which by defining itself within a fully persuasive environment immersed in digital data, registering the entire relations continuously, has crafted a set of clear formulas (numbers of clicks, likes, comments, shares, views, etc.) to calculate behavioural change: the engagement. We must, however, curb this approach in the interest of our research, in the sense that all this quantitative data is merely indicative and often misleading in the analysis (e.g. a campaign will not always be shared for the best reasons—it may contain a whole negative charge—but of course in the restricted area of marketing we know that no negative publicity exists).

2.1.3.1 Funology and Psychology of Interaction

For the purposes we seek, we looked to the most recent models capable of operating both modes, qualitative and quantitative. The number of models and frameworks has grown exponentially since Don Norman published the book *Emotional Design* in 2003, grounded in work of the previous decade on "emotional usability" (Kim & Moon, 1998; Logan, 1994). Therefore, more related to engagement, we could say that HCI has devoted great effort to the idea of "fun", with, for example, the book *Funology* (Blythe, Overbeeke, Monk, & Wright, 2003) being, in 2018, "the most downloaded book in the Springer HCI Series".[1] This notion was brought into HCI from the world of video games, being recognized as their main engagement component, not only by the players but also by game researchers (Fullerton, 2014; Koster, 2004; Romero & Schreiber, 2008; Salen & Zimmerman, 2003; Schell, 2008). However, this concept arouses much surprise among people working in the larger domain of interactive media (Harvey & Samyn, 2006), or in game criticism (Alexander, 2013; Portnow & Floyd, 2012), because as Ruberg (2015) states "there is

[1] Note at the Springer web page of the book *Funology 2. From Usability to Enjoyment* (2018) https://www.springer.com/gp/book/9783319682129.

much more to video games than fun (...) Video games have the power to communicate emotions as rich and difficult as befit the human experience".

Aren't we then restricting our research of user experience when we call for the study of such a limited set of experiences? The idea of a "fun appeal" seems to be no less restrictive than the so-called "seductive" (Anderson, 2011) or "evil" (Nodder, 2013) appeals. Note that these two proposals don't have merit: Anderson and Nodder used some good social psychology on attraction and desire to build their persuasive models. The problem is the narrowness of the models, the lack of an in-depth analysis of the human engagement process and consequent conceptual structuring and modelling.

Considering the larger domain of media arts, we know that Aristotle separated drama into tragedy and comedy, and both domains have always remained prevalent in discussions of cultural production. Feeling engaged in a fun, humorous or happy-ending experience is very different than feeling engaged in horror, drama, melancholic or traumatic ending experiences, because, even if we restrict the fun idea to the interaction design of a video game, it would be paradoxical, to ask the interaction to behave with a contrary emotional value to the message of the game. Cultural artefacts must be diverse, but we know that coherence between form and message is of the utmost importance for any artwork to affirm its relevance.

Looking into the funology movement in HCI, we can see that the book *Funology*, edited by Blythe, Overbeeke, Monk and Wright, was published in 2002 and was updated in 2018, as *Funology 2*, this time edited only by Blythe and Monk (2018). These two books presented funology as a new research possibility beyond usability, and even if the second book seems more closed in, stating as its main objective the "design for fun as a User Experience" (2018), in the first book, the statement of the book was wider: "fun, enjoyment, aesthetics and the experience of use" (2002). We believe the statement in the first book corresponds more correctly with the research presented in both books, because of the broad set of theories and authors, devoted to studying the entire user experience and not limiting the scope to fun.

From the first book, we would highlight the first section, dedicated to concepts, capable of offering us three different approaches: the articles "The Engineering of Experience" by Phoebe Sengers and "Making Sense of Experience" by Wright, McCarthy and Meekison that focus on the analytical, cultural and meaning components of experience; Overbeeke's article "Let's Make Things Engaging", which highlights the maker's approach and the doing as fundamental to the creation of engagement; and finally the articles "The Enchantments of Technology" by McCarthy and Wright; and "The Semantics of Fun" by Blythe and Hassenzahl, which focus on the specific domains of emotion and pleasure. We can see here the tripartite approach of Norman: the first chapters related to the reflective level; the second to the behavioural and the third to the visceral. On the other side, the second edition of the book tells us that the most downloaded and quoted article from the first edition was "The Thing and I: Understanding the Relationship Between User and Product" by Marc Hassenzahl, so this article was updated and republished in this second volume. We emphasize this article, not for relevance attributed by the community, but rather because it functions as a sort of synthesis of the three domains presented in the concept section of the first volume. Hassenzahl brings to the article his “hedonic/pragmatic model”, he had already discussed in his 2010 monograph, “Experience design: technology for all the right reasons”, which divides the user experience into three sections—“what”, “how” and “why”—working them in a way that becomes highly relevant to us by focusing on the “be goals” and “do goals” (see Fig. 2.5), based on the “activity theories” (Kaptelinin & Nardi, 2006) and the “needs” of users, based on Maslow (1943) and Sheldon, Elliot, Kim, and Kasser (2001). Hassenzahl states then that “understanding action in terms of motives fulfilled is crucial to an experiential approach to design” (2010, p. 45), with which we agree because we consider the subject’s motivations central to our model, as we will see in the next section.

This model by Hassenzahl and its tripartite dimensions “what”, “how” and “why” are a clear response to the essence of interactivity, which Overbeeke et al. (2002) defined as the “wholly trinity of interaction”, made of the cognitive, perceptual-motor and emotional skills, and which Bill Verplank (Moggridge, 2006, p. 127) defined as basic elements of interaction design: “Know”, “Do” and “Feel” (see Fig. 2.6).

As we can see, there are many models, but Norman’s model maintains its relevance. Because of its generic approach, it seems to be able to involve them all through the three categories: visceral, behavioural and reflexive (see Fig. 2.7). These categories were clearly derived from the theory of emotions presented by Damasio

Fig. 2.5 The three-level hierarchy of goals from the experience model of Hassenzahl (2010, p. 44)

Fig. 2.6 Bill Verplank’s interaction design sketch definition (2000)

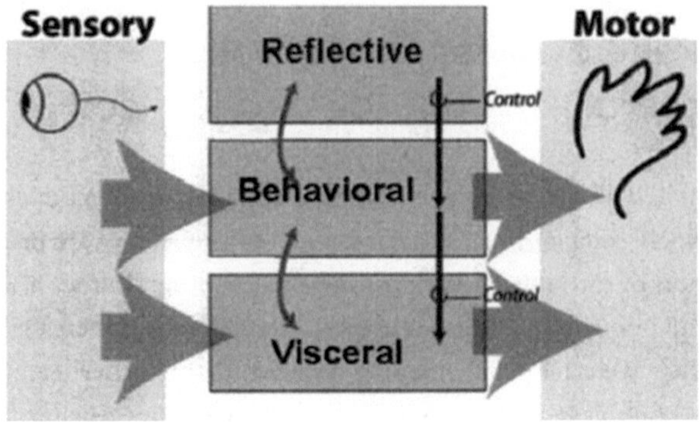

Fig. 2.7 The three levels of processing proposed by Norman: visceral, behavioural and reflective (2003, p. 22)

in 1994, which separated emotional processing into three phases: emotion, feeling and consciousness (see Fig. 2.8). Norman proposed that "visceral and behavioral levels are subconscious and the home of basic emotions. The reflective level is where conscious thought and decision-making reside, as well as the highest level of emotions".

The tripartite levels of processing by Norman may still be supported by the latest studies in the field of psychology. Daniel Kahneman, responsible for introducing a new set of concepts into psychology as well as in economics (he won the Nobel Prize in Economics, in 2002, after having created a whole new field of studies, Behavioural Economics), presented a new model to understand cognition, which differentiates the way we think into fast and slow (Kahneman, 2011). In the fast step, we have automatic responses, corresponding to Norman's viscerality; in the slow step, we find reflected and pondered responses, or Norman's reflexive component. Beyond this model, Kahneman has over the years demonstrated the existence of cognitive biases—human biased modes of evaluating reality, which defines the main studies of Behavioural Economics—dedicated to explaining how we make decisions and choices in a non-rationalizable mode—in essence, Norman's behavioural component.

2.1.3.2 Building the Framework

From a pragmatic perspective, Verplank is aligned with Hassenzahl, and Norman, Damasio and Kahneman are also aligned, all together building a ballast of knowledge capable of supporting the type of relation we expect to build between subjects and artefacts in the design of interactive media artefacts. We will then need to define in depth the elements of the experience responsible for producing engagement.

The framework discussion begins with the subjects, the element for which we have specific empirical data on their interactive playing motivations, collected by the large studies made by Yee which started with 3,000 players (2007), then 140,000 (2015) and have now reached more than 400,000 (2019). All that data, categorized by Yee as six main player motivations—"achievement", "immersion", "social", "mastery", "creativity", "action"—will permit us to start devising the first approaches

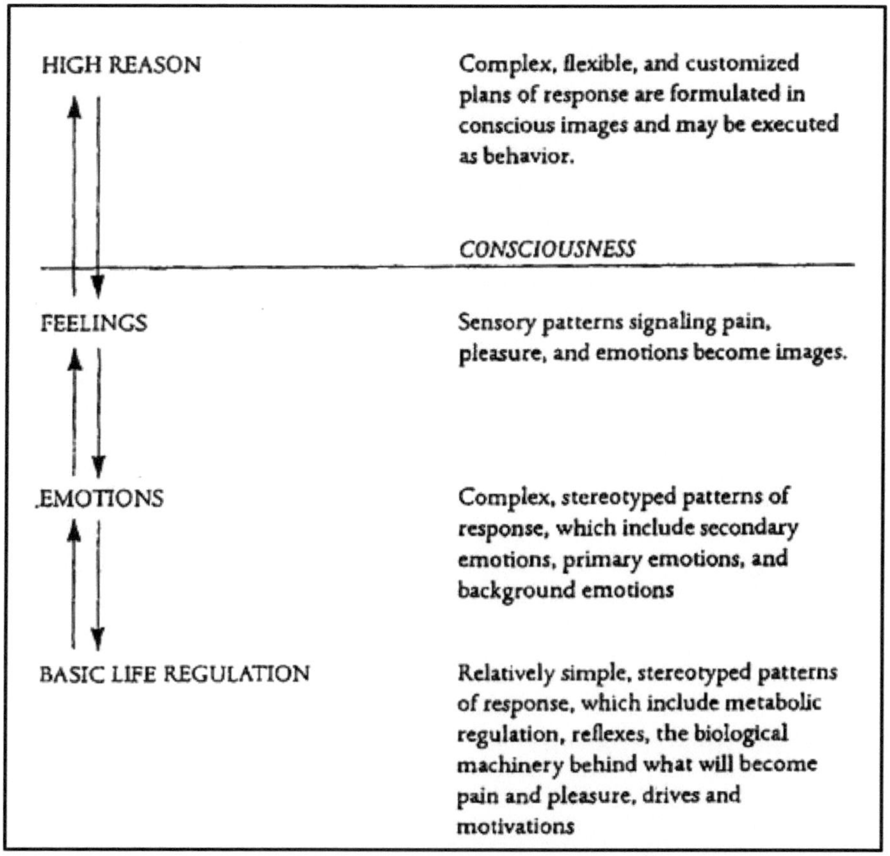

Fig. 2.8 The emotion effect on life regulation by Damasio (1999, p. 55), with emotions, feelings and consciousness

to the engagement streams. To help in the categorization we'll also bring into the discussion other interaction profiles, such as the ones used by Resnick (2017) to describe Scratch creators—"planners" and "tinkerers"—or the ones used by Gardener to distinguish the child's expressive drawing (1980, p. 90)—"patterners" and "dramatists"—or from the domain of video games, the Bartle taxonomy of gamers, which divides gamers into "achievers, explorers, killers and socializers" (Bartle, 1996). This profiling is the centre of the discussion of Chap. 3.

Following the context elements, we must be aware that we cannot define a priori the space–time in which artefacts will be used, because we have obtained the context from the perspective of the user's volition, following Hassenzahl's approach of understanding action through needs and motives (2010, p. 45). What motives then drive the subjects to interact, what are their needs to really go and interact with a reality made of artefacts? The most widely and accepted motivation theory is the "self-determination theory" by Deci and Ryan (1985), which divides intrinsic motivation into three levels—autonomy, competence and relatedness. Volition is also very dependent on the cognitive processes of curiosity, which can be mainly defined as a need to "fill in information gaps" (Loewenstein, 1994), an information gap that can arise from contexts of "uncertainty" (Litman, 2005), "novelty" (Litman & Spielberger, 2003) or "interpersonal information" (Litman & Pezzo, 2005, 2007). Each one of these contexts will be fully developed in Chap. 4.

Finally, for the artefacts, we considered media representation following a previous study we made on the multimodality of video games (Zagalo, 2019), in which we ended up defining the expressive domains favoured by each medium, using the modes of representation defined by Bruner (1966)—"symbolic", "enactive" and "iconic"—for the analysis of the learned, functional and natural forms. The forms were then approached though aesthetic theory (Eisner) and then deconstructed in their relationship with interactivity making use of game design (Salen & Zimmerman, 2003; Schell, 2008), play theory (Brown, 2009; Sutton-Smith, 2005) and cognitive film theory (Bordwell & Carroll, 1996; Smith, 2003; Tan, 2008). The media representation is fully detailed in Chap. 5.

Our framework is defined around a division of subjects' profiles that corresponds directly with specific contexts and specific types of media representations, as we'll see in the next chapters. Before that, let's see how the modelling of our engagement framework relates to experience.

2.1.4 The Model Approach

From the theoretical argumentation, which was based on proposals from communication and cybernetics (Watzlawick, McLuhan, Dubberly, Pangaro), design (Norman, Hassenzahl, Verplank, Resnick), psychology (Bruner, Kahneman, Csikzentmilhalyi, Deci, Ryan, Litman), game research (Yee, Zimmerman and Salen) and film studies (Tan and Bordwell), we reached a set of concepts on experience aligned with current interaction design triadic proposals but aimed specifically at engagement. For that, we propose a triadic approach to engagement design as a direct answer to the triadic experience—context, subjects and artefacts—and triadic interaction—know, do and feel—made of three non-hierarchical streams (see Fig. 2.9).

The streams will be summed up and characterized in Chap. 6 after the presentation of their internal components in Chaps. 3, 4 and 5, but just to present a quick overview of the modelling we'll produce, we used the lives of three of the greatest minds of our history: Descartes, Da Vinci and Shakespeare. Descartes dedicated most of his life to searching for answers in patterns and abstractions that could help him solving the rational puzzle of being alive, for which he achieved the response "Cogito ergo sum" (Descartes, 1637). During his interrogation of variables, he developed a method to guide him in the problem-solving process, which became known as "cartesian doubt": he felt the need to "know". Da Vinci didn't like books everything for him needed to be tested and experimented. He was an avid explorer of the world, conducting empirical studies into painting, sculpture, geometry, engineering and

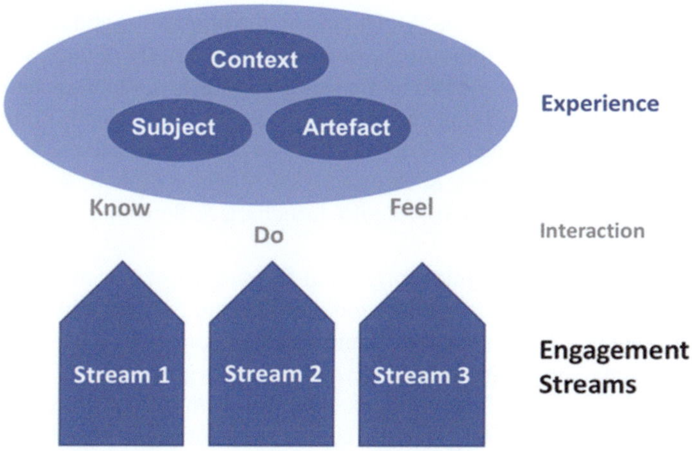

Fig. 2.9 Engagement streams serving the design of the interactive experiences

botany, as well in many other fields. To understand reality, Leonardo preferred the enactive approach. He dissected dozens of bodies and even opened a pig while its heart was still beating to see how the blood was being pumped (Isaacson, 2017) and to understand the internal functioning of a heart. Da Vinci used the world as his playground, following no playbook, using his full free will and autonomy to push the boundaries of existing knowledge, following his thirst "to do". Shakespeare invested all his life in dramatizing lives, in trying to understand how people act and react, putting them inside virtual dramas to test their emotions, motives and competences. We can see this approach working through the words of Hamlet "We know what we are but know not what we may be" (Shakespeare, 1600). However, Shakespeare knew he could only attain knowledge through social affinity: all his work, all his ideas, were performed live, opening his knowledge to society to learn from the feedback they would provide. In the end, he contributed highly to innovating language, drama and narrative (Hardy, 1997), which he learned by "feeling". All these three icons of our history lived all their lives doing these same activities, day after day. They were so engaged in experiencing it that nothing else would matter; their particular process of interacting with the world counted even more than the goal of their creations. Their mind models affected their interests and defined completely their engagement modes.

The model proposed here intends then to function as conceptual streams to help designers respond to the needs of the interaction. Nevertheless, models are not rules, not formulas, "Models are ideas about the world—how it might be organized and how it might work" (Dubberly, 2009, p. 54). And so, building models means building knowledge about what is still unknown, creating simulated hypotheses of the functioning of the problems we want to solve. We model to understand the world, creating hypotheses, not proofs, about how to grasp reality, the models "are not formed by deduction or induction but by abduction—inferring the most likely story to explain the evidence" (Dubberly, 2009, p. 54). Of course, the pragmatist abduction approach can't be done through mere literature review and some empirical data, so to help in diagnosis and interpretation we brought a set of approaches, methods and concepts developed over time through transdisciplinary research (Figueiredo, Pinto, Branco, Zagalo, & Coquet, 2013; Zagalo, 2009, 2017b; Zagalo & Gonçalves, 2013; Zagalo & Torres, 2008; Zagalo, Barker, & Branco, 2004; Zagalo, Branco, & Barker, 2003; Zagalo, Carvalho, & Araújo, 2016; Zagalo, Louchart, & Soto-Sanfiel, 2010; Zagalo et al., 2005).

Beyond the models, we cannot forget that the subject of our modelling is only in part about design. The messages (fictional or not) are created subjectively by the creators following their own intentions and world experiences. Therefore, it is not the goal of this model to become normative, but only to guide the design process, to help understand the realm of the complex experiences made possible by interactive media, presenting streams of engagement as structures for organizing the experiences and pushing engagement towards optimal directions.

References

Albert, W., Tullis, T., & Albert, W. (2008). *Measuring the user experience*. https://doi.org/10.1016/B978-0-12-373558-4.X0001-5.

Alexander, L. (2013). Playing outside. In *The new inquiry*. Retrieved from https://thenewinquiry.com/playing-outside/.

Anderson, S. P. (2011). *Seductive interaction design: Creating playful, fun, and effective user experiences (Google eBook)*. Retrieved from http://books.google.com/books?id=0nu3ZJDZOvkC&pgis=1.

Antonetti, J. V., & Garver, J. R. (2015). *17,000 classroom visits can't be wrong: Strategies that engage students, promote active learning, and boost achievement*. Alexandria: ASCD.

Bakhtin, M. (1979). *Estética da Criação Verbal*. São Paulo: Martins Fontes.

Bartle, R. (1996). Hearts, clubs, diamonds, spades: Players who suit MUDs. *Journal of MUD Research, 1*(1), 19.

Bateson, G. (1972). Steps to an ecology of mind: Collected essays in anthropology, psychiatry, evolution, and epistemology. In *Chandler Publications for health sciences*. Chicago: University of Chicago Press.

Bernhaupt, R. (2009). Evaluating user experience in games: Concepts and methods. In *Human-computer interaction series*. https://doi.org/10.1007/978-1-84996-272-8.

Blythe, M. A., Overbeeke, K., Monk, A. F., & Wright, P. C. (2003). *Funology. From usability to enjoyment*. https://doi.org/10.1007/1-4020-2967-5.

Blythe, M., & Monk, A. (2018). *Funology 2*. https://doi.org/10.1007/978-3-319-68213-6.

Bordwell, D., & Carroll, N. (1996). *Post-theory: Reconstructing film studies*. Wisconsin: University of Wisconsin Press.

Brodie, R. J., Hollebeek, L. D., Jurić, B., & Ilić, A. (2011). Customer engagement: Conceptual domain, fundamental propositions, and implications for research. *Journal of Service Research*. https://doi.org/10.1177/1094670511411703.

Brown, S. L. (2009). *Play: How it shapes the brain, opens the imagination, and invigorates the soul*. New York: Avery–Penguin Group.

Bruner, J. (1966). *Toward a theory of instruction*. Cambridge, MA: Harvard University Press.

Butin, D. W., & Seider, S. (2012). *The engaged campus*. https://doi.org/10.1057/9781137113283.

Damasio, A. (1999). *The feeling of what happens: Body and emotion in the making of consciousness*. San Diego: Harcourt.

Dewey, J. (1934). *Art as experience*. NY: Perigee Books.

Deci, E. L., & Ryan, R. M. (1985). *Intrinsic motivation and self-determination in human behavior*. New York: Plenum

Descartes, R. (1637). *A Discourse on the method. (Ian Maclean, Trans.)*. New York: Oxford University Press (2008)

Dubberly, H. (2009). Models of models. *Interactions, 16*(3), 54. https://doi.org/10.1145/1516016.1516029.

Dubberly, H., & Pangaro, P. (2015). Cybernetics and design: Conversations for action. *Cybernetics & Human Knowing*.

Duffer, M., & Duffer, R. (2016). *Stranger things*. Retrieved from https://en.wikipedia.org/wiki/Stranger_Things.

Figueiredo, A. C., Pinto, A. L., Branco, P., Zagalo, N. & Coquet, E. (2013). Bridging book: A not-so-electronic children's picturebook. In *ACM International Conference Proceeding Series*. https://doi.org/10.1145/2485760.2485867.

Fullerton, T. (2014). *Game design workshop*. Natick, MA: AK Peters/CRC Press.

Gardner, H. (1980). *Artful scribbles: The significance of children's drawings*. New York: Basic Books.

Hardy, B. (1997). *Shakespeare's storytellers: Dramatic narration*. London: Peter Owen Publishers.

Harmeling, C. M., Moffett, J. W., Arnold, M. J., & Carlson, B. D. (2017). Toward a theory of customer engagement marketing. *Journal of the Academy of Marketing Science*. https://doi.org/10.1007/s11747-016-0509-2.

Harrigan, P., Evers, U., Miles, M., & Daly, T. (2017). Customer engagement with tourism social media brands. *Tourism Management*. https://doi.org/10.1016/j.tourman.2016.09.015.

Hartson, R., & Pyla, P. S. (2012). *The UX book: Process and guidelines for ensuring a quality user experience*. https://doi.org/10.1016/C2010-0-66326-7.

Harvey, A. & Samyn, M. (2006). *Realtime art manifesto*. Retrieved from Gaming realities: The challenge of digital culture website: http://www.tale-of-tales.com/tales/RAM.html%0A.

Hassenzahl, M. (2010). Experience design: Technology for all the right reasons. In *Synthesis lectures on human-centered informatics*. https://doi.org/10.2200/S00261ED1V01Y201003HCI008.

Hodent, C. (2017). *The gamer's brain: How neuroscience and UX can impact video game design*. Boca Raton: CRC Press.

Hollebeek, L. D., Glynn, M. S., & Brodie, R. J. (2014). Consumer brand engagement in social media: Conceptualization, scale development and validation. *Journal of Interactive Marketing*. https://doi.org/10.1016/j.intmar.2013.12.002.

Isaacson, W. (2017). *Leonardo da Vinci*. New York: Simon & Schuster.

Kahneman, D. (2011). *Thinking, fast and slow*. New York: Farrar, Straus and Giroux.

Kaptelinin, V., & Nardi, B. A. (2006). *Acting with technology: Activity theory and interaction design*. Cambridge, MA: MIT Press.

Keller, P. (1999). *Husserl and Heidegger on human experience*. Cambridge University Press.

Kim, J., & Moon, J. Y. (1998). Designing towards emotional usability in customer interfaces—Trustworthiness of cyber-banking system interfaces. *Interacting with Computers, 10*(1), 1–29. https://doi.org/10.1016/S0953-5438(97)00037-4.

Koster, R. (2004). *A theory of fun for game design*. Sebastopol: Paraglyph Press.

Lehrer, J. (2007). *Proust was a neuroscientist*. New York: Houghton Mifflin Harcourt.

Litman, J. A. (2005). Curiosity and the pleasures of learning: Wanting and liking new information. *Cognition and Emotion*. https://doi.org/10.1080/02699930541000101.

Litman, J. A., & Pezzo, M. V. (2005). Individual differences in attitudes towards gossip. *Personality and Individual Differences*. https://doi.org/10.1016/j.paid.2004.09.003.

Litman, J. A., & Pezzo, M. V. (2007). Dimensionality of interpersonal curiosity. *Personality and Individual Differences*. https://doi.org/10.1016/j.paid.2007.04.021.

Litman, J. A., & Spielberger, C. D. (2003). Measuring epistemic curiosity and its diversive and specific components. *Journal of Personality Assessment*. https://doi.org/10.1207/S15327752JPA8001_16.

Loewenstein. (1994). The psychology of curiosity: A review and reinterpretation. *Psychological Bulletin, 1*(116), 75–98. https://doi.org/10.1037/0033-2909.116.1.75.

Logan, R. J. R. (1994). Behavioral and emotional usability: Thomson consumer electronics. In M. Wiklund (Ed.), *Usability in practice*. Cambridge, MA: Academic Press.

Maslow, A. H. (1943). A theory of human motivation. *Psychological Review, 50*(4), 370–396. https://doi.org/10.1037/h0054346.

Maturana, H., & Varela, F. (1984). *The tree of knowledge: The biological roots of human understanding*. Boulder, US: Shambhala.

McCarthy, J., & Wright, P. (2004). *Technology as experience*. Cambridge, MA: MIT Press.

Moggridge, B. (2006). *Designing interactions*. Cambridge, MA: MIT Press.

Moore, D. T. (2013). *Engaged learning in the academy*. https://doi.org/10.1057/9781137025197.

Morris, C. (1946). *Signs, language and behavior*. New York: Prentice-Hall.

Nielsen, J. (1994). Heuristic evaluation. In *Usability inspection methods*. https://doi.org/10.1089/tmj.2010.0114.

Nodder, C. (2013). *Evil by design: Interaction design to lead us into temptation*. New York: Wiley.

Norman, D. A. (2003). Emotional design—Why we love (or hate) everyday things. In *Basic books*. https://doi.org/10.1111/j.1537-4726.2004.133_10.x.

Overbeeke, K., Djajadiningrat, J. P., Hummels, C. C. M., & Wensveen, S. (2002). Beauty in usability: Forget about ease of use! In W. Green & P. Jordan (Eds.), *Pleasure with products: Beyond usability* (pp. 9–18). Taylor & Francis.

Pangaro, P. (2009). Designing for conversation. In *Cybernetics, conversation and applications for design*. Cambridge, MA: IDEO.

Pangaro, P. (2012). *What is cybernetics?*. US: Vimeo.

Peirce, C. S. (1931). The collected papers: Vol. 2: Elements of logic. In *Search*. https://doi.org/10.1038/135131a0.

Peirce, C. S. (1991). *Peirce on signs: Writings on semiotic*. Chapel Hill: University of North Carolina Press.

Portnow, J. & Floyd, D. (2012). *Beyond fun—Why games need to be more than fun*. Extra Credits.

Proust, M. (1913). *In search of lost time. Volume one: Swann's way* (C. K. S. Moncrieff & T. Kilmartin, Trans.). New York: The Modern Library.

Ren, X., Silpasuwanchai, C., & Cahill, J. (2019). Human-engaged computing: The future of human-computer interaction. *CCF Transactions on Pervasive Computing and Interaction*. https://doi.org/10.1007/s42486-019-00007-0.

Resnick, M. (2017). *Lifelong kindergarten. Cultivating creativity through projects, passion, peers, and play*. Cambridge, MA: MIT Press.

Rogers, Y. (2006). *Moving on from Weiser's vision of calm computing: Engaging UbiComp experiences*. https://doi.org/10.1007/11853565_24.

Romero, B., & Schreiber, I. (2008). *Challenges for game designers*. Newton: Charles River Media.

Rothmann, S. (2016). Employee engagement. In *The Wiley Blackwell handbook of the psychology of positivity and strengths-based approaches at work*. https://doi.org/10.1002/9781118977620.ch18.

Ruberg, B. (2015). No fun: The queer potential of video games that annoy, anger, disappoint, sadden, and hurt. *QED: A Journal in GLBTQ Worldmaking, 2*(2), 108.124.

Russon, J. (2010). *Human experience: Philosophy, neurosis, and the elements of everyday life*. New York: SUNY Press.

Saks, A. M. (2019). Antecedents and consequences of employee engagement revisited. *Journal of Organizational Effectiveness*. https://doi.org/10.1108/JOEPP-06-2018-0034.

Salen, K., & Zimmerman, E. (2003). *Rules of play: Game design fundamentals*. Cambridge, MA: MIT Press.

Sauro, J., & Lewis, J. R. (2012). Quantifying the user experience. In *Quantifying the user experience*. https://doi.org/10.1016/C2010-0-65192-3.
Saussure, F. (1915). *Cours de Linguistique Générale*. Paris: Payot.
Schell, J. (2008). *The art of game design: A book of lenses*. Morgan Kaufmann.
Seijts, B. G. H., & Crim, D. (2006). What engages employees the most or, the ten C's of employee engagement. *Ivey Business Journal*. https://doi.org/10.1306/D42695F3-2B26-11D7-8648000102C1865D.
Shakespeare, W. (1600). *Hamlet*. London: Cambridge University Press.
Shannon, C. (1948). A mathematical theory of communication. *The Bell System Technical Journal, 25,* 379–423. https://doi.org/10.1002/j.1538-7305.1948.tb01338.x.
Shedroff, N. (2001). *Experience design*. California: Waite Group Press.
Sheldon, K. M., Elliot, A. J., Kim, Y., & Kasser, T. (2001). What is satisfying about satisfying events? Testing 10 candidate psychological needs. *Journal of Personality and Social Psychology, 80*(2), 325–339. https://doi.org/10.1037/0022-3514.80.2.325.
Smith, G. M. (2003). *Film structure and the emotion system*. https://doi.org/10.1017/CBO9780511497759.
Steiner, R. (1996). *The foundations of human experience*. Herndon, VA: SteinerBooks.
Sutton-Smith, B. (2005). Play and ambiguity. In *The game design reader: A rules of play anthology*.
Tan, E. S.-H. (2008). Entertainment is emotion: The functional architecture of the entertainment experience. *Media Psychology, 11*(1), 28–51. https://doi.org/10.1080/15213260701853161.
Tomasello, M. (2008). *Origins of human communication*. Cambridge, MA: MIT Press.
Varela, F. J., Rosch, E. & Thompson, E. (1991). *The embodied mind. Cognitive science and human experience*. Cambridge, MA.
Verplank, B. (2000). *Interaction design*. Palo Alto.
Voorveld, H. A. M., van Noort, G., Muntinga, D. G., & Bronner, F. (2018). Engagement with social media and social media advertising: The differentiating role of platform type. *Journal of Advertising*. https://doi.org/10.1080/00913367.2017.1405754.
Watzlawick, P., Bavelas, J. B. & Jackson, D. D. (1967). *Pragmatics of human communication: A study of interactional patterns, pathologies, and paradoxes*. https://doi.org/10.2307/2798146.
Wiener, N. (1948). *Cybernetics: Or the control and communication in the animal and the machine*. Cambridge, MA: MIT Press.
Winograd, T. (1997). From computing machinery to interaction design. In *Beyond calculation the next fifty years of computing*.
Wolton, D. (2009). *Informer n'est pas Communiquer*. Paris: CNRS Éditions.
Yee, N. (2007). Motivations for play in online games. *CyberPsychology & Behavior*. https://doi.org/10.1089/cpb.2006.9.772.
Yee, N. (2015). Gaming motivations group into 3 high-level clusters. Retrieved April 12, 2019, from Quantic Foundry website: https://quanticfoundry.com/2015/12/21/map-of-gaming-motivations/.
Yee, N. (2019). *A deep dive into the 12 motivations: Findings from 400,000+ gamers*. Retrieved from https://quanticfoundry.com/2019/04/11/gdc2019/.
Zagalo, N. (2009). *Emoções Interactivas, do Cinema para os Videojogos* (*Interactive emotions, from film to videogames*). Retrieved from http://repositorium.sdum.uminho.pt/handle/1822/27674?locale=en.
Zagalo, N. (2017a). Narrative design, the case of "Horizon Zero Dawn." Retrieved from SlideShare website: https://www.slideshare.net/nzagalo/narrative-design-the-case-of-horizon-zero-dawn.
Zagalo, N. (2017b). Narrative design of sadness in heavy rain. *Journal of Science and Technology of the Arts, 9*(2 Special Issue). https://doi.org/10.7559/citarj.v9i2.246.
Zagalo, N. (2019). Multimodality and expressivity in videogames. *Observatorio (OBS*), 13*(86–101). https://doi.org/10.15847/obsOBS13120191411.
Zagalo, N., Barker, A. & Branco, V. (2004). Story reaction structures to emotion detection. In B. Barry & K. Brooks (Eds.), *Proceedings of the 1st ACM workshop on story representation, mechanism and context—SRMC '04* (p. 33). https://doi.org/10.1145/1026633.1026641.

Zagalo, N., Branco, V. & Barker, A. (2003). From the necessity of film closure to inherent VR wideness. In G. S. P. T. Olivier Balet (Ed.), *International conference on virtual storytelling 2003* (pp. 74–77). Retrieved from http://dblp.uni-trier.de/db/conf/storytelling/storytelling2003.html#ZagaloBB03.

Zagalo, N., Carvalho, A. A., & Araújo, I. (2016). Elementos do design de videojogos que fomentam o interesse dos jogadores. *Revista ESC—Educação, Sociedade & Culturas, 48,* 169–190.

Zagalo, N., & Gonçalves, A. (2013). Social interaction design in MMOs. In *Multiplayer: The social aspects of digital gaming*. https://doi.org/10.4324/9780203627488.

Zagalo, N., Louchart, S. & Soto-Sanfiel, M. T. (2010). Users and evaluation of interactive storytelling. In R. Aylett, M. Y. Lim, S. Louchart, P. Petta, & M. Riedl (Eds.), *ICIDS 2010* (pp. 287–288). https://doi.org/10.1007/978-3-642-16638-9.

Zagalo, N., & Torres, A. (2008). Character emotion experience in virtual environments. *The Visual Computer, 24*(11), 981–986. https://doi.org/10.1007/s00371-008-0272-6.

Zagalo, N., Torres, A. & Branco, V. (2005). Emotional spectrum developed by virtual storytelling. In G. Subsol (Ed.), *Virtual storytelling 2005* (pp. 105–114). https://doi.org/10.1007/11590361.

Chapter 3
Profiles of Engagement

Abstract In this chapter, we discuss the different types of personalities, their mental models and their motivations, in order to find universal users for our engagement design model. Empirical data from video game motivations is interpreted and discussed from different angles using diverse psychological theories. All is then confronted with real personas (historical figures) to collect more evidence and create an understanding as robust as possible of the different mindsets.

Creative content producers have always been keen to try to define their target audiences. From movies to music, from theatre to video games, they have all contributed in one way or another to trying to understand who the people are who buy, who consume, like and dislike artefacts and their variants. However, of all them, the video game industry is probably the one that has most devoted itself to understanding its users, not least because of the demands that interactivity places on the design of experiences. Also because it is the most recent and has an audience that uses the Internet as part of the experience, it has taken advantage of the medium to carry out the most diverse studies. Noteworthy is the work of Nick Yee, already praised by Nielsen (2016), that recently aggregated data from more than 400,000 players of video games (Yee, 2019).

For the purpose of this chapter, we are interested not only in understanding the ways in which player profiles have been realized, namely, in their relationship with interactive media, but especially in understanding the relationship of these profiles with the way they act, interact, seek information or understand the reality. At bottom, it is important to understand which mental models define the different types of interactors with interactive media, and **if these profiles are generalizable and in turn relatable to contexts and artefacts**.

3.1 Personality and Motivations

To answer the question, let's start with the empirical data from the video game industry (Yee, 2007, 2015b, 2019), from which we can extract some research categories. However, we should not forget the preponderance of the gaming component, which

N. Zagalo, *Engagement Design*, Human–Computer Interaction Series,
https://doi.org/10.1007/978-3-030-37085-5_3

can eventually contaminate other relevant variables of the overall interactive media domain. To accomplish this variable control, we will then match the game data with models already existing in the fields of personality (McCrae & John, 1992) and vocation (Holland, 1997), as well as some of the profile models and their motivations identified in previous studies on human interaction (Baron-Cohen, 2003; Caillois, 1958; Gardner, 1980; Resnick, 2017; Strauss, 1962; Turkle & Papert, 1990).

3.1.1 Player Motivations

Let us begin the analysis of psychological profiles with the most relevant domain, today, of interactive media video games. This is not the only domain in interactive entertainment, but because of its growth over the last 30 years it has managed to open so many different genre fronts, with games ranging from simple fights and races to interactive stories and simulators of various types, leaving virtually no known form of media interactivity out, which makes it the quintessential medium for our study.

The first study on player profiles was presented by Richard Bartle in 1996, at the time exclusively focused on MMO games, but with enough influence to be one of the most cited and respected papers over the years (Salen & Zimmerman, 2003). In it, Bartle proposes four major types of players: Killers ("to gain—a big reputation"), Achievers ("to succeed in the virtual world—to reach the highest level"), Explorers ("to find things out about the virtual world and how it works") and Socializers ("like talking, being part of a group, and helping others") (Bartle, 2009) (see Fig. 3.1).

Bartle's model was informally introduced, with little to no empirical evidence, and over time became challenged because of problems like the axial diagram promoting the exclusivity of each category or of overlapping, such as between "killers" and "achievers" (Yee, 2007). Throughout the last decade, many studies on game profiles have been promoted (Bateman, Lowenhaupt, & Nacke, 2011; Lazzaro, 2008;

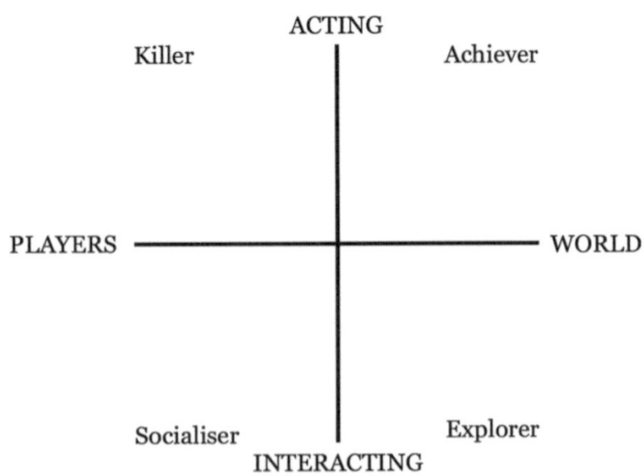

Fig. 3.1 The "Player Interest Graph" by Bartle (2009)

Nacke, Bateman, & Mandryk, 2014; Zammitto, 2010), but none as intensive and extensive as those carried by Yee, who started surveying and profiling gamers playing "EverQuest" in 2001 and in 2019 presented his latest study, made with more than 400,000 players from all over the world (Yee, 2019).

Yee started from Bartle's work, but not only did he expand it, he also built a full methodology to extract data and perform validation of parameters and categories through online questionnaires. Starting first with only three main categories—"achievement, immersion and social" (Yee, 2007)—he later expanded to six categories—achievement, mastery, creativity, immersion, social and action, each made of two motivational subcomponents (see Fig. 3.2). Beyond defining each subcomponent, in his last report, presented at GDC 2019, Yee proposed three big clusters combining the six categories. The first one, "action–social" stands for "immediacy and adrenaline (…) whether by the game itself or by interacting with other players"; then "mastery achievement", which defines "cool-headed, long-term gaming (…) seeks out gradual and cumulative mechanics"; and the third one, "immersion-creativity", defined by "play in the broadest sense of the word (…) seeks out expansive and expressive play styles (…) curious (…) testing the boundaries" (Yee, 2019).

Although we follow the six categories presented by Yee, we have doubts about the clusters presented in his latest talk. Yee has even felt the need to defend one of them, the "social–action" cluster (Yee, 2016a), stating that the social–action cluster has not been presented in any other study, albeit the categories appear, for example, in the Bartle model, but at opposite poles. Also, Yee defends this cluster as being "unintuitive", believing it to be well supported by the personality of "extraversion" (a personality trait defined in the Five-Factor Model see next section). However, we don't need much to see that something is wrong, principally if you put together highly opposed subcomponents as "community" and "destruction". We've dug a bit more into the research and found that Yee was also putting "competition" together with "community", so then looked into the research questions and found out why. For community, questions were about liking "being on a team, chatting, interacting

Fig. 3.2 The latest version of the motivation categories in the Diagram "Gamer Motivation" by Yee (2019)

with others"; and for competition they were about "duels, matches, being high on rankings", which explains the conclusion by Yee: "if Competition were the opposite of Community, team sports wouldn't make sense" (Yee, 2017). The problem is that being on a team is not, per se, a strong factor for socialization. Teams are created to achieve something, to compete, not to understand each other better or to create common or compassionate grounds. The problem with this mischaracterization is that the Yee model has no representation for the inner dimensions of the social aspects, which also explains why there is no relation with the immersion category, mainly the empathetic subcomponents. To clarify all this, we will now look into the dimensions of the most used psychological model of personality, the Five-Factor Model (McCrae & John, 1992).

3.1.2 Psychological Traits

To draw a psychological profile, we need to begin by defining the personalities of these profiles, knowing that personality is the term used by psychology to frame a set of behavioural, cognitive and emotional traits that serve to explain "psychological differences between individuals, that is, the relatively stable psychological attributes that allow us uniquely to characterize individuals and to distinguish them from each other" (Reisenzein & Weber, 2009, p. 54). To identify these differences, several models of subject analysis were created, among which the most used and referenced is undoubtedly the Five-Factor Model (FFM) or Big Five, consisting of five basic dimensions: "openness to experience", "conscientiousness", "extraversion", "agreeableness" and "neuroticism" (OCEAN) (McCrae & John, 1992). The FFM is not intended to be a definer of "universal characteristics" but rather a survey of "common characteristics of individual differences" (McCrae & John, 1992). Thus, the characterization of behaviours cannot be seen as limited to these dimensions, nor as single characterization dimensions of individuals, but rather as identifying the behavioural tendencies of individuals that can then be used to screen and support the identification of personal trends for academic and professional purposes (Fruyt & Mervielde, 1999). The robustness of the FFM should also be noted: various longitudinal studies have shown that the five individual differences are quite stable (Costa Jr. & McCrae, 1992; Roberts & DelVecchio, 2000), although data have been found to account for slight variation over time, such as the decline of neuroticism and extraversion and the rise of agreeableness and conscientiousness, and in the case of openness an increase until 20 years of age and then a decline (McCrae, 2009). In addition, its universality is supported by studies carried out all over the planet. This is only possible because the dimensions do not have a purely cultural basis, and biological evidence has been found in the field of genetics across different cultures (Yamagata et al., 2006) and with twin studies (Riemann, Angleitner, & Strelau, 1997).

Beginning (see Fig. 3.3) with neuroticism, it identifies subjects with a "tendency to experience stress", suffering "negative chronic effects" such as "depression", "anxiety" and "hostility" (McCrae & John, 1992) and is usually associated with

Low	<<<< Traits >>>>	High
Conventional Routine	**Openness** (Imagination & Action)	Curious Inventive
Impulsive Careless	**Conscientiousness** (Competence & Goal-driven)	Hardworking Organized
Quiet Reserved	**Extroversion** (Sociability & Emotional)	Outgoing Adventurous
Critical Uncooperative	**Agreeableness** (Cooperative & Trustworthy)	Helpful Empathetic
Calm Secure	**Neuroticism** (Emotional unstable)	Anxious Unhappy

Fig. 3.3 The basic dimensions of the FFM, and the variability between maximum and minimum scores. Table based on (Costa, McCrae, & Kay, 1995; McCrae & John, 1992)

"personality disorders" (Widiger & Costa, 2002). Extraversion, on the other hand, tends to predispose people to be happier (DeNeve & Cooper, 1998), presenting "active", "assertive", "enthusiastic" and "energetic" traits, tendentially positive traits (McCrae & John, 1992). In the case of "agreeableness", it is a dimension that "tends to involve the more humane aspects of humanity—characteristics such as altruism, nurturance, caring, and emotional support" (McCrae & John, 1992). On the other hand, conscientiousness accounts for thorough, neat, well-organized, diligent and achievement-oriented individuals (McCrae & John, 1992). They say that "agreeableness" and "extraversion" are approximate, which is also supported by the "Interpersonal Circumplex" model (Wiggins, Trapnell, & Phillips, 1988), on the "friendly" trend side. On the other hand, "agreeableness" and "conscientiousness" are inversely related, accounting for the classical dimensions of character used to describe opposing individuals—"good" versus "evil", or "strong-willed" versus "weak-willed"—while at the same time both can be easily observed and validated by peers and friends. Finally, "openness" tends to move closer to "conscientiousness" in the field of ideas but presents a need for "variety of experience", "fantasies, feelings, sensations", presenting "imaginative, original, curious, and artistic" traits (McCrae & John, 1992).

Before we even relate FFM to Yee's model, and taking into account some criticisms of the situational and ephemeral potential of personality dimensions (Spokane, Luchetta, & Richwine, 2002), let us deepen our understanding of behaviours and mental models a little further, analysing vocational psychology and talent development.

3.1.3 Vocational Psychology and Talent

Vocational psychology works almost in parallel to personality psychology, seeking to find models capable of more directly associating individuals' psychology with specific mental predispositions to interact with the world. While we are mostly talking about entertainment or knowledge content for interactive media, it may seem strange to evoke more work-related studies here, but what we seek is the deepening of the mental models that enable human interaction. See the following points from the study "A psychological theory of work adjustment: an individual-differences model and its applications" by René V. Dawis and Lloyd H. Lofquist: "Work is conceptualized as an interaction between an individual and a work environment"; "The work environment requires that certain tasks be performed, and the individual brings skills to perform the tasks" (1984, pp. 9–10). If we replace work with entertainment or knowledge, we have exactly the same kind of relationship that we are discussing here with the same actors, even though the motivations involved are quite different, since work aims at financial rewards. On the other hand, vocational studies move towards finding a perfect match between the motivations of the subjects and the type of work; thus we believe that there is relevant and correlated subject matter with FFM, something that has already been studied (Fruyt & Mervielde, 1999; Wille, De Fruyt, & Feys, 2010).

In vocational psychology, one of the most referenced works is the research of Holland (1997) which presents a list of six types of people—Realistic, Investigative, Artistic, Social, Enterprising or Conventional (RIASEC). The description of each type gives us (MU Career Center, 2010) the realists as "People who have athletic ability, prefer to work with objects, machines, tools, plants or animals, or to be outdoors"; the investigators or thinkers as "People who like to observe, learn, investigate, analyze evaluate, or solve problems"; the "artistic" or "creators" as "People who have artistic, innovative or intuitional abilities and like to work in unstructured situations using their imagination and creativity"; the "social" or helpers as "People who like to work with people to enlighten, inform, help, train or cure them, or are skilled with words"; the "entrepreneurs" or influencers as "People who like to work with people, influencing, persuading, leading or managing for organizational goals or economic gain"; and the conventional or organizers as "People who like to work with data, have clerical or numerical ability, carry out tasks in detail or follow through on others' instructions". According to Holland, each of these profiles will look for homonymous environments in order to "let them exercise their skills and abilities, express their attitudes and values, and take on agreeable problems and roles" (Holland, 1997, p. 4), and may adapt more easily if remaining at adjacent levels and avoiding opposites (see Fig. 3.4).

Vocational issues have been widely questioned, and one of the major contributors to that has been Ericsson's research on "deliberate practice" (Ericsson, Krampe, & Tesch-Römer, 1993), which claims the ability to enable anyone to achieve high-level skills in any domain. Over the years, Ericsson has argued that "The only innate differences that turn out to be significant—and they matter primarily in sports—are height and body size" (Ericsson, Prietula, & Cokely, 2007, p. 116), which if true would shatter any relevance of RIASEC or even OCEAN. This view has been widely popularized and disseminated, notably through works such as *Outliers: The Story of Success* (Gladwell, 2008), *Talent is Overrated: What Really Separates World-Class Performers from Everybody Else* (Colvin, 2008), *Drive: The Surprising Truth About What Motivates Us* (Pink, 2008) or *The Talent Code: Greatness Isn't Born.*

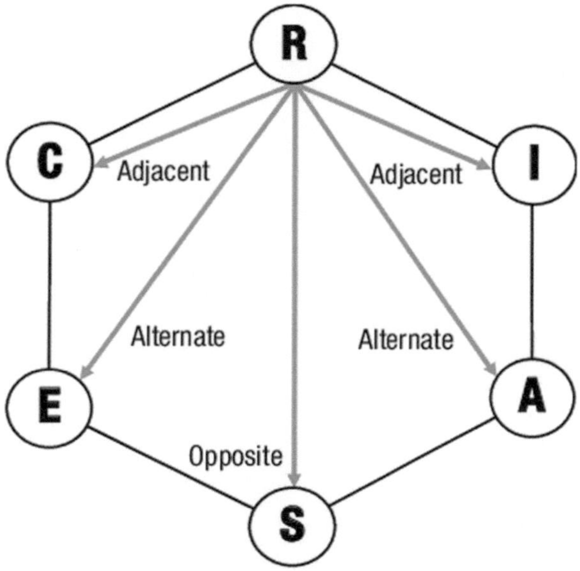

Fig. 3.4 The relationship between vocational profiles and vocational environments in the Holland Hexagon Model (1997) [diagram by (Nye, Su, Rounds, & Drasgow, 2012)]

It's Grown. Here's How (Coyle, 2009). All these works somehow try to defend the idea of the environment as primarily determinant, or of the individual above nature, fully disregarding the particulars of genetics (Plomin, DeFries, & McClearn, 1989). However, many studies presented in the meta-analysis by Hambrick et al. (2014) completely undermine the idea that practice is sufficient to achieve expertise and highlights the fact that "personality is an important part of the expert performance puzzle" (Hambrick et al., 2014).

3.1.4 Correlations

Going back to the FFM, we are interested in how it correlates with RIASEC, and that correlation has already been carried out by different studies (Armstrong & Anthoney, 2009; De Fruyt & Mervielde, 1997), suggesting a clear overlap with "openness" corresponding with the "artistic"; "conscientiousness" correlating with "conventional"; "extraversion" with "enterprising"; and "agreeableness" and "neuroticism" with "social". We can also bring together the correlations made by Yee (2016a) of his gamers' categories and the FFM, presenting the three models as in Table 3.1.

As can be seen from the table, there are several correlation problems, starting with the social component, related to empathy and friendship that is not represented in Yee's model. The relationship between games with the social component, friendship and help are not only cited in Bartle, but also in other studies (Zackariasson, Wåhlin, & Wilson, 2010) and are quite evident in a meta-study on player profiles (Hamari & Tuunanen, 2014), which from more than a dozen studies extracts the following player

Table 3.1 Correlation between FFM and RIASEC by (Armstrong & Anthoney, 2009; De Fruyt & Mervielde, 1997). On the FFM side, there is no correspondence with Neuroticism, and on the RIASEC side, there is no correspondence with Realist and Investigative. In the FFM's relationship with Yee's work (2016a, b), there is no relationship with Agreeableness or Neuroticism

Five-factor model	RIASEC Holland	Yee model
Conscientiousness (hardworking + organized)	**Conventional** (organizers + methodical)	**Mastery—Achievement** (challenge + completion)
Openness to experience (curious + inventive)	**Artistic** (creative + expressive)	**Immersion—Creativity** (fantasy + discovery)
Extraversion (outgoing + adventurous)	**Enterprising** (persuaders)	**Action—Social** (destruction + community)
Agreeableness (helpful + empathetic)	**Social** (helpers + friendly)	–
Neuroticism (anxiety + anger)	–	–
–	**Realist and investigative** (analytical + reserved)	–

profiles: "Achievement, Exploration, Sociability, Domination, and Immersion". The mischaracterization of Yee's "social–action" cluster also makes evident the mischaracterization of the "immersion-creativity" cluster, not only because it has no relation to the empathic component, but also because the domain of creativity represented by the components of Design and Discovery is unrelated with the components of Fantasy and Story, which is easily demonstrated by the player profile analysis of "Minecraft" (Yee, 2015a) (see Fig. 3.5), considered the quintessential creativity game.

Deepening the problem of "immersion-creativity" and analysing the map (Fig. 3.6) with the correlation between the two most relevant subcomponents "Story (elaborate narrative, interesting characters)" and "Discovery (explore, tinker, experiment)" as axes (Yee, 2016b), we can see the vast majority of elaborate storytelling games—such as *Uncharted*—are low on the "Discovery" scale (bottom of map). On the upside (top of map), we only have storytelling games with a strong component of abstract character control systems—such as *The Elder Scrolls*—that focus on "thoughtful, analytical gameplay" (Barton, 2019), which tend to distance players from the psychological components of the stories. On the other hand, when we look at the distribution of the game motivation components on the map (see Fig. 3.7) used by Yee to create the clusters (Yee, 2015b), we find that the "Discovery" component is completely removed from the components of "Story" and "Fantasy", which corroborates what we said above, lessening the relevance of the "immersion-creativity" cluster.

Nonetheless, the clusters created by Yee seem to us to be of little relevance, although we consider that the six broad categories presented continue to serve well the framing of the general motivations that various other game studies have also evidenced. By this, we do not mean that there are no potential clusters of interest, and this is what we will see next, by analysing different profiles and motivations

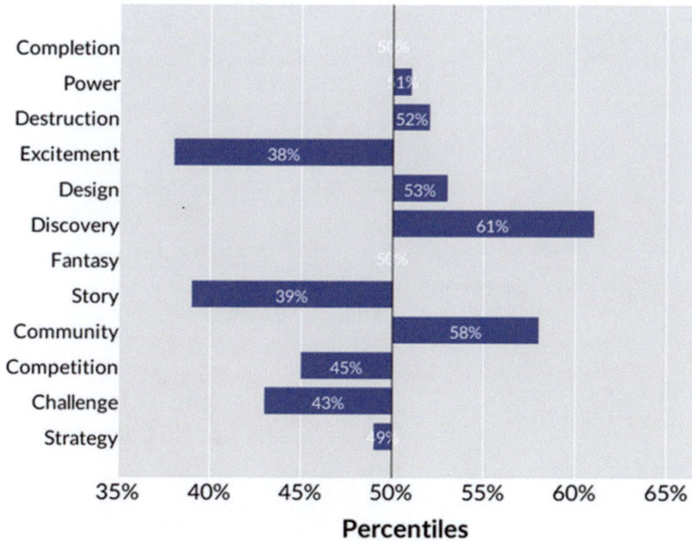

Fig. 3.5 Audience profile for *Minecraft* by Yee (2015a)

Fig. 3.6 Map of correlation between components story and discovery (Yee, 2016b)

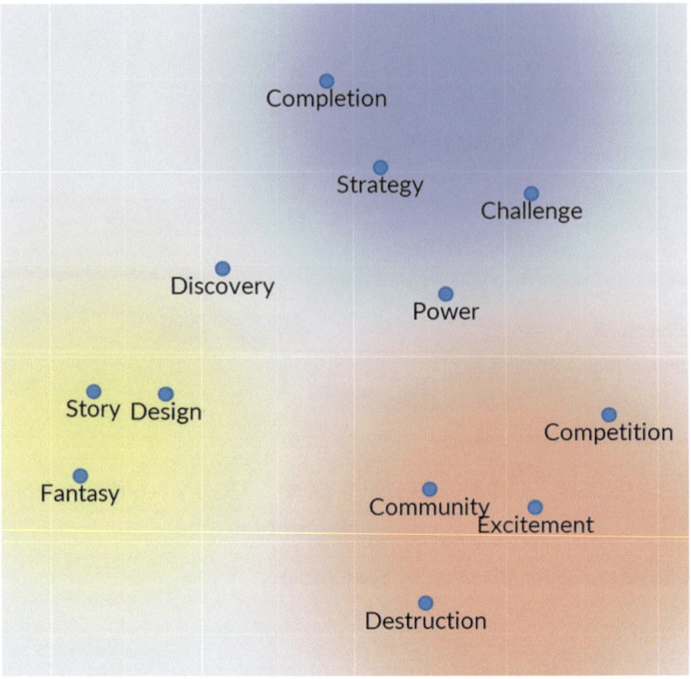

Fig. 3.7 Map of distribution of game motivation components (Yee, 2015b)

that have been found and discussed in other studies related to human interactive activities. The clustering problem is not exclusive to Yee's model: we have seen the same happening when using it to cast cluster configurations with FFM (Mueller & Tan, 2019). The results get more personal and less general, meaning it could serve well to analyse in more detail the personality of one individual, but it seems to help little when it comes to classifying groups.

Many other authors throughout the past few decades have developed categories to group people performing certain types of tasks not only in digital games, but also in traditional games (Caillois, 1958), in the ways they used tools (Strauss, 1962), the ways children draw (Gardner, 1980) and young adults coded apps or created stories (Resnick, 2017; Turkle & Papert, 1990) or just generally interacted with the world and others (Baron-Cohen, 2003). Some of these studies present only two types of people, others three. We looked into the definitions provided by each study, their labels and motives, and put them all together in three different columns in Table 3.2.

From the correlations made possible by the analysis in Table 3.2, it's easy to realize the existence of three great types of interactors: in the first column, those worried about patterns, structures and causation, who we can call **abstracters** because of their interest in defining the world through universal rules; in the centre, the **tinkerers**, moved by sensation and experimentation, willing to build, create and make; and on the right, those attracted to stories, socialization and feelings, who we can call **dramatists**. We now have enough information to define the profiles in our model. However,

Table 3.2 Categories used to qualify subject's profiles in different research studies on human interaction

Caillois (1958)	Agon (challenge, competition)	Ilinx (vertigo, visceral)	Mimicry (role-playing)
Strauss (1962)	Analytics (project, hierarchy)	Bricoleurs (trial-and-error, negotiable)	–
Gardner (1980)	Patterners (facts)	–	Dramatists (stories)
Turkle and Papert (1990)	Hard (logical)	–	Soft (relational)
Baron-Cohen (2003)	Systemizers (systems and maps)	–	Empathizers (relations and feelings)
Resnick (2017)	Planners (plan and programme)	Tinkerers (experiment and make)	–

prior to closing the discussion, we'll look into real examples of people who can demonstrate, as real cases, all these traits and behaviours as part of their mind models and how these approaches moved their existence to deliver their shared legacies.

3.2 Real Personas

To better understand and get to the base of the profiled personalities, we'll now look at real people, individuals known to us all because of the ways they interacted with the world and the ways they chose to leave their marks, analysing their behaviours, needs and motives. To help us, and to be able to do it in a manner accessible and comprehensible to all, the best approach is to look at successful people, if not for their personalities, at least for their legacies. For that, we give two short biographies for each profile. To widen our knowledge of types of people, we chose three from the Renaissance era, who have already served as brief eye-openers in the first chapter, and another three from the twentieth century.

3.2.1 Abstracters

René Descartes (1596–1650)

Descartes was one of the greatest geniuses of philosophy in history, comparable only, according to Russell (1945), to Aristotle. With his work *A Discourse on Method* (1637), he laid the foundations of what is now accepted as the scientific method, and it can be said that Descartes founded not only modern philosophy but also science, and laid the substratum for the emergence of the Enlightenment as well as the French and American revolutions. Descartes was shy and disliked social life. He was always well dressed but never married. He sought isolation in Paris, but not satisfied with the annoyance caused by his friends, would eventually enlist in the Dutch army, and because there was no war he could enjoy "two years of undisturbed meditation" (Russell, 1945). He was not a great reader but was someone who concentrated intensely to produce thought, theorizing about ideas and concepts.

> The first was never to accept anything for true which I did not clearly know to be such; that is to say, carefully to avoid precipitancy and prejudice, and to comprise nothing more in my judgment than what was presented to my mind so clearly and distinctly as to exclude all ground of doubt. (Descartes, 1637)

Descartes was strongly driven by the idea of understanding why we exist. As one of the founders of Rationalism, he lived in a dilemma: if everything has to have a reason for existing, if everything has a cause and a meaning, then everything cannot exist only in the void. Something else must exist beyond everything we see that can explain reality: a God, or some other force. From so much wondering he created what we now call "Cartesian doubt", which would lead him to the abstraction rule: "I think, therefore I am".

> The intellectual abstraction consists in my turning my thought away from one part of the contents of this richer idea the better to apply it to the other part with greater attention. Thus, when I consider a shape without thinking of the substance or the extension whose shape it is, I make a mental abstraction. Descartes in a letter of 1642 (Cottingham, 1992)

Not only was Descartes moved by intense uncertainty about the world in which he lived, but he felt an absolute need to solve the problem, for which he sought lifelong answers, always eager to master the subject, to reach the end of his quest. All this was driven by a widely conventional personality, obedient to the dictates of his time, always seeking to avoid affronting the church and the rest of society.

Stephen Hawking (1942–2018)

Hawking became known as one of the greatest astrophysicists in the world, having lived most of his life with "motor neurone disease", which kept him in a wheelchair, with great physical limitations, including communication and needing a computer to express himself, which made it impossible for him to have a normal social life. Having shown great intellectual abilities early on, it was from the moment he became aware of his illness and became more reclusive (Marsh, 2014), that his work began to be noticed. Hawking became one of the first proponents of the mathematical theory that explains the emergence of the Big Bang, based on a singularity, or black hole (Hawking, 1988).

His life would be devoted to the study of the properties of the cosmos, the particularities of time and black holes, more focused on theory than on empirical studies, probably also because of his physical limitations. Hawking would never abandon the scientific spirit, the search for demonstration, proof of causality and its conceptualization, as evidenced in the following excerpt:

> Any sound scientific theory, whether of time or of any other concept, should in my opinion be based on the most workable philosophy of science: the positivist approach (…) According to this way of thinking, a scientific theory is a mathematical model that describes and codifies the observations we make. A good theory will describe a large range of phenomena on the basis of a few simple postulates and will make definite predictions that can be tested. Hawking (2001, p. 31)

His illness, diagnosed in 1963, with an initial prognosis of only 2 years of life (which would not be fulfilled) led to depression in the first phase and gradually evolved into paralysis, beginning with loss of locomotion and loss of voice, until he was able to use only one face muscle to communicate with his computer. During his 50 years of living with the highly disabling disease, Hawking never gave up working, searching for answers to the emergence of the universe, for the reason supporting our own existence. He wrote more than two dozen books—popular, for children and for scientists—participated in dozens of conferences, gave hundreds of interviews and was awarded dozens of medals and doctorates, demonstrating a continuing eagerness for answers, always conjecturing new problems. He never stopped, so that when he died in 2018 at age 76, highly physically debilitated, he was still director of the Centre for Theoretical Cosmology at the University of Cambridge.

The relationship between Descartes and Hawking is complete, despite the 400 years that separate them, not only in the intensity of the search or in the need to reach their goals, removing any obstacles that lay ahead, but both always supporting their arguments via a mathematical language that permitted them to generalize, structure and organize thought, making of them true icons of the Abstracter profile.

3.2.2 Tinkerers

Leonardo Da Vinci (1452–1519)

Leonardo is one of the most recognized and admired characters in world history, essentially because of the diversity of his work, which made him the ultimate example of the polymath, and at the same time an example of the vigour and relevance of the European Renaissance. Without any particular training, given his status as a bastard son, Leonardo would follow his instincts and intuitions about everything that moved his interest.

> His quest for knowledge across all the disciplines of arts and sciences helped him see patterns. Occasionally this mode of thinking misled him, and it sometimes substituted for reaching more profound scientific theories. But this cross-disciplinary thinking and pattern-seeking was his hallmark as the quintessential Renaissance Man, and it made him a pioneer of scientific humanism. (Isaacson, 2017)

He started with painting, then sculpture, architecture and clothing design. He became an engineer and designed war machines, some functional, others completely impossible to build. He was interested in anatomy and autopsied dozens of corpses. He became interested in fluid mechanics and invested hundreds of pages in describing the movement and strength of water. He became interested in bird flight and designed various flight systems. He became interested in mathematics, but having some difficulties in calculus (Isaacson, 2017) devised an ingenious way to obtain answers through geometric drawing (see Fig. 3.8).

> He was mainly motivated by his own curiosity (…) He was more interested in pursuing knowledge than in publishing it. And even though he was collegial in his life and work, he made little effort to share his findings. (…) This is true for all of his studies, not just his work on anatomy. (…) when he died, Leonardo would leave — only piles of unedited notebook pages and drawings. (…) Over the years, and even centuries, his discoveries had to be rediscovered by others. (Isaacson, 2017)

We could say Da Vinci was the first Designer, someone who was deeply curious about how the world worked, searching to look, listen, feel and act to understand, to grasp the essence of functionality, and then through his mind and designs, transform and invent (Kemp, 2006).

> He had no taste for the abstractions of pure philosophy, which he scathingly characterized as a kind of pseudo-knowledge 'that begins and ends in the mind' (…) he was convinced that concrete knowledge could not reveal the nature of divinity itself. Rather, the role of human understanding was devoted to the revelations of the glories of natural design (…) No knowledge was valid if it could not be derived from 'experience'. He placed great value on experiment (…) apparently constraining in his insistent limiting of himself to the tangible

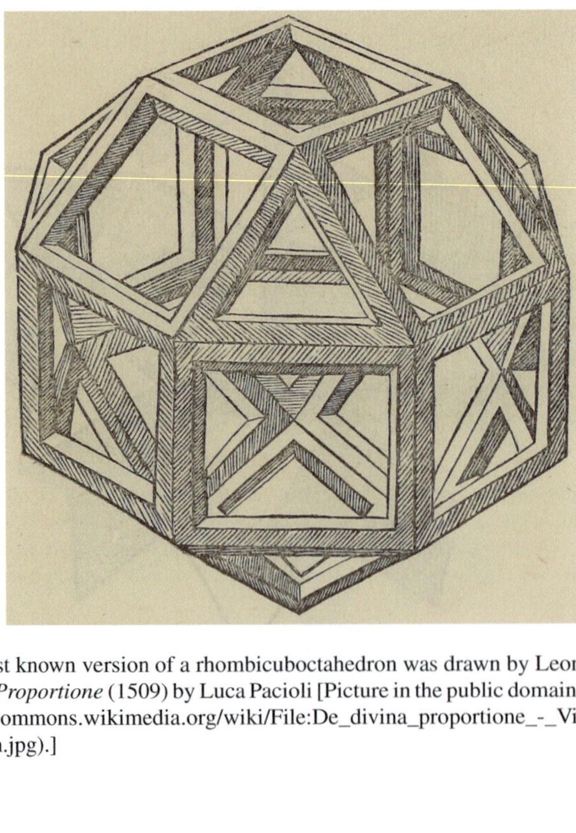

Fig. 3.8 The first known version of a rhombicuboctahedron was drawn by Leonardo Da Vinci for the book *Divina Proportione* (1509) by Luca Pacioli [Picture in the public domain, accessed at Wikimedia (https://commons.wikimedia.org/wiki/File:De_divina_proportione_-_Vigintisex_Basium_Planum_Vacuum.jpg).]

> facts of the physical universe as perceived through the senses. Yet such was the fertility of his imagination — what he called fantasia — that this ground-based enterprise took flight in a way that few creative artists and thinkers have ever emulated. (Kemp, 2004)

Da Vinci questioned the logic of reason and mere intuition, opposing them to empirical necessity, to pragmatism:

> They will say that being unskilled in letters I cannot find true expression for the matters of which I desire to treat; they do not know that in my subjects experience is a truer guide than the words of others, for experience was the teacher of all great writers, and therefore I take her for guide, and I will cite her in all cases.

> Although I may not be able to quote other authors, as they do, I can quote from a greater and more worthy source, namely, experience—the teacher of their masters.

> The eye, which is called the window of the soul, is the principal means by which the brain can most abundantly and splendidly contemplate the infinite works of nature; and the ear is the next in order, which is ennobled by hearing the recital of the things seen by the eye. If you, historians and poets, or mathematicians, had not seen things with the eyes, you could not report of them in writing. Da Vinci (1540)

Thomas Edison (1847–1931)

Despite Edison's enormous success, today being recognized as one of the main engines of technological invention of twentieth-century industrialization, he did not have access to a formal education, like Leonardo Da Vinci, simply because after a few months in school he was sent home on account of an alleged inability to learn. His mother took care of his minimal education, and soon Edison began to work. Due to his enormous intrinsic motivation and highly diversified interests, he would develop more than a thousand patents—including the phonograph, the film camera and the commercial light bulb (see Fig. 3.9)—and he managed to be the founder of *Science* in 1880, one of the world's top academic journals today. Before the age of 30, in 1876, he created Menlo Park, which would serve as an example for much of what would become America in the twentieth century: the applied research laboratories in which science was transformed into commercial products by following applied methodologies, predominantly trial-and-error, consequently forging the first "inventions factory".

For more than 50 years, Edison was dedicated to finding and transforming ideas, some abandoned by others as previously impossible to execute, and creating successful new commercial products. Much has been written about him, including good and bad stories about his obsession with success at all costs (see Edison quote below), sometimes causing harm to competitors, much like another well-known icon in the HCI domain, Steve Jobs. Over the years it has become clear that Edison invented nothing from scratch, just like Jobs. On the other hand, there is the undeniable volition to invent, of being able to make experiments where no other had taken them before, and thus produce solutions that could be made commercially available (Fessenden, 1940, p. 40). It was not intellectual genius, talent in the abstraction of complex processes, but his ability and talent to deal with multiple disciplinary environments,

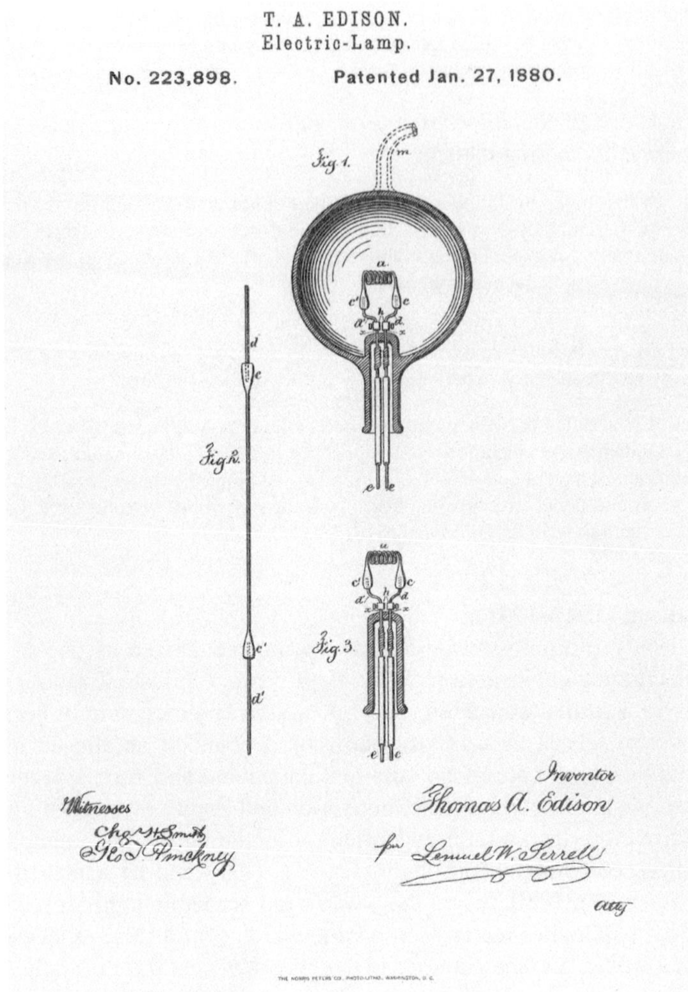

Fig. 3.9 The patent application of the "Light bulb" (1880) by Thomas Edison (Picture in the public domain, accessed at Wikimedia https://commons.wikimedia.org/wiki/File:Light_bulb_Edison_2.jpg.)

always searching, over and over, driven by continuous exploration and experimentation, that made him succeed. He had to work on many different fronts, from political interests to marketing and technological advancements, to guarantee conditions for the creation, innovation and production of his patents.

> After I have completed an invention, I seem to lose interest in it. One might think that the money value of an invention constitutes its reward to the man who loves his work. But (…)

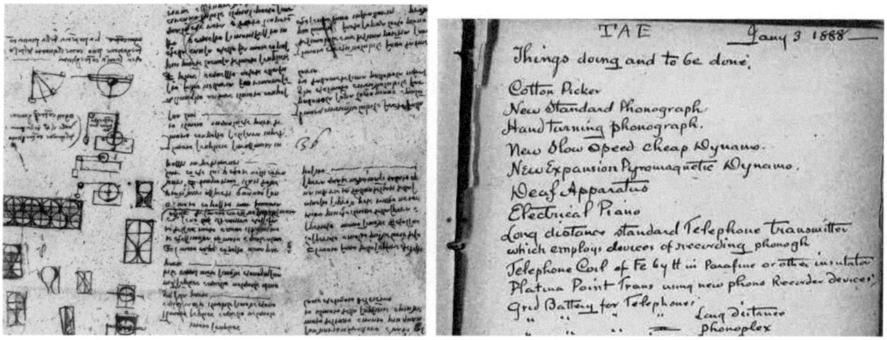

Fig. 3.10 Excerpts from the notebooks of Leonardo [left (Excerpt from picture in the public domain, accessed at Wikimedia https://commons.wikimedia.org/wiki/File:Reproduction_of_page_from_notebook_of_Leonardo_da_Vinci_LCCN2006681086.tif.)] and Edison [right (Excerpt from "Technical Note, Thomas Alva Edison, January 3rd, 1888" Edison Papers Digital Edition, accessed 27 July 2019 http://edison.rutgers.edu/digital/document/NA021AAF.)]

> now that I have all the appliances I need, and am my own master, I continue to find my greatest pleasure, and so my reward, in the work that precedes what the world calls success.
> Edison in interview (Marden, 1901, pp. 236–237)

Between Leonardo and Edison, there is in common a huge thirst for novelty and diversity, a constant quest to create and understand the workings of reality reflected in a legacy obsessively echoed in notes (see Fig. 3.10). In the case of Leonardo, 7,000 pages survived (Library, 2019; Suh, 2009); in Edison's case, there are millions of pages (many created by his assistants, but many from his own hand) that have been screened for 30 years by the State University of New Jersey (Israel, 1978). Both proceeded through tangible experimentation, following their intuition and ignoring the planning steps. They lived lives full of change, always open to facing difference and to being carried away by the nearest fantasy, albeit always with some degree of grounding. When we think of the ideal domains, we are in the absolute realm of Design, with the adjacent realms of Art and Engineering. They were the Tinkerers.

3.2.3 Dramatists

William Shakespeare (1564–1616)
Harold Bloom, one of the most high-profile literary critics of the twentieth century, said, on the assumption that he could directly question Shakespeare: "I would blurt out: did it comfort you to have fashioned women and men more real than living men and women?" (Bloom, 2002, p. 18). This question accounts for a large part of our interest in reviewing Shakespeare: his ability to present human nature in all its splendour, going deep inside each of its characters, pulling out what we intuit but

rarely have access to, in our daily life among humans. Not only did Shakespeare understand the workings of the human mind, he knew how to make it visible. This same capacity would be recognized in different human sciences, with Hooper saying that Shakespeare "With his understanding of the personality, behavior and the subconscious, the Bard has shaped our understanding of the mind throughout the ages" (2014), and the neuroscientist Damasio saying in an interview: "When I am asked who is the greatest scientist ever, I answer: in my area, it is Shakespeare" (Lucas, 2017). This may seem strange to many, but dramatists and novelists are above all scholars of human psychology, as Zola told his critics in the preface to the second edition of *Thérèse Raquin*:

> I have sought to study temperaments and not characters. In that lies the entire book. I have selected personages sovereignly dominated by their nerves and their blood, destitute of free will, led at each act of their life by the fatalities of their flesh. (Zola, 1868)

About Shakespeare's life and person we know little beyond the meagre records of that time (Holland, 2007; Shaw, 1996). Shakespeare was a mere commoner, and in his day, writers were disregarded, so there are no direct reports of his life and his person. Much of what has been written about the author has been done through speculation from his work (Bate, 2009; Greenblatt, 2016). However, from the many biographies that can be read about him, there are some common traits we can list: a person who could relate to people of all classes (Shaw, 1996), extremely sensitive to text and speech (Bloom, 2002), and demonstrating its agreeableness. Shakespeare lived for many years with a theatrical troupe and with direct responsibility for the financial maintenance of the theatre group (Greenblatt, 2016), which defines someone who was conscious and intelligent in the business field, but at the same time in love with the madness of bohemian life, with the intense and unstable relationship with others (Holland, 2007), without neglecting his family's social affirmation by acquiring a "coat of arms" (Bate, 2009).

Shakespeare fits all the broad social spectrum. On the one hand, there is the agreeableness, which allowed him to relate to everyone, to be affable and loved by all kinds of social strata, accounted for by his "neurotic elasticity". On the other hand, he had a capacity for control and management of business, to the point of becoming arrogant and demanding a coat of arms for his family, coping with the extreme of extroversion. Shakespeare was a social animal, playing on every possible relationship, only interested in what people felt, and somehow in controlling these feelings. In fact, his greatest weapon was exactly the theatre. His plays allowed him to develop real weapons of emotional manipulation and control of human nature. As Greenblatt says, "Theater, in Shakespeare's time as in our own, is a highly social art form, not a game of bloodless abstractions" (2016, p. 11).

Ingmar Bergman (1918–2007)

Bergman began in the theatre, as Shakespeare, but it was in the cinema he made himself one of the greatest artists of the human condition. His personal life was hectic, buzzing in the media, and he was not shy about baring it in his autobiography (Bergman, 1987). His personal life always clashed with his work, both his working method and the content of the texts, where everything had to be highly coordinated, rehearsed and perfect: "His private life was as randomly messy as his professional life was highly organized" (French, 2007). In an interview with the *New York Times*, he said, "I wanted to become a good director because I was a human being. In the studio and the theater, I could live happily" (Riding, 1995). The stage served him in controlling his ideas, in making sense of the world and others.

In a letter written to Ingmar Bergman in 1960, Stanley Kubrick, another of the great icons of world cinema, would say: "Your vision of life has moved me deeply, much more deeply than I have ever been moved by any films. I believe you are the greatest film-maker at work today. Beyond that, allow me to say you are unsurpassed by anyone in the creation of mood and atmosphere, the subtlety of performance, the avoidance of the obvious, the truthfulness and completeness of characterization" (Kubrick, 1960). And Martin Scorsese, in a 2010 interview, would say: "It's not that Bergman was the first film artist to confront serious themes. It's that he worked in a symbolic and an emotional language that was serious and accessible. He was young, he was setting an incredible pace, but he was looking at memory, old age, the reality of death, the reality of cruelty, and it was so vivid. So dramatic" (Björkman, 2010).

About his personal façade, Bibi Anderson said: Bergman "was so full of neuroses that if he took them away he would not be able to make films anymore" (Chilton, 2019), while Von Sydow argued, "He created a relationship between all the people he worked with. He was a very sensitive, intelligent man who knew a lot about human beings" (Chilton, 2019). In his films everything seems to boil down to the human, the feel and pulse of life, something that Bergman obsessively optimized through human expression, saying: "Faces are a big thing. The human face is the most cinematographic thing that exists. It is sensational and fascinating to look at a face" (Chilton, 2019) (see Fig. 3.11). In an interview given to Playboy in 1960, Bergman said:

> What matters most of all in life is being able to make that contact with another human. Otherwise you are dead, like so many people today are dead, but if you can take that first step toward communication, toward understanding, toward love, then no matter how difficult the future may be — and have no illusions, even with all the love in the world, living can be hellishly difficult — then you are saved. (Bergman, 1964).

Bergman had a long career, immensely respected as an artist, but always under suspicion as a person. That is, on the one hand, there were strong traits of agreeableness in the way he dealt with the actors and wrote the plays, a lot of extroversion in the way he dealt with the full weight of the professional component and also in the control and authority of his family life, but everything was permeated by neuroticism that kept him in an inconstant moral balance, between good and bad.

Shakespeare and Bergman shared more than the stage, in the theatre or the cinema, they needed the constant challenge of dealing with other humans, dealing with their unexpectedness, inconstancies and immense variabilities. They managed their own masks and façades very well, changing them according to whom they were speaking at each moment, and in each situation we can say they were true "social animals". But because of that, they also suffered from some imbalance, psychologically defined as

Fig. 3.11 Faces and relationship conflicts were the essence of Bergman cinema. Still from the movie "Wild Strawberries" (1957) by Ingmar Bergman

neuroticism, as changing façades is not a mechanical thing, and can affect internal balance. Approaching the others, and pushing always to make an effort to understand them, empathize and simulate their pains, their agonies and their problems, can transform itself into a burden (Bechtoldt & Schneider, 2016).

3.2.4 Synthesizing the Cases

It is inevitable to look at the psychological descriptions and associated personality descriptions and think about how they approach different epistemological currents developed throughout our history. Personality is a key element in the creation of our reasoning mental models (Fumero, Santamaría, & Johnson-Laird, 2010) and is therefore fundamental not only in how we respond to the needs of interaction with reality, but also in how we conceive that reality. On the one hand, obsession with logical problem-solving; on the other, the attempt to understand the organicity of nature and the way it does not obey simple rules, as well as the enormous social variability created by human beings. That is, we clearly have three distinct currents, one with logical–rational traits; another pragmatist; and one last, interpretivist.

In the first case—Descartes and Hawking—we can see how logical processes are used to achieve unquestionable results. This approach to human truth led the Greeks and later the rationalists to pantheism (Russell, 1945). The need to find a cause, a total explanation for our existence, and of the universe, compelled the need for a "causer", hence reality being seen as a whole: a deity. This problem was solved only by Darwin and the theory of evolution, which would eventually lead to the Big Bang that serves today as the main explanatory cause. On the other hand, by moving from the explanation of the universe to behaviour, following the same approaches, we ended up creating positivism. Processes that support logical modes require a set of precepts for which it is necessary to develop structured and deductible reasoning, making of it the main approach to the world, or as Louis Lee, Goodwin, & Johnson-Laird points out, "many people enjoy pure deduction, as shown by the world-wide popularity of Sudoku problems" (2008). One solution is not important for a particular case; what matters is the generalization of the deductive method. Hence, logic is only accepted when generalizable and replicable. It is in replication that the basis of modern science is based, on methodically structured patterns for the formation of logical systems that, interconnected, create the scientific knowledge.

But the world is not seen by all in the same way, as we can see in the case of the second group—Leonardo and Edison—since some doubt science as being the only way to access truth, rather characterizing it as part of the constituent illusion of the world in which we live (Kuhn, 1962). Hence, pragmatism (James, 1907) has its theorizing of knowledge based on empirical reality, although not in its causes, but in its effects. That is, the world does not exist as a model object, abstract and static, but rather as a constantly changing physical and organic system. Therefore, knowledge must be drawn from practical analysis, not from theoretical formulations. We learn by doing, drawing, creating and producing. After analysing the effects, we can, through abduction processes, even theorize the practice of what happens in each moment. Not only is the world real, it is in permanent flux (Dalsgaard, 2014), or as put by Rovelli (2017), even the "hardest stone (…) is in reality a complex vibration of quantum fields, a momentary interaction of forces, a process that for a brief moment manages to keep its shape, to hold itself in equilibrium before disintegrating again into dust". Creative minds, responsible for continuing exploration and creation approaches, conceive knowledge only through experience (Dewey, 1938).

Finally, we have the most particular worldview, situated at the level of persons, of Shakespeare and Bergman, who in this case are assumed as "indivisible" and "complete systems" (Herman, 2013). Hermeneutics began by giving us the world from the deepening of texts, their analysis and critical interpretation, eventually bringing us to interpretivism. In this perspective, logical abstraction does not exist; it is in the particular that we can find the essence of knowledge, the patterns derived from processes of induction, in which from the particular we can begin to conceive parts of the universal. Culture is strongly dependent on the individual, who is subjective, impossible to generalize. Hence, dramatic creators develop endless stories and dramas, and we have access to thousands of years of continuing literature without finding a pattern or formula that explains the foundation or the relevance of each new story. Interpretation allows us to understand the world, an interpretation that is not mere reading, but rather careful and methodical in order to understand the ramifications of the complexity of meanings.

The way of being in the world is conditioned by a set of inclinations traced by one's innate profile, but these are in turn accentuated by the culture in which they develop, namely, by the ways in which they develop their mental models of reality resolution, combining and expanding the potential of each human being, making the most of their intrinsic skills.

3.3 The Profiles

Given the profiles identified and the two persons described for each, moved by such different interests and ways of working, it is easy to understand that the kind of experiences that will be created in each one's subjective world from the same artefact will be quite different. In the foreground, we have well-defined problem-solving, following perfectly "planned" (Resnick, 2017), "systematized" (Baron-Cohen, 2003) and "logical" (Turkle & Papert, 1990) actions, completely focused on the "get to know". In the background, new approaches and unfamiliar environments are preferred, following "experimentation" (Resnick, 2017), "discovery" (Bartle, 1996) and "trial-and-error" (Strauss, 1962) approaches, pushing towards a "get to do"; The third plan, on the other hand, focuses on people, who in order to develop their work continually deepen the "relational" (Turkle & Papert, 1990) and the "communal" (Yee, 2007) aspects, all permeated with "feeling" (Baron-Cohen, 2003) and concretized in "stories" (Gardner, 1980), always searching for "get to feel". Like this, the three profiles engage with reality by following very different approaches, not only for their interests, but also for the ways in which they interact with the world.

Let's now put everything together and see how the profiles emerge (see Table 3.3).

Abstracters define themselves as the getters to know, objectifying at competence. Tinkerers are focused on getting to do, to seek for sensations. And dramatists just worry about getting to feel, to understand the others. The three profiles account for three distinct modes of engagement, and it is exactly these that we will focus on in the next chapters to determine the potential streams supporting engagement design in interactive media artefacts.

Table 3.3 Psychological and game motives definition of profiles

	Abstracters	Tinkerers	Dramatists
Historical characters	Rene Descartes Stephen Hawking	Leonardo Da Vinci Thomas Edison	William Shakespeare Ingmar Bergman
Five-factor model	Conscientiousness	Openness to experience	Agreeableness and extraversion
Holland codes	Conventional	Artistic	Social and enterprising
Yee model	Mastery and achievement	Creativity	Social and immersion
Profile definitions	Mentally focused in structuring and abstracting ideas to achieve goals and **get to know**	Insatiable curious and seekers of the novel, fluid discoverers to comprehend and **get to do**	Keen observers of behaviours, always comparing and using stories to **get to feel**

References

Armstrong, P. I., & Anthoney, S. F. (2009). Personality facets and RIASEC interests: An integrated model. *Journal of Vocational Behavior, 75*(3), 346–359. https://doi.org/10.1016/j.jvb.2009.05.004.

Baron-Cohen, S. (2003). *The essential difference: Men, women and the extreme male brain*. London: Penguin Press Science.

Bartle, R. (1996). Hearts, clubs, diamonds, spades: Players who suit MUDs. *Journal of MUD Research, 1*(1), 19.

Bartle, R. (2009). Understanding the limits of theory. In *Beyond game design: Nine steps to creating better videogames* (pp. 117–134). Charles River Media.

Barton, M. (2019). The YouTuber on a mission to save the classic RPG. *Wired*. Retrieved from https://www.wired.com/2019/06/youtuber-quest-save-rpg/.

Bate, J. (2009). *Soul of the age: A biography of the mind of William Shakespeare*. London: Random House.

Bateman, C., Lowenhaupt, R., & Nacke, L. E. (2011). Player typology in theory and practice. *Proceedings of DiGRA 2011*.

Bechtoldt, M. N., & Schneider, V. K. (2016). Predicting stress from the ability to eavesdrop on feelings: Emotional intelligence and testosterone jointly predict cortisol reactivity. *Emotion, 16*(6), 815–825. https://doi.org/10.1037/emo0000134.

Bergman, I. (1964). Ingmar Bergman, playboy interview. *Playboy*, 61–68.

Bergman, I. (1987). *The magic lantern*. Chicago: University of Chicago Press.

Björkman, S. (2010). Martin Scorsese on Ingmar Bergman. Retrieved from Philosophy of Science Portal website: http://philosophyofscienceportal.blogspot.com/2010/05/film-maker-on-film-makermartin-scorsese.html.

Bloom, H. (2002). *Genius: A Mosaic of one hundred exemplary creative minds*. New York: Warner Bros.

Caillois, R. (1958). *Les jeux et les hommes*. Paris: Gallimard.

Chilton, M. (2019). Ingmar Bergman: The messy life of a magic filmmaker. *Independent*.

Colvin, G. (2008). *Talent is overrated: What really separates world-class performers from everybody else*. New York: Portfolio.

Costa Jr., P. T., & McCrae, R. R. (1992). Trait psychology comes of age. In *Current theory and research in motivation, Vol. 39. Nebraska symposium on motivation 1991: Psychology and aging.* (pp. 169–204). Lincoln, NE, US: University of Nebraska Press.

Costa, P. T., McCrae, R. R., & Kay, G. G. (1995). Persons, places, and personality: Career assessment using the revised NEO personality inventory. *Journal of Career Assessment, 3*(2), 123–139. https://doi.org/10.1177/106907279500300202.

Cottingham, J. (1992). *The Cambridge companion to Descartes*. Cambridge: Cambridge University Press.

Coyle, D. (2009). *The talent code: Greatness isn't born. It's grown. Here's how*. New York: Bantam Books.

Dalsgaard, P. (2014). Pragmatism and design thinking. *International Journal of Design, 1*(8), 143–155.

Dawis, R. V., & Lofquist, L. H. (1984). *A psychological theory of work adjustment: An individual-differences model and its applications*. University of Minnesota Press.

De Fruyt, F., & Mervielde, I. (1997). The five-factor model of personality and Holland's RIASEC interest types. *Personality and Individual Differences, 23*(1), 87–103. https://doi.org/10.1016/S0191-8869(97)00004-4.

DeNeve, K. M., & Cooper, H. (1998). The happy personality: A meta-analysis of 137 personality traits and subjective well-being. *Psychological Bulletin, 124*(2), 197–229. Retrieved from http://www.ncbi.nlm.nih.gov/pubmed/9747186.

Descartes, R. (1637). *A discourse on the method*. London: Oxford University Press.

Dewey, J. (1938). *Experience and education*. Urbana: Kappa Delta Pi.

Ericsson, K. A., Krampe, R. T., & Tesch-Römer, C. (1993). The role of deliberate practice in the acquisition of expert performance. *Psychological Review, 100*(3), 363–406. https://doi.org/10.1037/0033-295X.100.3.363.

Ericsson, K. A., Prietula, M. J., & Cokely, E. T. (2007). The making of an expert. *Harvard Business Review, 85*(7–8), 114–121, 193. Retrieved from http://www.ncbi.nlm.nih.gov/pubmed/17642130.

Fessenden, H. (1940). *Fessenden—Builder of tomorrow*. Paris: Ramsay Press.

French, P. (2007). Twin visionaries of a darker art. *The Guardian*.

Fruyt, F., & Mervielde, I. (1999). RIASEC types and big five traits as predictors of employment status and nature of employment. *Personnel Psychology, 52*(3), 701–727. https://doi.org/10.1111/j.1744-6570.1999.tb00177.x.

Fumero, A., Santamaría, C., & Johnson-Laird, P. (2010). Ways of thinking: Personality affects reasoning. *Psicothema, 22*(1), 57–62.

Gardner, H. (1980). *Artful scribbles: The significance of children's drawings*. New York: Basic Books.

Gladwell, M. (2008). *Outliers: The story of success*. New York: Little, Brown.

Greenblatt, S. (2016). *Will in the world: How Shakespeare became Shakespeare*. London: W. W. Norton.

Hamari, J., & Tuunanen, J. (2014). Player types: A meta-synthesis. *Transactions of the Digital Games Research Association, 1*(2). https://doi.org/10.26503/todigra.v1i2.13.

Hambrick, D. Z., Oswald, F. L., Altmann, E. M., Meinz, E. J., Gobet, F., & Campitelli, G. (2014). Deliberate practice: Is that all it takes to become an expert? *Intelligence, 45,* 34–45. https://doi.org/10.1016/j.intell.2013.04.001.

Hawking, S. (1988). *A brief history of time*. London: Bantam Books.

Hawking, S. (2001). *The universe in a Nutshell*. London: Bantam Books.

Herman, D. (2013). *Storytelling and the sciences of mind*. Cambridge, MA: MIT Press.

Holland, J. L. (1997). *Making vocational choices: A theory of vocational personalities and Work environments*. Odessa: Psychological Assessment Resources.

Holland, P. (2007). *William Shakespeare*. Cambridge: Oxford University Press.

Hooper, R. (2014). Shakespeare: The godfather of neuroscience. *New Scientist, 222*(2965), 43–45. https://doi.org/10.1016/S0262-4079(14)60785-5.

Isaacson, W. (2017). *Leonardo da Vinci*. New York: Simon & Schuster.

Israel, P. (1978). *Thomas A. Edison papers*. Retrieved from http://edison.rutgers.edu/.

James, W. (1907). *Pragmatism. A new name for some old ways of thinking*. New York: Dover Publications.

Kemp, M. (2004). *Leonardo*. Oxford: Oxford University Press.

Kemp, M. (2006). *Leonardo Da Vinci: Experience*. Experiment and Design: Victoria & Albert Museum.

Kubrick, S. (1960). Letter to Ingmar Bergman.

Kuhn, T. S. (1962). *The structure of scientific revolutions*. Chicago: University of Chicago Press.

Lazzaro, N. (2008). The four fun keys. In *Game usability: Advancing the player experience*. https://doi.org/10.1201/b14580.

Library, B. (2019). Leonardo da Vinci's notebook. Retrieved from https://www.bl.uk/collection-items/leonardo-da-vinci-notebook.

Louis Lee, N. Y., Goodwin, G. P., & Johnson-Laird, P. N. (2008). The psychological puzzle of Sudoku. *Thinking & Reasoning, 14*(4), 342–364. https://doi.org/10.1080/13546780802236308.

Lucas, I. (2017). Entrevista a António Damásio. *Público*. Retrieved from https://www.publico.pt/2017/11/05/ciencia/entrevista/antonio-damasio-1791116.

Marden, O. S. (1901). *How they succeeded: Life stories of successful men told by themselves*. Boston: Lothrop Publishing.

Marsh, J. (2014). *The theory of everything*. New York: Universal Pictures.

McCrae, R. R. (2009). The five-factor model of personality traits: Consensus and controversy. In P. J. Corr & G. Matthews (Eds.), *The Cambridge handbook of personality psychology* (pp. 148–161). https://doi.org/10.1017/CBO9780511596544.012.

McCrae, R. R., & John, O. P. (1992). An introduction to the five-factor model and its applications. *Journal of Personality, 60*(2), 175–215. https://doi.org/10.1111/j.1467-6494.1992.tb00970.x.

MU Career Center. (2010). *Guide to Holland code*. Retrieved from http://www.wiu.edu/advising/docs/Holland_Code.pdf.

Mueller, S., & Tan, S. (2019, August). How many personality configurations exist? *Psychology Today*. Retrieved from https://www.psychologytoday.com/us/blog/seeing-what-others-dont/201908/how-many-personality-configurations-exist.

Nacke, L. E., Bateman, C., & Mandryk, R. L. (2014). BrainHex: A neurobiological gamer typology survey. *Entertainment Computing, 5*(1), 55–62. https://doi.org/10.1016/j.entcom.2013.06.002.

Nielsen, J. (2016). Games user research: What's different? In nngroup.com. Retrieved from March 20, 2016, from https://www.nngroup.com/articles/game-user-research.

Nye, C. D., Su, R., Rounds, J., & Drasgow, F. (2012). Vocational interests and performance: A quantitative summary of over 60 years of research. *Perspectives on Psychological Science, 7*(4), 384–403. https://doi.org/10.1177/1745691612449021.

Pink, D. (2008). *Drive: The surprising truth about what motivates us*. New York: Riverhead Books.

Plomin, R., DeFries, J., & McClearn, G. (1989). *Behavioral genetics: A primer*. London: WH Freeman & Co.

Reisenzein, R., & Weber, H. (2009). Personality and emotion. In G. Matthews & P. J. Corr (Eds.), *The Cambridge handbook of personality psychology* (pp. 54–71).

Resnick, M. (2017). *Lifelong kindergarten. Cultivating creativity through projects, passion, peers, and play*. Cambridge, MA: MIT Press.

Riding, A. (1995). The interview. Ingmar Bergman. *New York Times*. Retrieved from https://www.nytimes.com/2013/10/14/movies/the-interview-ingmar-.html.

Riemann, R., Angleitner, A., & Strelau, J. (1997). Genetic and environmental influences on personality: A study of twins reared together using the self and peer report NEO-FFI scales. *Journal of Personality, 65*(3), 449–475. https://doi.org/10.1111/j.1467-6494.1997.tb00324.x.

Roberts, B. W., & DelVecchio, W. F. (2000). The rank-order consistency of personality traits from childhood to old age: A quantitative review of longitudinal studies. *Psychological Bulletin, 126*(1), 3–25. https://doi.org/10.1037/0033-2909.126.1.3.

Rovelli, C. (2017). *The order of time*. London: Riverhead Books.

Russell, B. (1945). *A history of western philosophy*. New York: Simon & Schuster.

Salen, K., & Zimmerman, E. (2003). *Rules of play: Game design fundamentals*. Cambridge, MA: MIT Press.

Shaw, G. B. (1996). *Book reviews, Vol 2: 1884–1950*. New York: Penn State University Press.

Spokane, A. R., Luchetta, E. J., & Richwine, M. H. (2002). Holland's theory of personalities in work environments. In D. Brown (Ed.), *Career choice and development* (p. 560). Hoboken, NJ: Wiley.

Strauss, C. L. (1962). *La Pensée Savage*. Paris: Presses Pocket.

Suh, H. A. (2009). *Leonardo's notebooks*. New York: Black Dog & Leventhal Publishers.

Turkle, S., & Papert, S. (1990). Epistemological pluralism: Styles and voices within the computer culture. *Signs: Journal of Women in Culture and Society*, 1(16), 128–157. Retrieved from www.jstor.org/stable/3174610.

Da Vinci, L. (1540). *A treatise on painting (Codex Rurbinas Latinus)*. Roma: Vatican.

Widiger, T. A., & Costa, P. T. (2002). Five-factor model personality disorder research. In *Personality disorders and the five-factor model of personality* (2nd ed.pp. 59–87). https://doi.org/10.1037/10423-005.

Wiggins, J. S., Trapnell, P., & Phillips, N. (1988). Psychometric and geometric characteristics of the revised interpersonal adjective scales (IAS-R). *Multivariate Behavioral Research, 23*(4), 517–530. https://doi.org/10.1207/s15327906mbr2304_8.

Wille, B., De Fruyt, F., & Feys, M. (2010). Vocational interests and big five traits as predictors of job instability. *Journal of Vocational Behavior, 76*(3), 547–558. https://doi.org/10.1016/j.jvb.2010.01.007.

Yamagata, S., Suzuki, A., Ando, J., Ono, Y., Kijima, N., Yoshimura, K., Jang, K. L. (2006). Is the genetic structure of human personality universal? A cross-cultural twin study from North America, Europe, and Asia. *Journal of Personality and Social Psychology, 90*(6), 987–998. https://doi.org/10.1037/0022-3514.90.6.987.

Yee, N. (2007). Motivations for play in online games. *CyberPsychology & Behavior*. https://doi.org/10.1089/cpb.2006.9.772.

Yee, N. (2015a). Game audience profiles. https://quanticfoundry.com/2015/09/04/game-audience-profiles.

Yee, N. (2015b). Gaming motivations group into 3 high-level clusters. Retrieved April 12, 2019, from Quantic Foundry website: https://quanticfoundry.com/2015/12/21/map-of-gaming-motivations/.

Yee, N. (2016a). Gaming motivations align with personality traits. https://quanticfoundry.com/2016/01/05/personality-correlates.

Yee, N. (2016b). Mapping the open world genre: The 4 game quadrants. Retrieved July 25, 2019, from https://quanticfoundry.com/2016/02/24/open-world-genre-map/.

Yee, N. (2017). Competition is not the opposite of community. Retrieved July 25, 2019, from Quantic Foundry website: https://quanticfoundry.com/2017/03/23/competition-not-opposite-community/.

Yee, N. (2019). *A deep dive into the 12 motivations: Findings from 400,000+ gamers*. Retrieved from https://quanticfoundry.com/2019/04/11/gdc2019/.

Zackariasson, P., Wåhlin, N., & Wilson, T. L. (2010). Virtual identities and market segmentation in marketing in and through massively multiplayer online games (MMOGs). *Services Marketing Quarterly, 31*(3), 275–295. https://doi.org/10.1080/15332969.2010.486689.

Zammitto, V. (2010). *Gamers' personality and their gaming preferences* (Simon Fraser University). Retrieved from http://summit.sfu.ca/item/11349.

Zola, E. (1868). *Thérèse Raquin*. London: Penguin Classics.

Chapter 4
Contexts of Engagement

Abstract We discuss the environments that bring together subjects and artefacts, defining what motivates human curiosity and motivation, and how these two cognitive processes operate together to put subjects in will mode. Even if the willingness comes from inside, it is produced through stimulus, through cognitive triggers found in environments surrounding subjects, which we define here as patterns, and that we get to connect with the profiles defined in the previous chapter.

The process of interaction depends on a willingness of the interactor to act and interact, and this act is determined by a will of its own that can simply be defined as a mode of action. However, a more detailed definition of human action is less relevant to what is intended here, given its physiological bases and the interest we have instead in its psychological mode, to which we can call two central cognitive processes responsible for its creation: curiosity and motivation (Broeck, Vansteenkiste, Witte, Soenens, & Lens, 2010). These in turn contribute directly to the definition of the engagement processes that involve the context, concretizing the way the subjects act and seek to understand the artefacts.

The need to work on epistemic contexts is due to the impossibility of analysing each interaction situation in a design process. In this way, epistemic contextualization allows us to understand the functioning and internal pressures in the relationship with hypothetical real situations, and thus to create a generalization of potential interactional frameworks (e.g. problem-solving, making, empathizing).

In the next sections, we will determine how curiosity works and how it relates to motivation, and thereby obtain cycles that link willingness to engagement in the definition of supportive contexts, seeking at the end of the chapter to relate them to the defined psychological profiles defined in the previous chapter.

N. Zagalo, *Engagement Design*, Human–Computer Interaction Series,
https://doi.org/10.1007/978-3-030-37085-5_4

4.1 Epistemic Curiosity

What makes us *Homo sapiens*? Why do we keep asking: "What am I?", "Who am I?", "What do I know?", "Where am I?", "Who are they?" These are eternal questions that no other species on the planet poses, neither our dogs nor the most intelligent chimpanzees. Within our consciousness, there is something that impels us to question the world, others and ourselves, a certain need. We are not always thinking about this—we have many needs to be met. However, when the first levels of the "hierarchy of needs" (Maslow, 1943) are optimized, these issues start to emerge insistently. The great civilizations were formed only after from the agricultural revolution, because only then were the conditions established to meet basic needs, and thus give time and energy to questioning the needs at the top of the pyramid (see Fig. 4.1). These questions form a necessity driven by what we call human curiosity, a force that drives humans to act cognitively and to seek answers.

In the Loewenstein (1994) review of psychological curiosity, a short overview of definitions made throughout the history of ideas is given starting with Aristotle saying curiosity happens "not for any utilitarian end"; the Cicero defining it as "passion for learning"; Kant arguing about an "appetite for knowledge"; and on a less positive side, St. Augustine defining it more as an "ocular lust", attaching curiosity to human vices. But after this early period, some authors started talking about different forms of curiosity: Hume said there existed one related to the "love of knowledge" and another about "knowing the actions and circumstances of neighbours" (Hume, 1888, p. 453). James also talked about two: "scientific curiosity" and the "novelty of… environment" (James, 1890, p. 430). All these definitions serve us to start understanding curiosity, but neither of these authors pushed their studies on curiosity any further.

It was only in the 1950s that Berlyne attacked the subject of curiosity with all the psychological tools at his disposal from behaviourism to learning and motivational

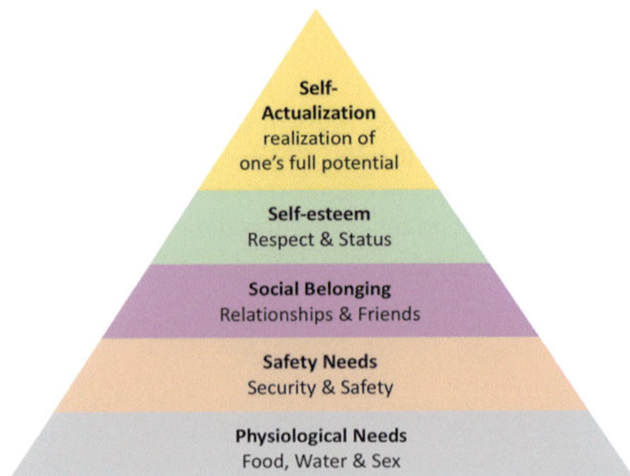

Fig. 4.1 The agricultural revolution created space and time for the development of epistemic curiosity and the development of an increasingly complex culture that would create the first great human civilizations. Diagram based on the pyramid of needs by Maslow (1943)

theories, and defended a supported need to separate the study of curiosity into two different categories: "perceptual" and "epistemic" (Berlyne, 1954, p. 180), with the perceptual defined as "a drive which is aroused by novel stimulus and reduced by continued exposure to these stimuli", a desire for "sensory experience" and the epistemic more concerned with the cognition, with the "desire for knowledge" (Powell, Nettelbeck, & Burns, 2016). Then in 1969, Piaget, according to Loewenstein (1994), defined curiosity as a "way of making sense of the world", because of an internal need for coherence, from which Loewenstein picked the idea of "violated expectations" (1994), after Berlyne had also talked about "conflict", a view that Leslie synthesized as "a person's curiosity is provoked when she perceives an incongruity between what she expects and what happens—when she feels there's a discrepancy between what she thinks she knows and what she sees" (Leslie, 2014, p. 64). This view was already supported by James's discussion: "The philosophic brain responds to an inconsistency or a gap in its knowledge, just as the musical brain responds to a discord in what it hears" (1890, p. 430).

Loewenstein then summarized all these ideas in what he called "information gap theory" (1994), as follows: "Information (…) fuels curiosity by creating awareness of ignorance, which gives rise to a desire to know more. As soon as we know something about a subject, we start to become uncomfortably aware of what we don't know, and that makes us want to close the gap (…) it's not simply the absence of information that creates curiosity, but a gap in our existing information" (Leslie, 2014, p. 67) (see Fig. 4.2).

Then, at the beginning of the 2000s, Litman refined curiosity, dividing Lowenstein's information-based concept into two types: intellectual interest, or "I-type" and informational deprivation, or "D-type" (Litman, 2005, 2010). In Fig. 4.3, we can see the activities responsible for producing I-Type (I) and D-Type (II). The I-type is stronger when there is an opportunity to "explore new ideas", to learn new and unfamiliar information, pushing for abstraction in order "to find out more" in order to extend existing knowledge. The D-type works better when conceptual problems

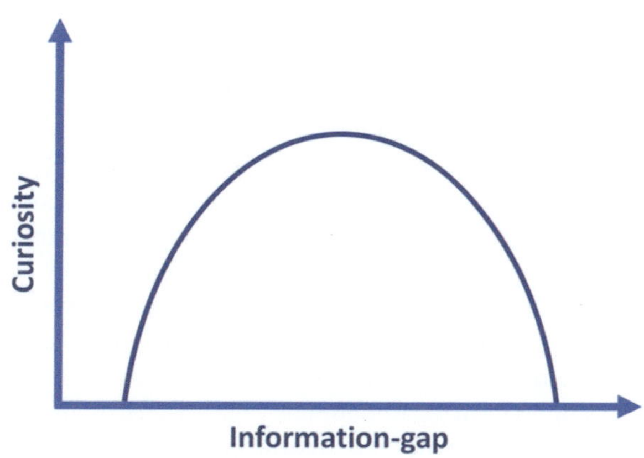

Fig. 4.2 At low levels of information gap, not much attention drives curiosity. At medium level, curiosity attains a peak, activating all means to find information missing, and be able to attribute meaning. At high levels of information gap, curiosity declines, losing interest. The diagram was made following the description of "information gap theory" by Loewenstein (1994)

I-type	D-type
1. Enjoy exploring new ideas.	6. Hours on a problem because I can't rest without answer.
2. Find it fascinating to learn new information.	7. Brood for a long time to solve problem.
3. Enjoy learning about subjects that are unfamiliar to me.	8. Conceptual problems keep me awake thinking.
4. Enjoy discussing abstract concepts.	9. Frustrated if I can't figure out problem, so I work harder.
5. Learn something new, like to find out more about it.	10. Work like a fiend at problems that I feel must be solved.

Fig. 4.3 Activities responsible for producing curiosity: I-Type (I) and D-Type (II). Excerpt from diagram by Litman (2008, p. 1593)

Curious about Emotions	Spying and Prying	Snooping
1. Attend to non-verbal messages people send	6. Think about interviewing others as a career	11. Look at things in people's rooms
2. Observe facial expressions to figure out feelings	7. Feel comfortable asking about private life	12. Going into houses to see how people live
3. Try to understand people's feelings	8. Would make a good private detective	13. Wonder what people's interests are
4. Figure out what others are feeling by looking	9. Wish I could turn invisible to spy on people	14. Shuffle through things because intrigued
5. People open up to me about how they feel	10. Think about being an investigative reporter	15. Like to know what other people do

Fig. 4.4 Activities responsible for producing interpersonal curiosity. Excerpt from diagram by Litman and Pezzo (2007)

are presented, making subjects work to find solutions without stopping, in order to reduce conflict and uncertainty (Litman, 2008).

These two types were then extended by Litman and Pezzo with the dimension of "interpersonal curiosity", which responds to "the desire for new information about people" (Litman & Pezzo, 2007) or knowledge about other's experiences, public and private (see Fig. 4.4). This dimension is especially relevant because humans need it for processes of social comparison (Festinger, 1954), a sort of continuous self-benchmarking, corresponding to the principal mode through which we understand ourselves (Bandura, 1986).

We can say then that we're curious and motivated to fill information gaps—about uncertain, novel and interpersonal situations—but what pushes us? Where does the motivation to continue come from? Is there a reward?

4.2 Motivation

Research on human motivation has divided its cognitive processes into two major variants, intrinsic and extrinsic (Deci & Ryan, 1985), qualifying the extrinsic as the most present in our Western society, in the form of immediately visible or quantifiable rewards such as "money" (Pink, 2008), which in the case of video games has been well evidenced by the "points, badges and leader boards" methodologies, closely associated with gamification (Carvalho, Zagalo, & Araujo, 2015). However, extrinsic motivation, although very effective in the short term, presents many problems, as presented in a refutation of Skinner's studies of behaviourism (1953), namely, the fact that stimuli need to be continually increased to maintain the same levels of motivation, which can lead to the complete disappearance of motivation in the absence of stimulus (Deci & Flaste, 1996; Robinson, Gallus, Lee, & Rogers, 2019).

Subsequently, in the 1980s, a new approach to human motivation emerged, proposed by Deci and Ryan (1985), entitled "self-determination theory" (SDT), based on so-called "intrinsically motivated behaviors" (Hunt, 1965; White, 1959). Recognizing the problems of extrinsic motivation, they sought to understand what intrinsically motivated human being to change, in order to seek lasting effects. As the name implies, the theory assumes that the intensity of our motivation is directly linked to our determination to achieve an objective (e.g. quitting smoking mostly only results in the long run when it comes from a will of one's own). Rather than differentiating extrinsic motivation—being motivated by something outside the goal itself (e.g. getting good grades at school to gain a game console)—from the intrinsic—doing something, because one wants to do that (e.g. learning to playing the piano because it gives us pleasure)—what this theoretical approach proposes is a change of focus to what determines action and fuels volition. The SDT approach sought to determine the basis of human will from a set of indicators—universal, adaptive and well-being oriented (Ryan & Deci, 2000). These studies showed an intrinsic motivation closer to the human process of curiosity, following the natural inclinations for mastery, exploration and social development, which became the basis of the three major conditions of SDT: "competence", "autonomy" and "relatedness" (Deci & Ryan, 1985).

The domain of "**competence**" arises from volitional behaviours that reward the subject with "pleasure in being effective" (White, 1959) and "satisfaction from learning" (Ryan & Deci, 2000). In this way, the subject seeks involvement with the challenge and at the same time seeks mastery of competence. From an evolutionary point of view, competence provides a set of skills that predispose the subject to a better ability to adapt to external changes. On the other hand, this motivation also serves to highlight "the unique talents of individuals in a group to become maximized in the niche-relevant way, and this differentiation may in turn produce benefits for all group members" (Ryan & Deci, 2000). Also, it ultimately explains how people can maintain the repetitive behaviours necessary for competency development in high-competition sport (Coyle, 2009).

In the domain of "**autonomy**", SDT argues for the existence of universal behaviour that tends towards self-organization, which relates to "a propensity for self-regulation of action and coherence of behavior" (Ryan & Deci, 2000). This need, or capacity for self-organization, relates to adaptation needs, so as to ensure in the subject the ability to process environmental variation, taking decisions and making choices, not automatically obeying the outside but rather capturing and re-organizing, what is being presented. At bottom, we are talking about capabilities that allow individuals to understand when a limit has been exceeded, such as spending too long watching a television series or playing games. This ability determines the level of control that subjects can have over seductive or persuasive external elements, acting to ensure priority to processes more relevant to them, to ensure the maintenance of an "inner coherence" avoiding "self-defragmentation" (Ryan & Deci, 2000). In a more informal language, we know this process as "willpower".

Finally, "**relatedness**" is the most easily recognized element, given its relationship to human behaviour and community building, fostered by our gregarious need. For the behavioural attachment expert Bowlby (1988), it is the existence of secure relationships that guarantees the subject's interest in the exploration of the environment. That is, the volition to look after children, to ensure the best conditions for their proper growth, would eventually become group behaviours, considering that the group tends to be more effective in maintaining the survival of all, both through food collection and protection, and above all through the transmission of information and knowledge within the group, enabling the advancement of well-being (Ryan & Deci, 2000).

The three conditions may come into conflict, such as individual autonomy versus social kinship, but when the three conditions are optimally managed they can guarantee the highest levels of motivation in subjects. An optimal motivational context will thus seek to offer the freedom to choose the path, ensure that the goal is within the reach and the possibility to connect and create bonds with others. When these three variables are met, the motivation level reaches its highest point, deteriorating whenever one of these variables is not met (Deci & Flaste, 1996).

4.3 Volition Cycles

Intrinsic motivation, described by self-determination theory, is in fact an upper level definition of the macrostructure that serves human reward systems. Biologically speaking, we are pushed by a balancing between feeling good and bad, belonging to the general homeostatic regulator (Damasio, 2018), regulated by hormones and neurotransmitters. Human curiosity is strongly regulated by one called dopamine, which is activated by what is defined as reward anticipation activity (Dubol et al., 2018). The anticipation of being rewarded activates the presence of dopamine in the brain. These systems can be hijacked by drugs, but naturally they are activated by just fulfilling our human needs (see Maslow above). In terms of experience, just think about a situation when you felt thirsty and had no water. Your brain starts firing dopamine to make you move and search for water. Dopamine is not responsible for the pleasure of then drinking the water. In the same manner, dopamine is released when you're preparing to eat a chocolate, but it is not responsible for the feeling, the tasteful pleasure of eating it. Instead, dopamine is responsible for making us move, making us seek, arousing our curiosity to look for.

When curiosity is abstracted from the subjective goals, the intellectual interest is just responding to the effect of novelty—number of times exposed to the stimulus; deprivation of the effect of uncertainty—the unknowability of results (Gottlieb, Oudeyer, Lopes, & Baranes, 2013); and the interpersonal is responding to the effect of comparison—the measuring of the self (Festinger, 1954). Remember the last time you were given a present (for your birthday, Christmas, a payment bonus, a job promotion, etc.). Do you remember the urge, the rush felt inside, previous to receiving it, previous to knowing what was inside, how it would change your well-being? The uncertainty of what would you receive, the expected novelty, the expected confirmation of your value? This was the reward anticipation brain regions being filled by dopamine, making you crave, or just naturally curious, till the disclosing of the

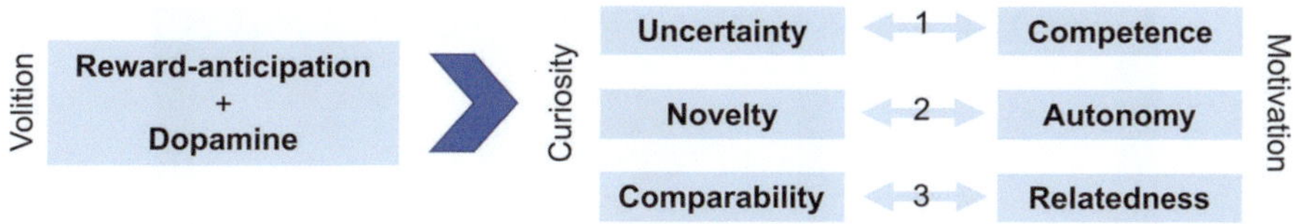

Fig. 4.5 The volition cycles arise from the urge to move and act pushed by dopamine, which is then controlled by the correlation between motivation and curiosity

surprise, when you moved from feeling anxious into feeling pleasure (or frustration if not as good as expected), as demonstrated by Kang et al. (2009) and reviewed by Sakaki et al. (2018).

We'll now look into each of the cycle dimensions (see Fig. 4.5) in order to understand the contextual situations that create their need.

4.3.1 Uncertainty/Competence

Litman defines the "deprivation of information" as "associated with setting performance-oriented learning goals, for which the correctness and relevance of newly acquired knowledge is critical to goal achievement" (2008, p. 1594), which points to situations of problem-solving but also to the competences needed. Missing information creates the uncertainty that it will be possible to achieve the desired result. Curiosity activates in us a search for information in order to suppress uncertainty and to achieve the desired solution, leading subjects to increase their levels of competence in the domain where there is a lack. To better understand the relationship between uncertainty and competence, let's start by analysing uncertainty.

Uncertainty is produced especially "when we make decisions" (Tannert, Elvers, & Jandrig, 2007). It is a fundamental process of agency. When I'm about to hit a golf ball, my uncertainty of getting the ball into the hole is connected with my competence at doing it. How much knowledge do I have: about the club—metal, wood, hybrid, putter; the ground where the ball will roll—grass, sand, water, relief, distance, etc.; about atmospheric elements that affect ball movement—wind, humidity, etc.; and about potential trajectories—force, impact, angle. Let us simplify the example by abstracting it to a decision of choosing to open door A or door B. The uncertainty about this choice stems from the information I have about each of the doors that allows me to proceed or not with a resolution process. In the absence of any information, the simple resolution process does not happen, because there are no variables to calculate or produce any strategy, only luck or chance (see Fig. 4.6).

The difference between playing games and gambling lies exactly in how we can act on the uncertainty that drives action. In a slot machine, we will act through chance, for without information about the rules driving each element in the screen there's no possibility to produce a thought-out choice: the uncertainty is absolute. In

Fig. 4.6 Slot machine asks for no strategy, only random luck (Excerpt of picture from OpenClipart, free to use, at: https://pixabay.com/vectors/slot-machine-casino-fruits-gambling-159972/. Accessed: 28.7.2019)

a chess game (see Fig. 4.7), at each new move indecision is bridged by the particular game data, which allows us, for example, to perform "reverse engineering" of moves (Ashley, 2013) and cases of similarly previously experienced and memorized moves, meaning that each move is anticipated by a whole cognitive process that we simply define as **problem-solving**. In gambling, the player's action is driven only by the extrinsic reward (e.g. money or otherwise). In game playing, the reward arises from within, through the increment of competence promoted by the problem-solving structure.

Mayer (1983), one of the most recognized problem-solving specialists, defines the cognitive process as "directed at achieving a goal for which the problem-solver does not initially know a solution method" (Mayer, 2013, p. 769). That is, first it takes a goal, something to achieve. The problem arises in the form of an obstacle or barrier that prevents us from reaching that goal. Without obstacles, there is no need to solve problems, or rather there would be no problem. The process itself "involves

Fig. 4.7 In chess you need a strategy to solve problems and win (Picture by Phil1256, free to use at: https://pixabay.com/photos/chess-chess-men-game-chess-pieces-982260/. Accessed: 28.7.2019)

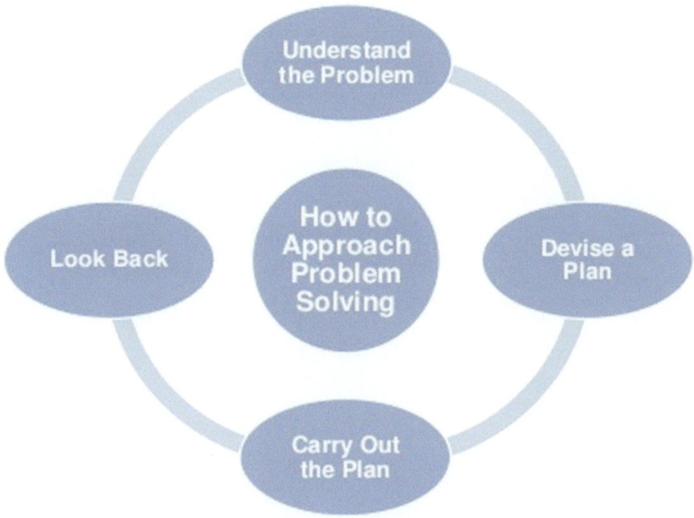

Fig. 4.8 The four-step model to solve problems presented by Polya in 1945

mental computations in which some operation is applied to a mental representation, sometimes resulting in the creation of a new mental representation". In terms of thinking, problem-solving concerns only one type of thinking, "direct thinking", which can then make use of different thinking methods, such as deductive or inductive. The problem-solving process has been widely discussed, and there are a large number of approaches to it, yet two of the most cited models are the Polya model with four steps (1945)—"Understand the problem; Devise a plan; Carry out the plan; Review/extend" (see Fig. 4.8); and the McKinsey approach with seven steps (Davis, Keeling, Schreier, & Williams, 2007)—"Define problem; Structure problem; Prioritize issues; Plan analyses & Work; Conduct analyses & work; Synthesize findings; Develop recommendations" (see Fig. 4.9).

It is all too clear that this approach to thinking requires concrete capabilities of mental representation or abstraction, of "planning", "execution" and "monitoring" (Mayer, 2013), using for that purpose a kind of concrete knowledge consisting of "facts, concepts, procedures, strategies and beliefs" (Mayer, 2013). All of these elements can then be operated on by a set of heuristics as advocated by Polya (1945) such as "analogy", "generalization", "induction" and "decomposition", among others, which correspond to the set of "associative approaches, processing information and Gestalt" advocated by Mayer (2013). All of these approaches and actions proceed to achieve the resolution of a problem, which may have a practical implication, or as Polya says "there may be a deeper curiosity, a desire to understand the ways and means, the motives and procedures, of solution", which totally differentiates the process from the mere pull of the lever of the slot machine.

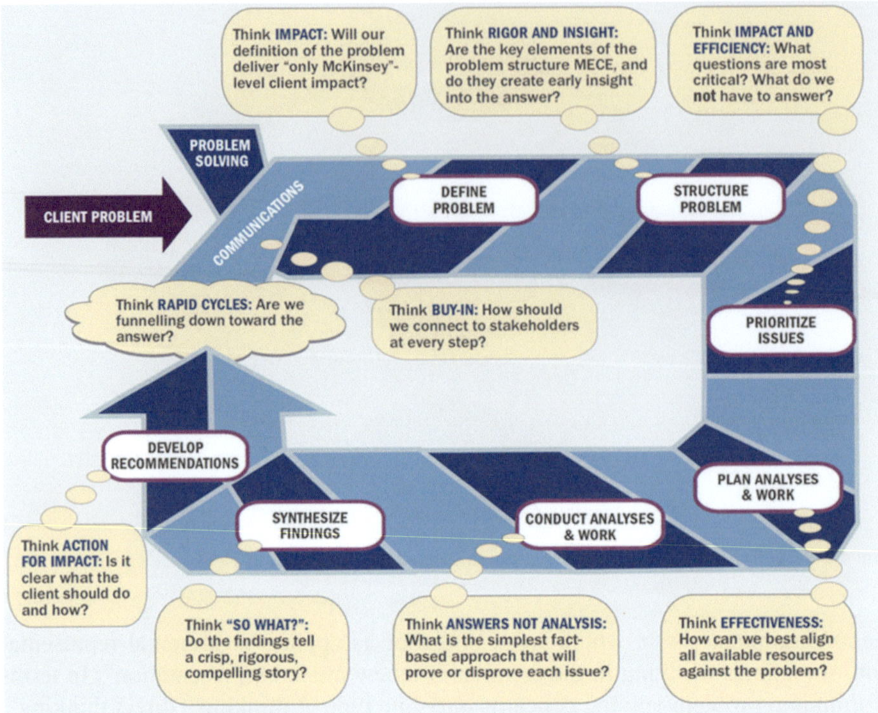

Fig. 4.9 The seven-step model presented by McKinsey in 2007

In McKinsey's diagram, questions arise as the demand for "rigor", "efficiency" and "effectiveness". In Polya's work, "order", "care", "patience" and "persistence" are mentioned. In another recent study (García, Boom, Kroesbergen, Núñez, & Rodríguez, 2019), concerning problem-solving phases, references are made to linearization and hierarchization as being associated with success, and recursiveness with failure. This points to a type of processing driven by focus and a sense of progress, assessed by increasing competence and mastery. Problem-solving is thus the domain of scientific thinking, of the exact sciences, logical reasoning and decision-making.

Problem-solving may be the domain par excellence of mathematics, but not only. We can find it in any place made of logic, which traverses almost all our existence, because everything in our society is done based on some kind of reasoning. Otherwise, no justice system would work and be respected by people. For each action done, we request a justification, which must be sustained by logical arguments. It is this need that explains the "deprivation of information", because we need to know why, and if there's no logical explanation, we work to find it. This is integrated in depth in our biology, in our pattern-seeking behaviours. When patterns are not evident, the level of uncertainty rises, calling for curiosity to maintain us seeking for the information missing that will help us see the pattern.

Fig. 4.10 In this illustration, we use the prägnanz—its ordering processes—through inductive reasoning, to make sense of the visual elements presented (Illustration by the author)

Throughout human evolution, this pattern seeking has evolved, providing us with some tools to work around the information that is missing, like deduction and induction. This can be seen in the "principles of grouping" (Rock, 1985), or the gestalt prägnanz (see Fig. 4.10), as in the "filling in the gaps" approach we take to interpret texts, following Umberto Eco's method (1989), or in Bordwell's "hypothesizing theory" (1985) about how we pick cues to anticipate "what will happen next" in a suspense or mystery movie sequence. When some action or description is missing, we "invent" it in our minds to make sense and continue the reading and watching until we can confirm whether the filling in or the hypothesizing we made was correct. This is the puzzle effect, which presents us with a full meaning that is fragmented and dispersed, for which we have to work to put back together all the pieces, to reach the hidden meaning.

Problem-solving can occur anywhere with anything, but it is strongly dependent on competence, not only pushing for curiosity to become more competent, but also of being able to understand and really enjoy the process. Vygotsky defined what is known today as the theory of the "zone of proximal development" (ZPD) (1930), which defines "the distance between the actual developmental level as determined by independent problem-solving, and the level of potential development as determined through problem-solving under guidance or in collaboration with more capable peers" (Vygotsky, 1978, p. 88) meaning that in order to maintain volition, the requested solution must be in the immediate next step of existent competences. If the level of complexity is too high or too low, subjects will give up. This is very similar to the process of curiosity as described in the "information gap theory" of Loewenstein (1994).

Curiosity as uncertainty is strongly based on the competence variable of self-determination motivation. The ZPD has served as the main design method for creating learning settings, which Bruner described as processes of "scaffolding" (Wood, Bruner, & Ross, 1976), consisting in the laying of new knowledge supported by previously known knowledge. The curiosity through uncertainty, or full engagement, arises only in optimal ways if the motivation of competence is operated through processes of progressive rising of difficulty. Or, simply said, **contexts of mastery**.

4.3.2 Novelty/Autonomy

Having novelty as one of the pillars of curiosity (Litman, 2008, p. 1594), the main points of engagement appear in the form of "intellectual interest", "fun of learning" and "the exploration of new knowledge" (Litman, 2012, p. 1163). In this sense, the novelty or the new awakens in the human a need to discover, explore and experiment, which manifests as "sensation seeking" (Zuckerman, 2001), pushing for personal desires and previous experiences, correlating directly with the need of autonomy.

Unlike uncertainty, novelty arouses less desire to deepen the artefact and obtain missing information, acting more through "exploratory pursuit" (Cloninger, 1987), producing, instead of focusing attention, "impulsive, exploratory, fickle and excitable" behaviours (Cloninger, 1987; Zuckerman, 2001). While uncertainty drives people to worry about detail, dwelling on careful analysis of information to make the best decisions, novelty works almost antithetically, leading people to jump from theme to theme, from element to element, so as to avoid boredom (Cloninger, 1987; Zuckerman, 2001). An example that has already become a classic of this phenomenon is Instagram's "endless scroll" (see Fig. 4.11), qualified by some as "behavioral addictive" (Alter, 2017), in which subjects take too little time to analyse each image and are very quickly impelled to move on to the next, the new, the always newer. This effect has been widely exploited by tourism promoters, selling the idea of the new and never seen as promoting "positive emotions" (Mitas & Bastiaansen, 2018). The same effect can also be seen in the extreme increase in consumer choices (Iyengar, 2010) (see Fig. 4.12), something that seeks to respond to the desire to try different,

Fig. 4.11 Instagram's endless scroll is recognized as being able to create behavioural addiction, and it relies on the novelty effect (Picture by Daria Shevtsova, licensed free to use at: https://www.pexels.com/photo/person-holding-space-gray-iphone-x-1440722/. Accessed: 28 July 2019)

Fig. 4.12 The novelty effect can be seen in the apparent innovation of infinite consumer choices (Picture by Fancycrave, licensed free to use at: https://www.pexels.com/photo/assorted-bottle-and-cans-811108/. Accessed: 28 July 2019)

new and appealing things, but also the need to differentiate in the market by mere novelty. That is, curiosity is triggered by the presentation of previously unseen patterns, which in turn encourages autonomic motivation in the hope of individualizing, moving away from the already existing within the collective, fully supporting the creative desire to reach the original and different.

It is clear from this opposition of elements of curiosity (uncertainty—novelty) driven by motivation (competence—autonomy) that we may be facing subjects who will privilege different tendencies in their approach to reality, and we can see this, for example, in the way they approach risk situations. Studies on the relationship between dopamine and novelty seeking (Calvey, 2017) report behaviours founded on extraversion and impulsivity that foster greater openness to risk, prioritizing immediate sensation over future impacts. In this way, the inner thirst for autonomy, exploration and experimentation dominates the decisions to be made, without looking at external reality control that continually circumscribes the boundaries, whether social, physical or cognitive, providing space for optimal contexts of invention and creativity (Zagalo & Branco, 2015).

This propensity, or inability, to follow rules in thinking goes, once again, against the problem-solving method of the previous section, following a non-direct or divergent logic of thinking—linked to dream, fantasy or play—in which ideas are given full freedom to flow without direction. Munari (1977) sought to illustrate this process (see Fig. 4.13) from the deconstruction of thought and memory. In it, we can see how reasoning through the associative model of ideas uses a database (memory) to fantasize or remix the imagination. In this sense, Munari argues that the larger this database, the more diverse knowledge you have, the easier it will be to develop

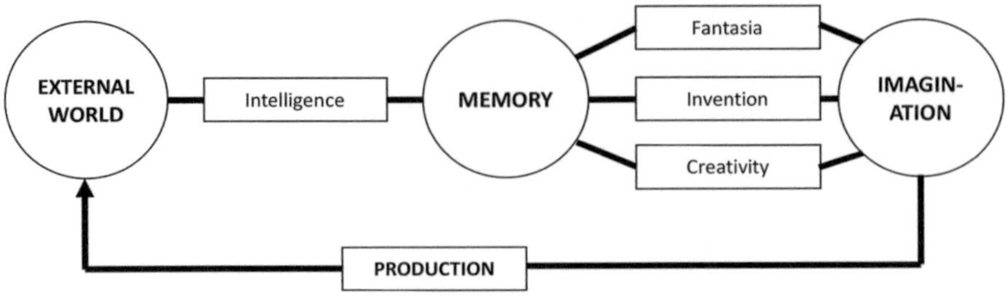

Fig. 4.13 The model of creativity purposed by Munari (1977) (The model has been rebuilt to be translated to English from the original version)

creativity. However, this database is not enough: there is something else happening in associative processing, as we will see.

The best way to understand what happens in creative processing is to differentiate between inventive and innovative approaches, based on the idea that the former seek difference and novelty, while the latter seek to optimize earlier inventions that require a much more comprehensive approach, close to the previous uncertainty/competence cycle. Thus, the processes necessary for the invention proceed much more dynamically, based on a context of creativity driven by continuous forward and backward cycles of exploration and creation (Maggitti, Smith, & Katila, 2013) (see Fig. 4.14), driven by the association and disassociation of concepts, by divergence, laterality and variability of options. Notice how this discontinuity is totally opposed to the hierarchization and linearization of problem-solving contexts (García et al., 2019).

The invention can be described through the example of the revolutionary conception of "Les Demoiselles d'Avignon" (1907) (see Fig. 4.15) with Picasso not only

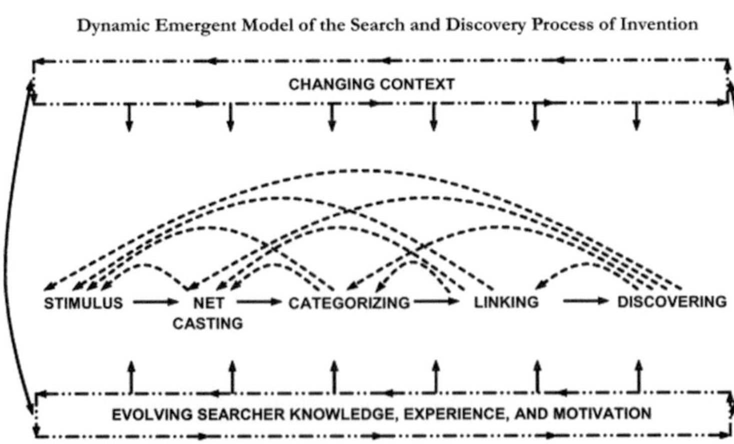

Fig. 4.14 The process of invention takes place in an environment of permanent flow between actions, unlike the focused and planned modes, privileging autonomy and creativity to reach the invention (Maggitti et al., 2013)

Fig. 4.15 The search for new (through strangeness) visual patterns, never before seen, by Picasso in "Les Demoiselles d'Avignon" (1907) (Picture in the public domain, https://en.wikipedia.org/wiki/File:Les_Demoiselles_d%27Avignon.jpg, used under the "fair use" law. Accessed: 28 July 2019)

drawing hundreds of sketches looking for something new, erasing and redrawing on the canvas itself, letting his mind wander, drawing on El Greco, Gauguin, Cezanne, primitivism, African tribal art and even the mathematics of Maurice Princet, that gave him the celebrated cubist effect, to achieve an unprecedented remix, a totally new thing.

In this context of creativity, the novelty/autonomy relationship works driven by the fluidity of the processes, which is enhanced by a fickle attention leading to jumping between elements, an effect produced by the search for newness without restraints and also supported by autonomy. The gratification of anticipation that drives subjects to search for more and more works on the basis of novelty, thereby also optimizing the creation of the new. This is not something simply developed, or worked as a method, but rather is inherent in the sensibilities of the creators, as we have seen with Da Vinci or Edison, and we can see it when revisiting Proust, who was known for having built one of the greatest works of literature, a seven-volume book with over 3,000 pages, in a process that took 10 years to develop. In order to put it into practice, Proust shut himself at home during the last 10 years of his life and insulated the entire room with cork lining (see Fig. 4.16). Why? Because he needed to control himself, he needed to focus, to follow a linear and controlled writing process, which was extremely difficult

Fig. 4.16 In the replica of Proust's bedroom, at Museé Carnavalet (Paris), it is possible to see the walls insulated with the cork (Picture by the author)

for him, as his ability to maintain attention was greatly reduced. This is evidenced in a study (Zabelina, O'Leary, Pornpattananangkul, Nusslock, & Beeman, 2015) in which is demonstrated an enormous sensitivity to stimuli or "breadth of attention" (Kasof, 1997) that predisposes to greater thinking fluency (Dumas, Schmidt, & Alexander, 2016) in the most creative people. Proust needed to shut down his external sensitivity, to evoke and analyse internal memories and experiences.

This fluidity of the creative process also explains Csikszentmihalyi's already famous concept of "flow" (1990), as it is through this fluidity that the subject can stand on the fine line between frustration and anxiety. Although the theory proposes a single, focused and regulated activity, it is mainly just talking about the external process made by the interactor since, as we have seen above, excessive focusing restricts the openness and associativity of ideas, requiring persistence and patience, contrary to what flow is based on. That is, the flow does not happen during the mere cognitive solving of the problem, but rather during the creative process of autonomic undirected thinking. It is at this point of action, "to do", in constant reaction to feedback, not compulsory or controlled, with mental representations swarming among various, always new, interesting and engaging choices, that we feel the loss of self-awareness; that is, we lose our awareness, the notion of conscious thought control, and we move on to unconscious, daydreaming thinking.

All this points to a set of needs dear to the fields of artistic creation and design. There may be focuses and goals, but the way to get there is different, original, nonlinear and poorly standardized. In this sense, it is common to find some confusion between problem-oriented processes and outlined objectives and those that novelty–autonomy seeks. Even in design, a more systematized discipline than the arts, more aimed at processes of innovation rather than originality, the basis is distinguished from engineering, as the design process is not moved to respond to one goal, but rather to find alternatives to the goal itself, which requires completely different ways of focusing and insisting on the same spot, or just: **contexts for creativity**.

4.3.3 Comparability/Relatedness

Unlike uncertainty and novelty, which by focusing on problem-solving and creativity contexts operate on more accessible and potentially stable external information, information about humans is "extraordinarily complex" (Fiske, 1995), given the need to access private and subjective experiences—in their behaviour, thoughts and feelings—that make information less easily accessible and at the same time less reliable. For this purpose, "interpersonal curiosity" (Litman & Pezzo, 2007) is a fundamental behaviour that guarantees the activation of the search for knowledge about others, being strongly motivated by the volition of "social comparison" (Festinger, 1954).

Without strong knowledge of each other, it is not possible to guarantee the creation of affiliation processes between people. Family ties foster an intrinsic basis of closeness and relationship (Bowlby, 1988) that cannot be replicated by mere affiliation groups due to lack of biological relationship, forcing the continued comparative processes between us and the others, searching to identify affinities and sympathies. These comparative processes do not serve only to understand others, they are also fundamental in understanding ourselves (Dunning & Hayes, 1996) and this perspective intensifies through Mead's symbolic interactionism (Mead, 1982) which argues that we exist only insofar as we socially interact with others. That is, our individuality depends on the common symbolic aspects that occur in the interaction with other individual beings. From this relationship emanates a set of shared references that allow each of us to understand the contexts in which we are inserted, the others and ourselves.

This same approach was deepened through Bandura's "theory of social learning" (Bandura, 1962), which argued empirically, that human beings learn essentially by imitating each other. Working on the social relationship, the subjects observe and compare in order to create their own behavioural models of action in the world. These same models can be amplified not only by behaviourist punishment and gratification, but by visualizing these processes in others, that is, through imitation learning or mere observation, which Bandura refers to as "enactive" or "vicarious" (Bandura, 1977). The case of enactivity is fundamental in the field of "tacit knowledge" (Polanyi, 1966), knowledge that cannot be described, which we access only by visualizing others doing and imitating, learning by doing—e.g. cycling or surfing. For Varela, Rosch and Thompson, the enactivism goes beyond the mere imitation and:

> emphasize the growing conviction that cognition is not the representation of a pre-given world by a pre-given mind but is rather the enactment of a world and a mind on the basis of a history of the variety of actions that a being in the world performs. (Varela, Rosch, & Thompson, 1991, p. 9)

Fig. 4.17 Tourism is one of the greatest social phenomena of the twenty-first century, attracting crowds of people who want to experience what millions of others have experienced before (Picture licensed free by Pxhere at: https://pxhere.com/en/photo/868996. Accessed: 28 July 2019)

Of course, the dominant culture is mostly attached to the idea of mimetic representation. As Baudrillard stated, we are already living in a "simulacrum" (Baudrillard, 1981), with the representation controlling our knowledge of the real. For that, the vicarious case is much broader, serving us all the time in real-time relationships, but most of all explaining the charm and power of the traditional media—e.g. television and film—in building the social fabric and symbolic-cultural mechanism that later offers us phenomena such as the effects of current tourism (see Fig. 4.17).

But the tourism effect is really twofold, vicarious and enactive. It can be seen both in the imitation of visiting tourist sites and as symbolic role models in creating images of these sites, as can be seen in the work done by the Instagram account, @insta_repeat.[1] In this account, the unknown author has dedicated herself to searching the Instagram flow for similar photos, finding pictures of enormous mimicry, where the same places give rise to final images with almost equal framing, light, poses and expressions. The anonymous author said, in interview: "I think they became 'templates' when they grew in popularity, thus creating the cycle of familiarity and repetition. Now, in this photography genre, these templates are the gold standard for what a 'successful' image should look like. It's a self-fulfilling prophecy" (McGeary, 2018) (see Fig. 4.18). These templates were created through the enactment of the world and the minds, and not through mere imitation, they appear through the performing process. Even if for Harari they are nothing more than imaginary order:

> people do not wish to accept that the order governing their lives is imaginary, but in fact every person is born into a pre-existing imagined order, and his or her desires are shaped from birth by its dominant myths. (Harari, 2014; Chap. 6)

---

[1]The account is public assessable through the URL: https://www.instagram.com/insta_repeat. Accessed: 28 July 2019.

Fig. 4.18 We tend to recreate photographs that our minds recognize, enacting actions that mimic our imagination of others like us (Pictures reproduced from the account @insta_repeat (https://www.instagram.com/insta_repeat); the author maintains anonymity.)

A final example, immensely cited, of this phenomenon of extreme comparison and social imitation, appears in DeLillo's *White Noise* (1985), in which the author demonstrates how the simple existence of others can make the artefact dispensable, taking us to believe just through the knowledge of the cultural symbolic (see excerpt below). Taking into account that DeLillo's discussion is about an American barn, we can even connect it to Fig. 4.18, which elevates the symbol presented in text and images to the level of iconic, extrapolating its physical meaning into the abstract level.

> "Several days later Murray asked me about a tourist attraction known as the most photographed barn in America
>
> (…)
>
> Soon the sign started appearing. THE MOST PHOTOGRAPHED BARN IN AMERICA. (…)
>
> All the people had cameras; some had tripods, telephoto lenses, filter kits. A man in a booth sold postcards and slides — pictures of the barn taken from the elevated spot. We stood near a grove of trees and watched the photographers.
>
> (…)
>
> "No one sees the barn," he said finally.
>
> A long silence followed.
>
> "Once you've seen the signs about the barn, it becomes impossible to see the barn." (…)
>
> "We see only what the others see. The thousands who were here in the past, those who will come in the future. We've agreed to be part of a collective perception.
>
> (…)
>
> "They are taking pictures of taking pictures",
>
> Excerpt from *White Noise* (DeLillo, 1985)

Festinger argues that "social comparison" is fundamental in the process of "self-evaluation" (1954, p. 135), which ensures the maintenance of individual internal coherence. So, when we want to know how we are, what we can and cannot do, we draw on comparison with others, looking at their weaknesses and strengths to understand how they solve problems. On the other hand, it is this need for self-regulation that promotes the gregariousness of the species, its need for the group and at the same time the search for groups that share the same values and principles (1954, p. 136). Corcoran and colleagues (2011) consider "self-regulation" a comparison with equals, adding to it two other levels: comparison with alleged inferior, and superior subjects. Thus, we have the "self-image" responsible for looking for inferior traits in others in order to create a more positive image of oneself; and "self-improvement", looking for superior traits, looking for tips for improvement and progress (2011, p. 121). Bringing together the three comparative processes, we find that we are facing the whole basis sustaining the contexts of "empathy", in which the subjects actively compare, understanding the other through themselves. In the contemporary world, the comparative act is no longer only done through face-to-face groups, given the individualistic tendency of society that tends to consider talking about others, gossiping, as something harmful (Litman & Pezzo, 2005), but can be done by means of artefacts, thanks to the invention of media—novels, plays and films. This also explains why cinema was seen by film studies in the 1960s and 1970s as a voyeuristic artefact (Morrisson, 1970; Mulvey, 1975), a definition that was later replaced by empathy.

Empathy in cinema began with the simplest common sense—"putting oneself in the shoes of the other"—and evolved with Zillmann, who worked on conceptualization in the field of Media Psychology, defining empathy as a state in which it is not just "feeling for" but also "feeling with" (1991) (see Fig. 4.19). In the field of neuroscience, Gallese and Goldman (1998) discovered the so-called "mirror neurons" that allowed us to advance our knowledge of the neurological processes behind empathy. Mirror neurons are responsible for our mimicking activity of the other and in some ways explain more basic affective processes such as "emotional contagion". Baron-Cohen (2003) divided empathy into two components—cognitive and affective. The first defines the ability to "predict another person's behavior or mental state", while the affective component defines the "appropriate emotional response to the other person's emotional state". Summing this up:

> The process of empathy is a complex process that is closely related to theories of mind or mental simulation about our ability to construct one model of another's mind either through simulation or imagination, which enhances the competence to anticipate actions, the other and thus not only perceive and feel the other, but also act by adjusting emotionally to the other. It is one of the strong pillars of social interaction… (Zagalo, 2009, p. 62)

But De Waal (2009) takes this definition even a little further because it establishes a more direct relationship between the mental image of empathy and our physiological action, connecting common sense to mirror neurons:

> empathy and sympathy start not in the higher regions of imagination, or the ability to consciously reconstruct how we would feel if we were in someone else's situation. It began

Fig. 4.19 *The Shawshank Redemption* (Darabont, 1994) was not the biggest box office hit, but it has been the highest rated IMDB movie for over a decade. The film fully offers the comparative idea on three fronts: self-regulation, self-image and self-improvement. The conflicts presented offer empathic contexts that allow the viewer to effectively learn more about others and about themselves. In the picture, we can see the characters' relationship responsible for the spectator's comparisons and empathy (Picture reproduced from the movie *The Shawshank Redemption* (1994))

> much simpler, with the synchronization of bodies: running when others run, laughing when others laugh, crying when others cry, or yawning when others yawn. (De Waal, 2009, p. 51)

The "synchrony of bodies" turns out to be the key to empathy and the foundation of interpersonal curiosity or comparative need: a physiological process, the result of the evolution of species and through which we have succeeded over millennia to develop social systems of such great complexity. In fact, Rizzolati, in a 2004 article, goes further by raising the importance of gregariousness processes to the basic human condition:

> If we want to survive, we must understand the actions of others. Furthermore, without action understanding, social organization is impossible. In the case of humans, there is another faculty that depends on the observation of others' actions: imitation learning. Unlike most species, we are able to learn by imitation, and this faculty is at the basis of human culture. (Rizzolatti & Craighero, 2004, p. 169)

This leads us to a greater assumption about the context of artefact production, since over the last decade many studies have been defending our absolute need for stories, referring to them as the main way to reach knowledge, as a central way of human understanding (Boyd, 2010; Gottschall, 2012; Herman, 2013). But when we look at the stories—whether oral, written or audiovisual—what we always see in them, centrally and high above any other element, is people and their conflicts. Bodies, faces, expressions, examples and cases. That makes us consider that what makes humans like stories so much is not the stories themselves—plot or *fabula*—but the windows they open to the comparison with and understanding of others like us, and above all feeling these others. Cinema, literature and narrative media in general are empathetic machines, simulators of human conflicts that we can peer into without being seen, as voyeurs or gossip lovers. As Storr puts it:

> Stories are us. It's story that makes us human. Recent research suggests language evolved principally to swap 'social information' (Dunbar, Lycett, & Barrett, 2005, p. 133) back when we were living in Stone Age tribes. In other words, we'd gossip. We'd tell tales about the moral rights and wrongs of other people, punish the bad behaviour, reward the good, and thereby keep everyone cooperating and the tribe in check. Stories about people being heroic or villainous, and the emotions of joy and outrage they triggered, were crucial to human survival. We're wired to enjoy them. (Storr, 2019, p. 2)

Social comparison explains the success of the media, serving as mirrors of humanity, presenting us with processes that have adaptive and utilitarian foundations. Empathy contexts are thus volitional processes of searching for feelings, fulfilling needs, that activate curiosity. Social comparison produces the emotional information needed to create **contexts of affinity** and thus motivates subjects to action.

4.4 Epistemic Contexts and Profiles

From the analysis of the processes of activation of human curiosity as well as the intrinsic behaviours that promote motivation, three pairs were identified—Uncertainty/competence; Novelty/autonomy; Comparison/relatedness—promoters of human volition that led us to identify three major areas of action, or contexts: **Mastery**, **Creativity** and **Affinity**. These three contexts then correlate directly with the profile identified in the previous chapter (see Fig. 4.20).

In all three, there's always a need for the interactor to comprehend and explain the reality of the artefact presented to him or her, or to find patterns that satisfy the information gap that triggered this curiosity. The search for patterns is something founded deep within us, inscribed in our biology: "the human mind delights in finding pattern—so much so that we often mistake coincidence or forced analogy for profound meaning" (Gould, 1985). Bor (2012), following the evolutionary work of Gould, based on studies of neuroscience and the formation of consciousness processes, further highlights the fundamental aspects of this cognitive obsession:

Fig. 4.20 The interaction motives of the profiles correlate with the action areas defined by the volition cycles

> The process of combining more primitive pieces of information to create something more meaningful is a crucial aspect both of learning and of consciousness and is one of the defining features of human experience. (…) Perhaps what most distinguishes us humans from the rest of the animal kingdom is our ravenous desire to find structure in the information we pick up in the world. We cannot help actively searching for patterns. (Bor, 2012)

However, the patterns sought are not the same for everyone, and we can refer here to Hayakawa's "Ladder of Abstraction" (see Fig. 4.21), used by Hart (2007) to account for the descriptive variability of the real. For Hayakawa, the more we place speech at the top of the stairs, the harder it becomes for our receiver to create mental images. At the top, the elements present too many variables and possibilities, making the images fuzzy. On the other hand, the brain uses the imagery produced by the senses—visual, aural, smell and touch—to create mental images. But if we think of our profiles, we realize that in terms of the patterns sought, they are in the antipodes. What moves the interest of the abstracter is precisely the mastery of the whole, for whom the particular individual is irrelevant, but rather the symbol, capable of framing categories to model explanatory equations of wholes.

Fig. 4.21 The ladder of abstraction. In Hart (2007, p. 170)

Fig. 4.22 The patterns developed by contexts

Dramatists, on the other hand, are more focused on understanding the individual subject, because empathy needs human emotional comparison, without which we cannot put ourselves in the other's shoes, needing the effect to mentally recreate the concrete feelings of that other to arrive at affinity. On the other hand, the tinkerer is much more focused on the properties and features of elements, so he or she does not depend so much on generalization or particularization.

Let us then look, using some examples, at the different patterns sought in each of the above contexts. In the case of **mastery**, the patterns sought are **problem-solving** structures that, based on causality, allow for generalization and replication of the process or response (e.g. a method for solving a mathematical calculation; understanding what differentiates animal species; understanding how waves are produced in oceans). In the case of **creativity**, we seek **unfamiliar** patterns to obtain original mechanics (e.g. painting with new materials; creating drink from a never tried mix; adding weird features to an existent system/tool). And, in the case of **affinity**, one looks for the particular and concrete, human-centred and emotional to build empathy (e.g. when a parent loses a child; when a couple separates; when a child goes away to study) (see Fig. 4.22).

The function of these contexts and patterns will be used to frame the relationship between interacting subjects and artefacts. In this sense, and not being able to anticipate the final real contexts for which each artefact will be designed, it is possible to use these three approaches in the analysis of effective contexts and to define in which of them they fit. The choice of either of these contexts cannot be seen as exclusive, but rather as a tendency. Contexts, by their multifactorial dependence, are never closed. A movie can offer unfamiliar contexts, just as the problem-solving process may depend on comparative social information. We should not restrict contextual patterns to the vehicles of information transmission, nor types of discourse.

References

Alter, A. (2017). *Irresistible: The rise of addictive technology and the business of keeping us hooked.* New York, USA: Penguin Press.

Ashley, M. (2013). Working backward to solve problems. Retrieved July 27, 2019, from TEDed website: https://ed.ted.com/lessons/working-backward-to-solve-problems-maurice-ashley.

Bandura, A. (1962). Social learning through imitation. In M. R. Jones (Ed.), *Nebraska symposium on motivation, 1962*. Oxford: University Nebraska Press.

Bandura, A. (1977). *Social learning theory*. Upper Saddle River: Prentice-Hall.

Bandura, A. (1986). *Social foundations of thought and action: A social cognitive theory*. Upper Saddle River: Prentice-Hall, Pearson.

Baron-Cohen, S. (2003). *The essential difference: Men, women and the extreme male brain*. London: Penguin Press Science.

Baudrillard, J. (1981). *Simulacres et Simulation*. Paris: Éditions Galilée.

Berlyne, D. (1954). A theory of human curiosity. *British Journal of Psychology. General Section, 45*(3), 180–191. https://doi.org/10.1111/j.2044-8295.1954.tb01243.x.

Bor, D. (2012). *The ravenous brain: How the new science of consciousness explains our insatiable search for meaning*. New York: Basic Books.

Bordwell, D. (1985). *Narration in the fiction film*. Wisconsin: University of Wisconsin Press.

Bowlby, J. (1988). *A secure base: Parent-child attachment and healthy human development*. New York: Basic Books.

Boyd, B. (2010). *On the origin of stories*. Cambridge, MA: Harvard University Press.

Broeck, A., Vansteenkiste, M., Witte, H., Soenens, B., & Lens, W. (2010). Capturing autonomy, competence, and relatedness at work: Construction and initial validation of the work-related basic need satisfaction scale. *Journal of Occupational and Organizational Psychology, 83*(4), 981–1002. https://doi.org/10.1348/096317909X481382.

Calvey, T. (2017). *The extended evolutionary synthesis and addiction: The price we pay for adaptability*. https://doi.org/10.1016/bs.pbr.2017.07.004.

Carvalho, A. A., Zagalo, N., & Araujo, I. (2015). From games played by secondary students to a gamification framework. In *Society for Information Technology & Teacher Education International Conference*, pp. 737–744.

Cloninger, C. R. (1987). A Systematic method for clinical description and classification of personality variants. *Archives of General Psychiatry, 44*(6), 573. https://doi.org/10.1001/archpsyc.1987.01800180093014.

Corcoran, K., Crusius, J., & Mussweiler, T. (2011). Social comparison: Motives, standards, and mechanisms. In D. Chadee (Ed.), *Theories in social psychology* (pp. 119–139). Hoboken, NJ: Wiley-Blackwell.

Coyle, D. (2009). *The talent code: Greatness isn't born. It's grown. Here's how*. New York: Bantam Books.

Csikszentmihalyi, M. (1990). *Flow: The psychology of optimal experience*. New York: Harper and Row.

Damasio, A. (2018). *The strange order of things: Life, feeling, and the making of cultures*. New York: Pantheon.

Darabont, F. (1994). *The Shawshank redemption*. Culver City: Columbia Pictures.

Davis, I., Keeling, D., Schreier, P., & Williams, A. (2007). *The Mckinsey approach to problem solving* (No. 66).

De Waal, F. (2009). *The age of empathy: Nature's lessons for a kinder society*. New York: Random House.

Deci, E., & Flaste, R. (1996). *Why we do what we do: Understanding self-motivation*. London: Penguin Books.

Deci, E., & Ryan, R. M. (1985). *Intrinsic motivation and self-determination in human behavior*. https://doi.org/10.1007/978-1-4899-2271-7.

DeLillo, D. (1985). *White noise*. New York: Viking Adult.

Dubol, M., Trichard, C., Leroy, C., Sandu, A.-L., Rahim, M., Granger, B., … Artiges, E. (2018). Dopamine transporter and reward anticipation in a dimensional perspective: A multimodal brain imaging study. *Neuropsychopharmacology, 43*(4), 820–827. https://doi.org/10.1038/npp.2017.183.

Dumas, D., Schmidt, L. C., & Alexander, P. A. (2016). Predicting creative problem solving in engineering design. *Thinking Skills and Creativity, 21,* 50–66. https://doi.org/10.1016/j.tsc.2016.05.002.

Dunbar, R., Lycett, J., & Barrett, L. (2005). *Evolutionary psychology: A beginner's guide*. Oxford: Oneworld Publications.

Dunning, D., & Hayes, A. F. (1996). Evidence for egocentric comparison in social judgment. *Journal of Personality and Social Psychology, 71*(2), 213–229. https://doi.org/10.1037/0022-3514.71.2.213.
Eco, U. (1989). *The open work*. Boston: Harvard University Press.
Festinger, L. (1954). A theory of social comparison processes. *Human Relations, 7*(2), 117–140. https://doi.org/10.1177/001872675400700202.
Fiske, S. (1995). Social cognition. *Advanced social psychology* (pp. 149–194). New York: McGraw-Hill.
Gallese, V., & Goldman, A. (1998). Mirror neurons and the mind-reading. *Trens in Cognitive Sciences, 2*(12), 493–501. https://doi.org/10.1016/S1364-6613(98)01262-5.
García, T., Boom, J., Kroesbergen, E. H., Núñez, J. C., & Rodríguez, C. (2019). Planning, execution, and revision in mathematics problem solving: Does the order of the phases matter? *Studies in Educational Evaluation, 61,* 83–93. https://doi.org/10.1016/j.stueduc.2019.03.001.
Gottlieb, J., Oudeyer, P.-Y., Lopes, M., & Baranes, A. (2013). Information-seeking, curiosity, and attention: Computational and neural mechanisms. *Trends in Cognitive Sciences, 17*(11), 585–593. https://doi.org/10.1016/j.tics.2013.09.001.
Gottschall, J. (2012). *The storytelling animal: How stories make us human*. Boston, MA: Houghton Mifflin Harcourt.
Gould, S. J. (1985). *The Flamingo's smile: Reflections in natural history*. New York: W. W. Norton.
Harari, Y. N. (2014). *Sapiens: A brief history of humankind*. New York: Harper Collins.
Hart, J. (2007). *A Writer's coach: The complete guide to writing strategies that work*. New York: Pantheon.
Herman, D. (2013). *Storytelling and the sciences of mind*. Cambridge, MA: MIT Press.
Hume, D. (1888). *A treatise of human nature*. London, Oxford : Clarendon Press.
Hunt, J. (1965). Intrinsic motivation and its role in psychological development. In *Nebraska symposium on motivation* (pp. 189–282).
Iyengar, S. (2010). *The art of choosing*. New York: Twelve.
James, W. (1890). *The principles of psychology* (Vols. 1 & 2). New York: Holt. https://doi.org/10.1037/10538-000.
Kang, M. J., Hsu, M., Krajbich, I. M., Loewenstein, G., McClure, S. M., Wang, J. T., et al. (2009). The wick in the candle of learning. *Psychological Science, 20*(8), 963–973. https://doi.org/10.1111/j.1467-9280.2009.02402.x.
Kasof, J. (1997). Creativity and breadth of attention. *Creativity Research Journal, 10*(4), 303–315. https://doi.org/10.1207/s15326934crj1004_2.
Leslie, I. (2014). *Curious: The desire to know and why your future depends on it*. New York: Basic Books.
Litman, J. A. (2005). Curiosity and the pleasures of learning: Wanting and liking new information. *Cognition and Emotion*. https://doi.org/10.1080/02699930541000101.
Litman, J. A. (2008). Interest and deprivation factors of epistemic curiosity. *Personality and Individual Differences*. https://doi.org/10.1016/j.paid.2008.01.014.
Litman, J. A. (2010). Relationships between measures of I- and D-type curiosity, ambiguity tolerance, and need for closure: An initial test of the wanting-liking model of information-seeking. *Personality and Individual Differences*. https://doi.org/10.1016/j.paid.2009.11.005.
Litman, J. A. (2012). Epistemic curiosity. In N. M. Seel (Ed.), *Encyclopedia of the sciences of learning* (pp. 1162–1165). https://doi.org/10.1007/978-1-4419-1428-6_1645.
Litman, J. A., & Pezzo, M. V. (2005). Individual differences in attitudes towards gossip. *Personality and Individual Differences*. https://doi.org/10.1016/j.paid.2004.09.003.
Litman, J. A., & Pezzo, M. V. (2007). Dimensionality of interpersonal curiosity. *Personality and Individual Differences*. https://doi.org/10.1016/j.paid.2007.04.021.
Loewenstein. (1994). The psychology of curiosity: A review and reinterpretation. *Psychological Bulletin, 1*(116), 75–98. https://doi.org/10.1037/0033-2909.116.1.75.
Maggitti, P. G., Smith, K. G., & Katila, R. (2013). The complex search process of invention. *Research Policy, 42*(1), 90–100. https://doi.org/10.1016/j.respol.2012.04.020.

Maslow, A. H. (1943). A theory of human motivation. *Psychological Review, 50*(4), 370–396. https://doi.org/10.1037/h0054346.
Mayer, R. E. (1983). *Thinking, problem solving, cognition*. New York: W.H. Freeman.
Mayer, R. E. (2013). Problem solving. In *The Oxford handbook of cognitive psychology*. https://doi.org/10.1093/oxfordhb/9780195376746.013.0048.
McGeary, K. (2018, October). Wander, roam, replicate: A conversation about copy-cat culture in the travel space With @Insta_Repeat. *Passion Passport*. Retrieved from https://passionpassport.com/insta_repeat/.
Mead, G. H. (1982). *The individual and the social self: Unpublished essays by G. H. Mead* (D. L. Miller, Ed.). Chicago: University of Chicago Press.
Mitas, O., & Bastiaansen, M. (2018). Novelty: A mechanism of tourists' enjoyment. *Annals of Tourism Research, 72,* 98–108. https://doi.org/10.1016/j.annals.2018.07.002.
Morrisson, J. (1970). *The lords and the new creatures*. New York: Simon & Schuster.
Mulvey, L. (1975). Visual pleasure and narrative Cinema. *Screen, 16*(3), 6–18. https://doi.org/10.1093/screen/16.3.6.
Munari, B. (1977). *Fantasia*. Coimbra: Edições 70.
Pink, D. (2008). *Drive: The surprising truth about what motivates us*. New York: Riverhead Books.
Polanyi, M. (1966). *The tacit dimension*. Chicago: University of Chicago Press.
Polya, G. (1945). *How to solve it*. Princeton, NJ: Princeton University Press.
Powell, C., Nettelbeck, T., & Burns, N. R. (2016). Deconstructing intellectual curiosity. *Personality and Individual Differences, 95,* 147–151. https://doi.org/10.1016/j.paid.2016.02.037.
Rizzolatti, G., & Craighero, L. (2004). The Mirror-Neuron System. *Annual Review of Neuroscience, 27*(1), 169–192. https://doi.org/10.1146/annurev.neuro.27.070203.144230.
Robinson, C. D., Gallus, J., Lee, M. G., & Rogers, T. (2019). The demotivating effect (and unintended message) of awards. *Organizational Behavior and Human Decision Processes*. https://doi.org/10.1016/j.obhdp.2019.03.006.
Rock, I. (1985). *The logic of perception*. Cambridge, MA: MIT Press.
Ryan, R. M., & Deci, E. L. (2000). Self-determination theory and the facilitation of intrinsic motivation, social development, and well-being. *American Psychologist, 55*(1), 68–78. https://doi.org/10.1037/0003-066X.55.1.68.
Sakaki, M., Yagi, A., & Murayama, K. (2018). Curiosity in old age: A possible key to achieving adaptive aging. *Neuroscience & Biobehavioral Reviews, 88,* 106–116. https://doi.org/10.1016/j.neubiorev.2018.03.007.
Skinner, B. (1953). *Science and human behavior*. Oxford: Macmillan.
Storr, W. (2019). *The science of storytelling*. Croydon: Harper Collins.
Tannert, C., Elvers, H.-D., & Jandrig, B. (2007). The ethics of uncertainty. In the light of possible dangers, research becomes a moral duty. *EMBO Reports*, *8*(10), 892–896. https://doi.org/10.1038/sj.embor.7401072.
Varela, F. J., Rosch, E., & Thompson, E. (1991). *The embodied mind. Cognitive science and human experience*. Cambridge, MA: MIT Press.
Vygotsky, L. (1930). *Imaginação e Criatividade na Infância*. Lisboa: Dinalivro.
Vygotsky, L. S. (1978). *Mind and society: The development of higher psychological processes*. Harvard University Press. https://doi.org/(Original manuscripts [ca. 1930-1934]).
White, R. W. (1959). Motivation reconsidered: The concept of competence. *Psychological Review, 66*(5), 297–333. https://doi.org/10.1037/h0040934.
Wood, D., Bruner, J. S., & Ross, G. (1976). The role of tutoring in problem-solving. *Journal of Child Psychology and Psychiatry, 17*(2), 89–100. https://doi.org/10.1111/j.1469-7610.1976.tb00381.x.
Zabelina, D. L., O'Leary, D., Pornpattananangkul, N., Nusslock, R., & Beeman, M. (2015). Creativity and sensory gating indexed by the P50: Selective versus leaky sensory gating in divergent thinkers and creative achievers. *Neuropsychologia, 69,* 77–84. https://doi.org/10.1016/j.neuropsychologia.2015.01.034.

Zagalo, N. (2009). *Emoções Interactivas, do Cinema para os Videojogos* (*interactive emotions, from film to videogames*). Retrieved from http://repositorium.sdum.uminho.pt/handle/1822/27674?locale=en.

Zagalo, N., & Branco, P. (2015). *Creativity in the digital age*. https://doi.org/10.1007/978-1-4471-6681-8.

Zillmann, D. (1991). Empathy: Affect from bearing witness to the emotions of others. In J. B. D. Zillmann (Ed.), *Responding to the screen: Reception and reaction processes* (pp. 135–167). New Jersey: Lawrence Erlbaum Associates Inc.

Zuckerman, M. (2001). Sensation seeking: Behavioral expressions and biosocial bases. In *International encyclopedia of the social & behavioral sciences* (pp. 13905–13908). https://doi.org/10.1016/B0-08-043076-7/01772-1.

Chapter 5
Artefacts and Representation

Abstract In this chapter, we enter the discussion of the design of artefacts, their representational possibilities and approaches connected with our profiles and contexts. We present the representation divided into three main categories—symbolic, enactive and mimetic—from which we then build a discussion on the different impacts they have on interaction. The artefact analysis gets deeper with the analysis of the pleasure motives and stimuli and its correlation with the different types of interaction with representation. All is supported by illustrative examples, made of situations, diagrams and pictures.

Interactive media are part of the large media domain that involves all types of media used to record and distribute information. Their origin is confused with the origin of human culture, in the sense that culture as we recognize it exists only as an externalization of ideas, and these always need some means of recording as well as distributing, making known to others. We can think of the Lascaux cave walls and charcoal, which served as a record of the ideas and mental creations externalized by our ancestors, but they also served to distribute them, and they did so well that we still have access to those same records. Until the emergence of the digital sphere, the media had their borders with art well defined, since they labelled the means of registration and distribution, while art labelled the process of creation and production, but could not exist without the media. On the other hand, with the migration from analog to digital, the sense of media as defining the practical and specific components of recording, and thus the conditioning of artistic creation, lost relevance, for everything is digital: the media became all of one type. However, in order to maintain their logic of differentiation, they began to use art to define themselves. Thus, today it has become common to denominate literature, cinema or music as media, using their expressive beacons, artistic languages, which allow us to create a framework of specific information, not through the material object, but through the way they manipulate the digital surface. On the other hand, given the miscegenation and explosion in digital content creation, art came to be used to define objects that were once just media elements—e.g. commercials, humour programmes, informational texts, games or comic strips. Thus, Bolter is very straightforward, and claims

N. Zagalo, *Engagement Design*, Human–Computer Interaction Series,
https://doi.org/10.1007/978-3-030-37085-5_5

what many of us have been saying for some time: "Art and Media are now the same thing" (2019, p. 15).

Therefore, and bearing in mind this book's focus on interactive media, before defining its interactive specificity it must be understood that what is at stake is no longer the media. Then, in order to work out its minimum expressive units, complying with the media as art, we have to move to another semiotic level of understanding the objects of communication. Going down to a biological level, we could look at the ways related to our senses—visual, aural, gestural, spatial, etc.—or look at a level of the basic elements of the creative process—letters, numbers, shapes, faces, bodies, volume, sound, movement, etc.—yet for their elementarity and lack of meaning-making per se, they would be of little use. Thus, it is important to work at an intermediate level, with possibilities for semantic production, that is, capable of producing meaning in a social context (Kress, 2009), called modes—text, graphic, image, audio, video—and, in the case of interactive media, interactivity.

Given the undifferentiated relationship between media and art, we are now able to speak of the artefacts that make up the spectrum of interactive media in a simpler way, as we can use both media and art designation to delimit the expressive mode, simply by, for example, adding the interactive component—e.g. interactive audio, interactive video—or listing already established media definitions—e.g. new media, digital media, hypermedia, multimedia—or some established artistic designations—e.g. hypertext, video games, virtual reality. New designations for the type of artefacts produced by interactive media are always emerging, notably because of the regular technological development in this area, but using the above-mentioned approach, in a way, gives us conditions to frame the scope of the design approach that we want to propose in this book.

Hence, retrieving the listing of interactive media modes—text, graphics, image, audio, video and interactivity—the focus of this book is exclusively on interaction design, as the discussion is made within the general HCI framework. That is, although we are faced with artefacts made up of plastic aesthetic components that mix different expressive modes, the design dealt with here does not concern any mode other than interactivity. This is not to disregard the remaining components of interactive media artefacts, because interactivity does not exist in isolation. Indeed, as will be seen in the next section, in order to understand the impact of interactivity on the production of different meanings, representation in other media arts will have to be evaluated, along with their non-interactive modes, and their expressive capacities compared with the different artefacts produced by interactive media.

5.1 Representation

In order to build the categorization of interactivity to artefact design we need to begin by defining artefacts in their form, and in order to do so it is inevitable to understand how that form is given to human understanding, which takes us to define the artefacts representation, for which we've mixed the phenomenological approach by Peirce and the cognitive by Bruner, discussed then through a media and arts point of view grounded in Dale and Eisner.

For Peirce, representation refers to the act of representing, of "being in place of", or being considered "like being this other" (Peirce, 2000, p. 61), turning representation into a synonym for sign (Fisch, 1986, p. 352), and therefore making of representation the core of semiotics, the philosophical branch responsible for the study of signs developed by Peirce. For Peirce, "the most important division of signs" (Peirce, 2000, p. 64) could then be split into three main categories: indexes, icons and symbols. By indexes, Peirce defines representations bearing physical or existential relation with the object being represented. Like smoke being connected with fire, a barometer being connected with humidity or the "wooden metre" demonstrating physically the real dimension of the metre preserved in Paris. Indexes are representations, but bear in them some physical or tangible condition that directly connects to the real object. Then for icons, Peirce brings the idea of semblance: an image or portrait presents strong resemblance with the object, or the metaphor which serves the representation of ideas through "a parallelism". Finally, the symbols only get connected with the object through conventional rules or norms: they must be learned. Daniel Everett then states that Peirce not only divided the representation into three main categories, but he also indicated "a progression of signs from natural signs (indexes), to icons, to human-created symbols" (2017, p. 16). This means that indexes get to be the basic level of representation, icons the middle ground and then symbols the most complex, and only developed lately in human cognitive evolution, which can be related to the cognitive vision of representation laid out by Jerome Bruner, as we'll see.

On Bruner's cognitive side we have a concern with representation that does not focus on the traditional sense of an external object, but rather on how cognition shapes and memorizes representations. In his theorizing about instruction, Bruner (1966) attempted to find the best model for instructing subjects to get knowledge, for which he tried to define the kind of experiences necessary for the learning process. To this end, it presented what he called "three modes of representation"—symbolic, enactive and iconic—that established ways of memorizing and interpreting the representation of lived experiences. Bruner looks at these modes from a learning perspective as sequential, following the progression stated by Everett about Peirce's categories. He states that a child begins to interpret the world through touch, action and reaction, and then moves to picture comprehension, and is only at a later stage able to deal with symbols, which requires the ability to translate them internally into concepts. The approach to representation is not seen as a mere development theory; Bruner uses it to optimize the instruction of subjects, including adults, which is particularly relevant for us because it could open new ways to optimizing human engagement.

In Bruner's iconic mode we have the creation, preservation and cataloguing of mental images formed from the real presented by the sensory system of vision. This mode allows us to record changes in shape, light and colour, and thus understand the difference between objects—e.g. between a door and a window. Iconic representation works through similarity (the Peircean semblance), that is, what is preserved is a copy as true as possible to the reality presented to our eyes, serving as a database of cases in support of the interpretation of reality—e.g. if we have windows and doors, we are potentially facing a case that configures the existence of a house. Of the three modes presented by Bruner, it is in principle the simplest, since there is no transduction of what is felt for what is preserved. What we bring to mind, as representation, is the image of what we have seen before.

Already, in the enactive mode, we have the whole constellation of information related to human action, mechanical aspects of action. These are not amenable to mere description, as they function as a somatic whole understandable only at the level of the relationship between consciousness and the body (which we can relate directly to the object relation of indexes discussed by Peirce). When we learn to play the violin, our focus and retention of information, or creation of internal representation, happens more by the aspects of pose, gestures, strength and movement of the body than by the symbolic learning of a musical score. It is in the field of enactive representation that constant training is used to optimize the mechanical representation of the body's action to ensure the best execution possible, or the most perfect representation. Enactivity thus corresponds to the particular representation of internal mechanisms, their configurations and variations.

Finally, the symbolic demands from the subject a whole set of skills of abstraction and association of ideas that require the presence of previous concepts in memory, so-called conventions, without which representation cannot become meaningful. That is, the preservation of graphic words or symbols happens to the extent that the subject can assign them a meaning, even though that meaning, unlike images and enactions, may vary. The symbolic thus produces a whole level of representation much more complex by its immense flexibility and adaptability to the changes of the real. For example, we can learn to read an "A" with Portuguese phonetic intonation, and then understand that English phonetic intonation is distinct, yet preserve the symbolic representation of both, and use each one in the appropriate contexts.

This progression or evolution of representation is also supported by the "Cone of Experience" proposed by Dale in 1946 (last revision made in 1969) (see Fig. 5.1, left). In it, Dale defined a kind of scale of the learning experience, presenting a set of activities that would respond to each of Bruner's modes of representation: symbolic—"verbal symbols", "visual symbols"; iconic—"still pictures", "motion pictures", "television" and enactive—"contrived experiences", "direct purposeful experiences". The top of the cone accounts for less world experience, or, following Bruner, greater difficulty in experimenting because it works at a more conventional level. At the bottom, we get the opposite, with enactivity or direct experiencing of activity. The cone has since been updated in the multimedia domain by Baukal and colleagues (2013), as we can see in Fig. 5.1 (right). The update concerns not only the contextualization of each medium in the function of its modes, but also the proposition of an axis of abstraction, moving from symbolic to enactive, or in the case modes—from Text to VR.

Following closely, Eisner (2002) refers to the existence of a set of cognitive processes in the production of representation artefacts, which work "from idea or image, through the hand, into the material, and then into the head of an eager reader of text or image, sound, or movement" (2002, p. 7). That is, the representations developed and transformed inside our minds somehow desire to become artefacts, to

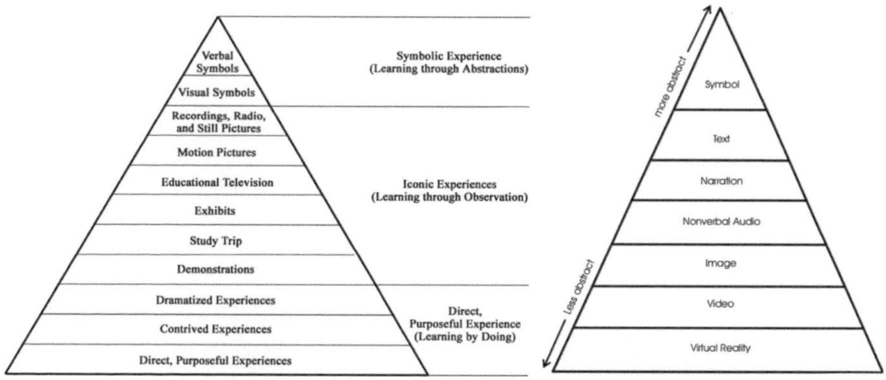

Fig. 5.1 On the left, the "Cone of Experience" by Edgar Dale, in its version of 1969, with the relations with Bruner modes of representation. Reproduced from West (2017) (Book published in Open Access. Direct https://lidtfoundations.pressbooks.com/chapter/edgar-dale-and-the-cone-of-experience/, 1 August 2019). On the right, the "Cone of Abstraction". Reproduced from Baukal and colleagues (2013)

be able to communicate with others. But then a question arises in direct relation to the aspects mentioned by Bruner: how do these representations arrive at the point of even making sense to others? Eisner proposes three modes to answer—conventional, mimetic and expressive—that we can relate to Bruner's categories, following closely the proposed models by Dale and Baukal (see Fig. 5.2).

From the relationship between the two systems of representation, Bruner and Eisner, we can say that the conventional highlights the learning component necessary for a symbolic interaction; the mimetic magnifies the need for realism of the iconic interaction and the expressive pervades the psychomotor domain with emotional components. That is, the representation applied to interactive media does not account for mere aspects of interaction, but seeks to fit this with the representation and its engagement needs. In order to better understand this relationship, let's look at how representation relates to contexts.

5.2 Representation and Contexts

When confronting contexts with the potential representation of artefacts, we find that the patterns defined for each of the contexts—problem-solving, unfamiliar and empathy—are in line with the expected action patterns. That is, on the symbolic side, the construct presented is abstract, requiring logic for its understanding, that is, the meaning and explanation of the symbolic is achieved through finding causality within the explanation of its convention. On the enactive representation, the direct relation with the object and understanding of its functioning makes for the mechanical understanding needed by the unfamiliar patterns of the creative production. Finally, on the

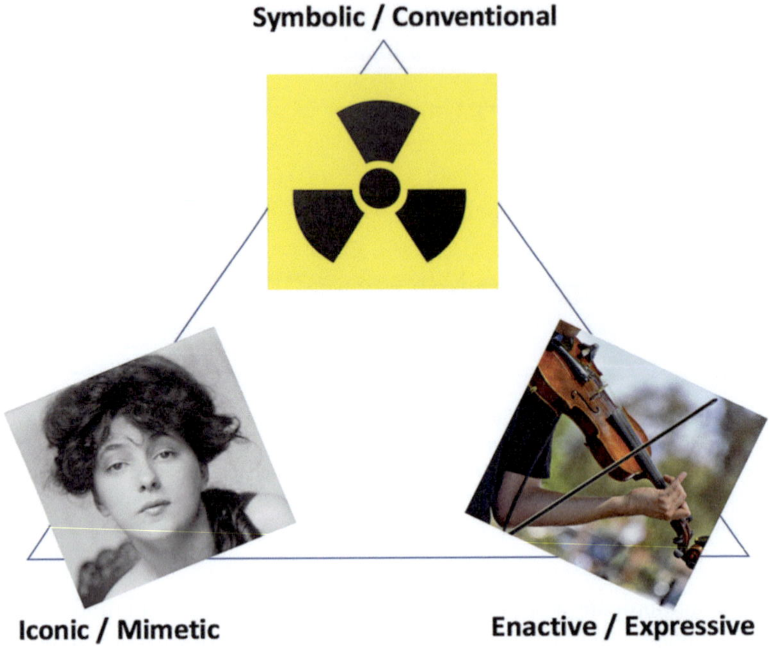

Fig. 5.2 Representation of the artefact can be carried out from three different perspectives. Each triangle vertex brings together the concepts of Bruner and Eisner (The picture used for "iconic/mimetic" is a portrait of Evelyn Nesbit done in 1900 by James Carroll Beck, in the public domain (https://www.loc.gov/pictures/item/2006684222/, 1 August 2019). The picture used in "enactive/expressive" is CC0 Public Domain (https://www.publicdomainpictures.net/en/view-image.php?image=239925, 1 August 2019))

mimetic side, the patterns are locked around concrete perspectives, the particular aspects of emotionality in individuals, which are presented through iconic modes, making use of mimicry (see Fig. 5.3).

Let us then try to understand what forms of interaction could guarantee this relationship between contexts and representations.

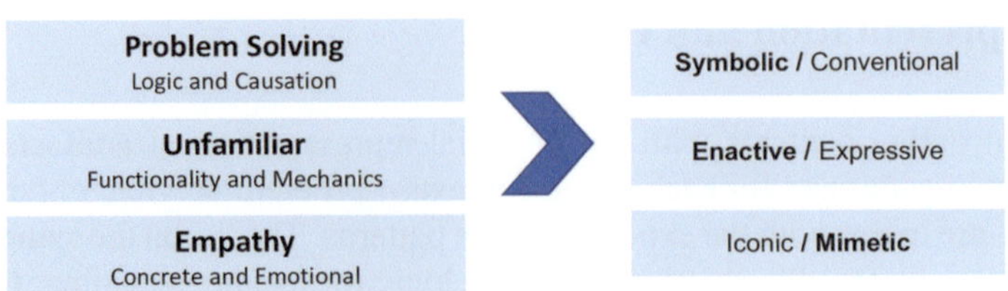

Fig. 5.3 The correlation between contexts and patterns with modes of representation

5.2.1 Symbolic Interaction

Starting from the relationship between context and symbolic representation we find that we are facing a particular type of artefact, an artefact that is not easily given to meaning by the subject, which requires the understanding of previous conventions in order to be able to offer sufficient substrate to the construction of logical deductions. We leave behind the mere visual symbols to pick on the interactive symbolic, that is, the formal mechanics of games (Aarseth, 1997; Schell, 2008). If we look at Katie Salen and Eric Zimmerman's more consensual definition that the "game is a system in which players engage in an artificial conflict, defined by rules, that results in a quantifiable outcome" (2003, p. 96), we can see how they determine the game based on a system. A "system" is by definition an abstraction of symbolic and conventional rules that need to obey logic and causality. As for the "quantifiable", it means concrete results, that is, it needs to present a problem and demand a solution.

Looking more concretely at the problem and solution, we realize that the essence of the game artefact tends to the mastery of puzzles, the building of meaning through form (see Fig. 5.4). Cognition, pushed by gestalt, requires the resolution of the puzzle, calling for the production of a final and abstract form as preferred by Plato. The puzzle is a no more than a structure of obstacles that prevents immediate access to the goal, the resolution, which is completely evident in Kuhn's (1962) description of the scientific investigation process:

> Perhaps the most striking feature of the normal research problems we have just encountered is how little they aim to produce major novelties, conceptual or phenomenal. But if the aim of normal science is not major substantive novelties — if failure to come near the anticipated result is usually failure as a scientist — then why are these problems undertaken at all? (…) Bringing a normal research problem to a conclusion is achieving the anticipated in a new way, and it requires the solution of all sorts of complex instrumental, conceptual, and

Fig. 5.4 The symbolic interaction is best exemplified by the problem-solving action that is determined to find solutions for puzzles. The *Rubik's Cube* is one of the most successful examples of problem-solving as a puzzle. The interaction is physical but purely symbolic (Picture licensed by PixaBay at https://pixabay.com/pt/photos/quebra-cabe%C3%A7a-jogo-cubo-1243091/, 1 August 2019.)

> mathematical puzzles. The man who succeeds proves himself an expert puzzle-solver, and the challenge of the puzzle is an important part of what usually drives him on. (Kuhn, 1962)

On the other hand, and following Kuhn, Joi Ito mentions the fact that this mode of interaction does not per se lead to any innovation, as it focuses exclusively on solving the problem, just looking for the gratification offered by the puzzle:

> "And I think one of the problems with just straight engineering is you sort of assume that the person who gave you the problem knows what the problem is and your job is just to solve it. (..) You actually have to keep asking the question, "Is this even the right question?" Joi Ito in interview (Johnson, 2019)

Symbolic interaction is focused on the puzzle and its resolution, the process of obtaining answers. The complete definition of the structure responding to the final form is the goal. For video game interaction formalists, ludologists (Aarseth, 2001; Costikyan, 2000; Eskelinen, 2001; Juul, 2001), anything that goes beyond symbolic interaction—characters, scenarios or narrative—is just part of a "theme" that even when changed keeps on being "the same game" (Aarseth, 2004, p. 48). That is, there is no space or interest in the discussion of content, message or meaning, because everything is abstract, everything is symbol, and therefore dependent on conventions at each moment. The engaged mental model excels at modelling abstract systems, by being disconnected from concrete matter, without any connotation with the particular, let alone the human, with all cognitive focus directed only at solving the puzzle, overcoming obstacles.

5.2.2 Symbolic Interaction: Obstacles and Challenges

Problem-solving games, or puzzles, appeal to the skill of the player, who develops while searching for mastery, which as we saw in Chap. 3 is the basis of the Abstracters. We can even camouflage the symbolism of *Alquerque*, replacing circles with queens, kings and bishops, and create a *Chess* game of two armies, with one male king and one female queen (see Fig. 5.5), but if there is a problem to solve, all that is completely irrelevant to the game action. For players, only the piece moves are interesting: how these moves translate on the board and the overall game impacting the next moves. The game is a complete abstraction from the physical domain, the theme is mere decoration, it is irrelevant, as is the visual aspect, as Pinker says:

> Visual thinking is often driven more strongly by the conceptual knowledge we use to organize our images than by the contents of the images themselves. Chess masters are known for their remarkable memory for the pieces on a chessboard. But it's not because people with photographic memories become chess masters. The masters are no better than beginners when remembering a board of randomly arranged pieces. Their memory captures meaningful relations among the pieces, such as threats and defenses, not just their distribution in space. (Pinker, 1997, p. 295)

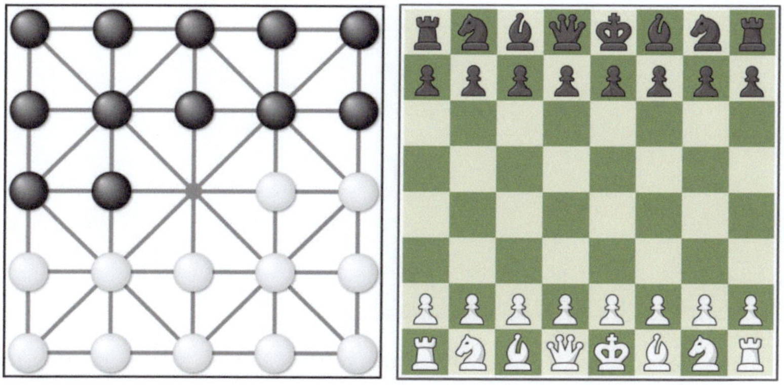

Fig. 5.5 *Alquerque* (left) and *Chess* (right) are two of the oldest games mentioned in the *Book of Games* (1284) by King Alfonso X of León & Galicia [The picture from *Alquerque* is licensed under CC 4.0, (https://commons.wikimedia.org/wiki/File:Alquerque_ board_at_starting_position_2.svg, 4 August 2019). The picture of chess is a screen capture from https://Chess.com.]

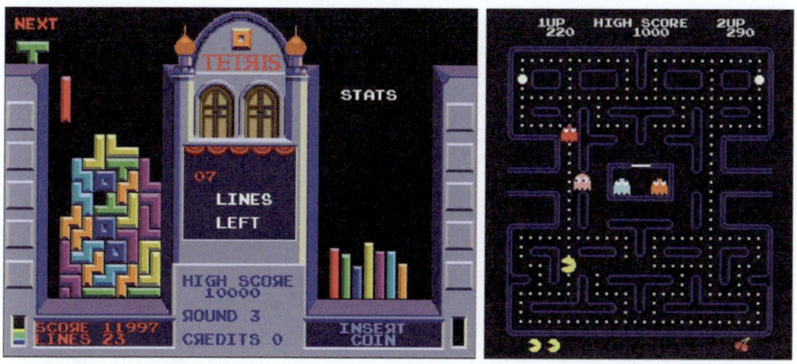

Fig. 5.6 *Tetris* (left) and *Pac-man* (right) can be seen as digital evolutions of chess

The same description of cognitive play by Pinker can also be applied to *Tetris* (Pajitnov, 1984) (see Fig. 5.6). What drives Tetris players is pattern recognition and the ordering of the pieces, which due to the uncertainty of the next piece forces the player to move between inductive and deductive reasoning in search of the best puzzle solutions. These same modes served as the ground for the design of games like *Pac-Man* (Iwatani, 1980) (see Fig. 5.6), and most of the FPS (first-person shooter) and shoot-em-up action games, where it's up to the player to recognize the space, to deduce the best strategy for searching and completing these spaces, and while uncertain use induction to make quick decisions (see Fig. 5.7). Because of the markedly analytical and demanding basis of such games, they have always had trouble dealing with narrative insertion, with one of the leading creators of *Doom* (Hall, 1993), John Carmack, even saying that "Story in a game is like a story in a porn movie. It's expected to be there, but it's not that important" (Kushner, 2003).

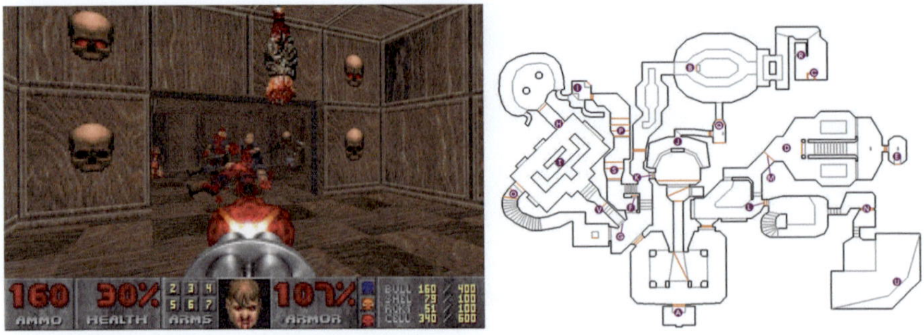

Fig. 5.7 *Doom* (left) can be seen as a 3D evolution of *Pac-man*. The map (right) of one level of the game *Doom*, demonstrating the player's need to search and go beyond the obstacles in space to solve the problem and win (Picture licensed by Doom Wiki under Fair Use. https://doomwiki.org/wiki/File:E1M3_walkthrough.png.)

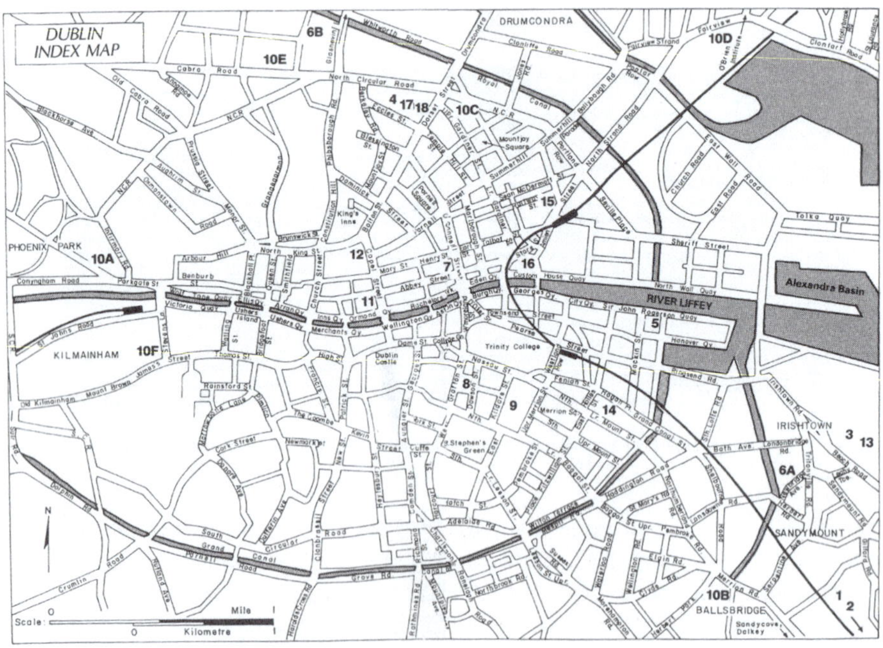

Fig. 5.8 Map of Dublin with the locations marked where Stephen Dedalus and Leopold Bloom pass during the single day of action, 16 June 1904. Reproduced from (McCarthy & Rose, 1991, pp. 8–9)

This symbolic interaction approach, based on puzzle design, is not unique to the domain of video games. Some of the most relevant examples have emerged in modernist literature, with such works as James Joyce's *Ulysses* (1922), which uses the map of Dublin (see Fig. 5.8) to locate all of the book's actions, and the reader is supposed to reconstruct the whole puzzle of what really happened by the end of the book. Nabokov said about the work of interpretation of *Ulysses* that "Instead of perpetuating the pretentious nonsense of Homeric, chromatic, and visceral chapter headings, instructors should prepare maps of Dublin with Bloom's and Stephen's intertwining itineraries clearly traced" (1973, p. 156). Joyce chose the puzzle approach on purpose, as he says:

> I've put in so many enigmas and puzzles that it will keep the professors busy for centuries arguing over what I meant, and that's the only way of insuring one's immortality. Joyce interview in (Ellmann, 1982)

After Joyce, others went even further with works such as *Rayuela* (1963) by Julio Cortázar or *La Vie Mode d'Emploi* (1978) by Georges Perec, which are true games in the guise of stories. These approaches have also been used in film, albeit less explicitly: with stream of consciousness approaches by Jean-Luc Godard; metaphors by Andrei Tarkovsky or symbols with David Lynch. Buckland defines this type of cinema as "puzzle films" (2009), while Elsaesser speaks of "mind-game films" (Elsaesser, 2009), using "Memento" (Nolan, 2000) as the ultimate exponent of this approach, a film in which the story is presented in reverse mode, but being practically secondary, with the only thing that matters the unravelling of the structure, the connecting of the puzzle pieces. Therefore, we have traditionally narrative media arts, such as literature and cinema, adopting game design techniques to draw their narratives and engage receptors.

Despite the narrative tendency of these media, the fact that they pull through the mastery of puzzle solving ultimately makes the dimensions of storytelling—such as characters, their moral behaviours and implications—more like props. The readers and viewers are focused above all on the effort to understand what they are reading or seeing, searching to understand what is happening. The focus is on reasoning, deduction and induction, and this is what we are interested in highlighting: the demonstration that the primary mode of engagement of symbolic interaction is focused on the "get to know".

5.2.3 Enactive Interaction

In the case of enactive interaction, expressiveness follows the enactivity of tasks, searching for new mechanics and functionalities that tend to result in unfamiliar new modes of operation. This mode of interaction is evident in humans from childhood and is called play (not gaming, but unstructured play). Unlike playing a game, unstructured play is "free and spontaneous" and "self-motivated" (Lopes, 2004, p. 70).

The act of play, both in humans and in other species, comes almost automatically without external or goal imposition. Play begins in the early hours of life by exploring the space outside the mother's belly, and is based, especially in the early years, on exploring not only the outside world, but above all the senses' capacities to feel that outer environment. Given the needs of cognition to assign meaning to what the senses experience, a constant exploration of the senses and their relationship with the outside are sought, in what Sutton-Smith defined as "dialectics of play" (1978). Play is something deeply concrete and tangible, requiring the direct action of the senses—touch, smell, taste, sight and hearing. Later, as adults, physical play tends to drown by saturation of sense perception and sufficient understanding of the outside, giving preference to more symbolic play. However, an adult fringe, notably tinkerers, still keep the flame of the physical relationship with the real alive, evolving it into more abstract and complex domains, as the artist Elina Brotherus argues:

> Art is the only occupation that allows the adult to continue playing. On the other hand, if you watch the children play you will see that it is a serious activity that requires concentration. In this sense, it resembles the process of artistic creation. One defines the rules of the game wondering: what happens if…? And then follows them. When that person is an artist, the result is called art. In *El País*, 21 June 2019.[1]

Think then, that if as a child we built a house with little stones, drew aliens on a piece of paper or created a rhythm with two wooden sticks, it was all just playing, with no concrete purpose or expected results. But as adults, this play opens ideal spaces for the production of creativity, allowing the emergence of design and art (Boyd, 2010). The creative play that happens in the use of tools, objects and materials (Gauntlett, 2011)—such as LEGO (see Fig. 5.9)—through verbs like play, build, manufacture and make in their own environments—reality simulators like sheets of paper, boxes of sand or virtual worlds—is a type of play that leaves traces and produces artefacts, creating space for enactive interactivity.

Fig. 5.9 LEGO pieces continue to be recognized as one of the greatest inspirations of human creativity (Gauntlett & Thomsen, 2013), being used with particular commitment by tinkerer profiles (The picture is one frame from the video "LEGO Drawing Machine (Spirograph)" by JK Brickworks, published in YouTube on 24 June 2016, at https://www.youtube.com/watch?v=1Ihjh_F7jn0, 6 August 2019.)

[1] "Elina Brotherus: 'El arte es la única ocupación que permite al adulto seguir jugando'", *El País*, 21 June 2019, Gloria Crespo MacLennan. https://elpais.com/cultura/2019/06/20/babelia/1561029777_123564.html (6 August 2019).

There is, in this profile and in its creations, a rather mechanistic worldview (Darwin, 1859), leading to the sense that the world is a construct, an assembled system of multiple functional parts, and our action can change the way in which these parts are arranged and make the world work. The resulting artefacts do not seek to solve major problems, nor do they offer great interpretations of the world or human beings, but rather provide new mechanics and functionalities, and new organizational structures of form, innovations, inventions and recreations. All interaction searches and results in a constant flow of action over reality.

5.2.4 Enactive Interaction: Simulation and Functionality

In the digital domain, the simulation component becomes even more evident, but only because simulation is an integral part of the world of play, without which we could not have these "magic circles" (Huizinga, 1938) that guarantee the safety and non-affectation of lives while playing (Brown, 2009; Sutton-Smith, 2005). We can think of children's playgrounds, and then on to Disneyland, eventually finding that video games are just digital extensions of physical simulations. We must also note that these simulations, in the case of theme parks and many video games, tend to be only navigable and manageable (e.g. *Dear Esther* (Pinchbeck, 2012) and *Gone Home* (Gaynor, 2013)), for the most part preventing their users from really participating. The player can move in space, can perform various verbs—run, jump, fly (see Fig. 5.10)—but the world remains unchanged. As in most theme park attractions, we can only experience the offered closed-in system and repeat, hoping that randomized variability will make the second experience interesting again.

However, when it is possible to customize the experiences, the user is called upon to act and to participate effectively in the creation. That's exactly what Thomas Edison did when he set up his lab at Menlo Park in 1876, known as "The Invention Factory", with Edison being nicknamed "The Wizard of Menlo Park" (Israel, 2016), which almost looks like a designation taken from the worlds of Walt Disney. This laboratory, acting as a simulator, sought above all to ensure the safety of experimentation, to free the creator of the danger from actions never tried before. In this way, one could make mistakes and fail tens or hundreds of times without consequence. This is the enactive interaction, a process in which the user actively and creatively participates in the construction of the simulation itself.

Since the era of the ZX Spectrum, some video games have come up with "mod makers"[2] (Zagalo, 2013), some simpler, some more complex, and evolving into systems similar to the creators' tools with the emergence of *Doom* in 1993, and

[2]"Mods" is the term used for games, or game excerpts, still playable, changed by users. The "mod makers" are the tools offered to make these changes in some games.

Fig. 5.10 In *Super Mario Bros.* (Miyamoto, 1985) we can navigate the space and manipulate the objects, the main character and its interaction with other characters and objects, but we cannot participate in building Mario's experience, transforming the challenge or experimenting with different scenarios

lately evolving into offering complete game engines (e.g. Unreal) that can be used today at no cost if for non-commercial purposes. However, it is not these engines that we are talking about, as they are more like complete solutions for effective game production. Next to this approach we saw distinct tools appear, sort of "creative games" or parts of games that allowed a user's creations, such as the possibility to create game levels such as in *Super Mario Maker* series (Oshino, 2015, 2019) (see Fig. 5.11). In these we have the intersection between playing and creating. In

Fig. 5.11 In *Super Mario Maker* 2 (2019) we can participate in building the simulation of *Super Mario Bros.*, effectively experimenting with all possibilities, including creating a full final game and sharing it, creating "a haven of player creativity" (Muncy, 2019)

Fig. 5.12 "Minecraft" took the simulator to level zero and "forced" players to build almost everything with cubes, in a clear move to imitate the LEGO system

fact, we are not trying to solve problems or make money, we are just seeking to simulate ideas, try possibilities and share them with others. If we wanted to create a *Super Mario Bros.* to sell, we would be better by choosing other tools, like Unity or Unreal, but the goal here is different: the aim is to increase interaction with the game world, and what the player seeks is to feel the sensation of novelty. We push forward something that we've tried to do before in the game, experimenting and changing the functionalities and mechanics of something we know very well, working to build that very something we have wanted to try before, but which the artefact didn't permit.

In the same vein, there emerged a multitude of other game tools, among which the most famous is *Minecraft* (Persson, 2009) (see Fig. 5.12), going much further than the likes of *Super Mario Maker*. Because there was absolutely nothing predetermined beyond the raw materials and tools, it was up to the experimenter to invent and imagine everything from scratch. The game works as a pure simulator, like a blank sheet of paper with materials like pencils and pens, now all depending on the creator's imagination. In the field of video games, these are also known as "sandboxes", i.e. free creation spaces. But this play can result in effective actions in the real world, *Minecraft* projects have been used in schools for teaching (Lane & Yi, 2017; Nebel, Schneider, & Rey, 2016) or to imagine and reconfigure urban spaces (Elmerghany & Paulus, 2017; Ertiö & Bhagwatwar, 2017; Rexhepi, Filiposka, & Trajkovik, 2018).

Although in these latter scenarios there may occur predetermined goals and objectives, and problems to be solved (in the domains of learning, urbanism, collaboration and participation), Minecraft is not used as a mere task solver, but rather as an exploration tool for new ideas and concepts, as an innovation guider. For this specific purpose, game tools like *Minecraft* make available to users the experimentation and manipulation of functionalities, with the possibility to test, contrast and compare approaches. These artefacts work directly on the imagination, from where constructions then emerge, which may or may not become inventions or innovations. The focus is on experimenting and exploring, and that's what matters in the enactive interaction engagement: the "get to do".

5.2.5 Mimetic Interaction

In the mimetic field, we are looking for similarities, visual and relational, with emotional traits particularized by individual subjects to serve in the creation of empathy contexts. Unlike the symbolic domain, there is no conventional learning here, but rather the capabilities built by experience in daily relationship with others. The basis of this type of interaction is the simple everyday social interaction of any human being, in which, according to Goffman (1959), we assume a facade and play a distinct role depending on the need of each situation. According to Goffman, in a face-to-face interaction we are as if in the middle of a theatre stage, in which we try to manipulate the impression produced on the other of the person we are, because we assume ourselves to be what others see in us. On the other hand, in most daily stages, there are roles that we have to play that require a certain kind of performance from us—being a parent, teacher, boss, client, husband, son, etc. In this sense, the mimetic interaction depends on the context of each stage, i.e. the drama and the actors involved (see Fig. 5.13).

In these processes, our skills in mind theory and mental simulation are triggered (Cruz & Gordon, 2003), which guarantee us the ability to construct one model of the other's mind, enhancing our competence to anticipate the actions of the other and thus not only to perceive and feel the other, but also to act by adjusting to the other. As Decety says, "We belong to a gregarious species and virtually all our

Fig. 5.13 Human body behaviours are part of the most significant tools of mimetic interaction. In this scene from "Who's Afraid of Virginia Woolf?" (1962), the body language of the characters serves as the main communication of what is really happening in the room

actions and thoughts are directed toward others or produced as responses to real or imagined interactions with them" (2005). But we are not just looking at each other: interaction occurs at the interpersonal and intergroup levels, with mimicry supporting the synchronization of our behaviours—in conversation, dance, march, show audience, etc.—being rewarded for cooperation and well-being (Wiltermuth & Heath, 2009). This explains our obsession with anthropomorphizing the other that is different than us. We have more difficulty in synchronizing with the behaviours of a mouse or duck, but a humanized rat or duck is different (e.g. Disney's Mickey Mouse and Donald Duck), which also makes difficult for us to imagine non-humanoid extraterrestrials, explaining why movies insist on portraying them in that form.

On the other hand, the face has become the main attribute of cinema. Given all the manipulative power that film has in using the camera to control framing and the emotional facet that cinema tends to exacerbate, we have seen in recent years a continual increase in facial close-ups, with David Bordwell even saying that "In the studio years, the filmmaker would rely on the actor's whole body, but now actors are mainly faces" (2006, p. 134). The face is the body's greatest communicative and mimetic attribute and is capable of producing the "greater 'involvement'" (Branigan, 1984, p. 6) and "attraction" (Gunning, 1994, p. 384) (see Fig. 5.14), largely because of its capabilities (Ekman, 1997) (see Fig. 5.14). Several studies cited by Wallenstein in the book *The Pleasure Instinct* (2008) have demonstrated the importance of the face by placing its attractiveness at the level of the most effective stimulus, with the most extreme example given being:

> Neonates a mere nine minutes old were shown different drawings before having ever seen a face — any face. They looked significantly longer (a common measure of preference) at a stylized pictogram of a normal human face, than at pictograms with exactly the same features but scrambled (a nose, mouth, eyes, and brows situated randomly on a circular "face"), suggesting they enter the world searching for kith and kin. (Wallenstein, 2008, p. 23)

However, the power of drama and characters does not show only through audiovisual images, despite the recognition of the strength of close-ups. Our mental and imaginary simulation capabilities allow us to work through all these processes, even though not watching but just reading. Contrary to Fodor's hypothesis of mentalese[3] (1975), Bergen proposed the "Embodied Simulation Hypothesis" (2012) which tells us that we perceive language through the simulation in our minds of the experiences being described, reactivating previous sensory and motor experiences (García et al., 2019). That is, we really don't need to see, for just reading the description of a dramatic scene brings us face to face with the characters, and their feelings, fears and joys, allowing us to empathize with them.

> embodied simulation makes use of the same parts of the brain that are dedicated to directly interacting with the world. When we simulate seeing, we use the parts of the brain that allow us to see the world; when we simulate performing actions, the parts of the brain that direct physical action light up. The idea is that simulation creates echoes in our brains of

[3]Fodor put forward a theory called "language of thought hypothesis", which would work as compositional structure, language-like, capable of ordering thoughts.

1. The antecedents, the events that brought about the expression;
2. The person's thoughts: plans, expectations, memories;
3. The internal physical state of the person showing the expression;
4. A metaphor;
5. What the expresser is likely to do next;
6. What the expresser wants the perceiver to do;
7. An emotion word.

Fig. 5.14 It's impossible to look at a face without questioning: what is this person thinking about? (Picture licensed by PixaBay at https://pixabay.com/photos/kid-child-portrait-sad-poor-2529907/.) Contrast the picture of the face with the "seven kinds or domains of information" provided by face expressions, defined by (Ekman, 1997, p. 318)

> previous experiences, attenuated resonances of brain patterns that were active during previous perceptual and motor experiences. We use our brains to simulate percepts and actions without actually perceiving or acting. (Bergen, 2012, pp. 14–15)

This is what happens when we read a scene in a novel, because that is what the writer aims at, as Joseph Conrad tells us, "My task which I am trying to achieve is, by the power of the written word, to make you hear, to make you feel—it is, before all, to make you see. That—and no more, and it is everything" (1910). Experiment with the following excerpt from Hemingway's *A Farewell to Arms* (1929), in analysing how our mind creates the space, people and their actions:

> In the late summer of that year we lived in a house in a village that looked across the river and the plain to the mountains. In the bed of the river there were pebbles and boulders, dry and white in the sun, and the water was clear and swiftly moving and blue in the channels. Troops went by the house and down the road and the dust they raised powdered the leaves of the trees. The trunks of the trees too were dusty and the leaves fell early that year and we

> saw the troops marching along the road and the dust rising and leaves, stirred by the breeze, falling and the soldiers marching and afterward the road bare and white except for the leaves. (Hemingway, 1929)

As we can see, in mimetic interaction, the presentation of forms ready for our understanding and analysis also occurs, eliciting the search for meaning or the attempt to reach the intended form of communicative intention. However, unlike symbolic interaction, here the form is of the Aristotelian type rather than Platonic, that is, individual and ephemeral. That which is felt and expressed by a character is unique in that space and time, has meaning only for the understanding of that individual, and therefore requires particular action to be taken at the moment.

5.2.6 Mimetic Interaction: Choose to Bond

Storytelling in interactive environments has been widely studied over the last four decades, with several dedicated conferences—VS, TIDSE, ICIDS, ELO, NarraScope[4]—looking for new solutions to allow an easy relationship between interaction and drama. The problem was identified in the early days of multimedia, with dedicated research groups arising and disappearing—e.g. Interactive Cinema at Media Lab—then becoming a research problem of the video games industry. For decades, the introduction of interaction in dramatic scenes has been centred on the plot, the choices to be given to the always unsuccessful interactors. Even before these digital experiences we had had paper experiences like the "Choose Your Own Adventure" series and "Fantastic Adventures", which suffered from the same problem: excessive focus on interaction with the plot. This problem was fuelled by the theoretical basis used, grounded in Aristotle's *Poetics* (335BC) that claims the plot is the most important element of tragedy, an idea that we see reflected throughout history in theories on narrative and storytelling (Barthes, 1966; Genette, 1966; Metz, 1966), with many of the current studies on the scientific relevance of stories focused on plot elements (Buckland, 2009; Gottschall, 2012; Herman, 2002; Ryan, 2001), the so-called "knowing what comes next" (Bordwell, 1985; Branigan, 1992), which has even been addressed as a "narrative problem-solving" (Black & Bower, 1980; Varotsis, 2018). However, this is an immensely problematic approach, especially when it comes to the domain of interaction, which as we have already seen here enters directly into the realms of human mimicry.

Lajos Egri (1946) had no doubts about going against Aristotle, because, in fact, the plot is a mere structure of events, a mere experimental and non-concrete space for the presentation of human beings or anthropomorphized beings. What really drives

---

[4]In the first decade of 2000, the conferences "Virtual Storytelling" and "Technologies for Interactive Digital Storytelling and Entertainment" were organized as intercalated bi-annual series. Then, by the end of the decade, they merged into the "International Conference on Interactive Digital Storytelling". More recently, the Narrascope has focused more into the narrative design and ELO on the specifics of interactive fiction.

story lovers are the characters who show an other, a similar one, with whom one can measure affinities, and experience how they react at any given moment, to feel and understand who it is, how it is and why it is. What matters is the comparative, the feeling like them, projecting their own future, looking at the past and measuring themselves on a social scale, to gauge whether they behaved better, worse or simply well enough. All this discussion becomes more entrenched when seen from the writer's perspective. Writers usually get classified, or classify themselves, as plot-driven or character-driven creators, meaning that they prefer to write with some predefined goal for the story, drawing a master plan grounded in a problem-solving structure. On the other supposed side, writers create characters in depth and then "let them decide" the outcoming of the conflicts and ending. These approaches are normally attached to genre fiction—Adventure, Thriller and Suspense–which follow the plot-driven type, whereas Drama follows the character-driven mode. Using this binary point of view underlines the idea that stories, mainly plot-driven, follow problem-solving patterns. This would represent a problem for the model outlined in this book, because when we split up the interactive engagement process, we put problem-solving outside the realm of dramatists. The first point to make is that plot-driven and character-driven are not two different genre styles or writer preferences, but instead are both needed to create a good and meaningful story (Stevens, 2009). Or as Straubel puts it, following the suggestion that narratives can be plot-driven only takes us to "inevitability and the foregone conclusions", and because of that we need the character's depth to "have creative and humanistic series of choices that can support the construction of believable stories" (2006).

With regard to problem-solving, let's have a look at what happens in a movie or book and compare it to what happens in a puzzle or video game of detectives. In the game or puzzle, it is up to the participant to make the effort to connect the evidence, look for similarities, contrast them, come up with analogies and structure preferences for what happens after planning all the answers, and consequently a step-by-step resolution. None of this happens in a traditional narrative. It is true that mentally we are guessing, but at no time do we launch plans for their resolution. Assumptions are mere speculation, not problem-solving, about the futures of the characters: the receptor is only attempting to understand who they are, what they want and why they want it from its own personal perspective, developing an interpretation. This is what critical thinking means for a receptor: to speculate on scenarios through what is being read or being told, throughout past experiences, creating meaning at a personal level, for which we empathize and mentally negotiate a character's relationships.

Note that the apparent desire is only to try to solve a problem, since what is wanted is to encounter the person who fits into the human envelope of that guilt: the hero, our saviour. This is never forced, as we are not solving but imagining, feeling the experience while receiving more and more data offered by the story, always hoping for the story to unravel itself, not for us to unravel it. Herman discussed narrative as an instrument of the mind, saying it is used by receptors as a scaffolding tool, a problem-solver helper, because "stories provide means for balancing expectations against outcomes, general patterns against particular instances" which helps in making the processes of problem-solving intelligible (Herman, 2013, p. 240). Stories get to "be used to redress problems that arise when anticipated experiences, projected to be similar to those encountered in the past, do not materialize" which then ends in providing "context of typicality in terms of which unexpected occurrences can be interpreted, enabling various modes of problem-solving" for the receptor's future use (Herman, 2013, p. 240).

Note also how, in a game like *Cluedo* (Pratt, 1949) we have to connect the gun and the place, and we have to follow rules and solve the mystery presented, and how this all turns characters into mere pawns, as relevant as any other piece of the scene. While playing we never care for characters, we just want to solve the problem. Hence, trying to translate a narrative into an interactive environment by evoking problem-solving will truncate narrative engagement. This only began changing in the early 2000s, when some new types of dramatic artefacts—e.g. *Galatea* (Short, 2000) or *Façade* (Mateas & Stern, 2005)—began to emerge, moving the interaction emphasis from plot to characters, creating the first moments of mimetic interaction, where our choices would impact and transform the characters. This approach would be followed later by commercial video games, not fully changing the games, although it could be felt in some design mechanics—for example, in video games such as *Mass Effect* (Hudson, 2007), *Heavy Rain* (Cage, 2010) or *The Walking Dead* (Vanaman, 2012)—with the narrative choices presented impacting the lives of the characters in stories. Game players were then held responsible for what would happen to the characters, interacting to create empathic relationships with the characters, instead of merely advancing the story plot or solving the game problem. The interaction became mimetic, drawing players into a "get to feel".

5.3 Preferences and Outcomes

Having listed a number of elements that allow us to look more clearly at the patterns and design of artefacts according to the contexts and profiles presented in the previous chapters, before closing this chapter, preferences and tastes must be discussed: what can be offered by each profile pleasure in the contextual experiences and how these pleasures are mirrored by artefacts. For this purpose, studies in the field of pleasure sciences were sought, even though such studies suffer from the presence of a high degree of subjectivity. However, not only was a focus on the component of the subjects attempted, but also on the component of what we know most concretely about artefacts, and, in particular, their successes and popularizations. Obviously, the success metric is too vague, yet within the framework being exposed here it is not irrelevant and may help in understanding in more depth the relation between artefacts and subject profiles. For this purpose, works by Paul Bloom, Derek Thompson and Seth Godin have proven useful.

Bloom (2010) argues for the existence of two great modes of human pleasure elicitation, which are also central in the design of cultural production: essentialism and familiarity. On the side of essentialism, we have a tendency to see in artefacts not only their form and content, but also their supposed essence. We assume that a painting signed by Vermeer or Matisse is worth much more than a perfect copy of that painting. Because we believe in the so-called "original", we believe there is some kind of authentic essence, put there by the author, touched by him or her. We don't believe the copy, even if 100% similar, possesses any of that essence. There are multiple studies and examples in which people, after discovering that a painting they had at home was a copy of the work of a famous painter, report that this information drastically altered the way they looked at the painting. Even though they were conscious of the fact that the picture on the wall was exactly the same, the pleasure they took from it had been completely transformed (Bloom, 2010). A contrary example can be achieved when we are given to drink water from a sterilized bedpan: we know and believe that the water is fit to drink, but essentialism produces a belief in our imagination that makes us feel very uneasy (Bloom, 2010).

> things have an underlying reality or true nature (…) and it is this hidden nature that really matters (…) What matters most is not the world as it appears to our senses. Rather, the enjoyment we get from something derives from what we think the thing is. (Bloom, 2010, pp. xii, 9)

Essentialism works based on the processes of imagination, which according to Gendler (2008) produces states of "alief", that is, of belief in a reality that only exists in our imagination. Alief is part of the set of mental simulations that we are producing and recording about reality that later become responsible for our imagination, but also for creating expectations of and reactions to illusion. Gendler defines it as follows:

> A paradigmatic alief can be characterized as a mental state with associatively-linked content that is representational, affective and behavioral, and that is activated — consciously or unconsciously — by features of the subject's internal or ambient environment. (Gendler, 2008, p. 642)

Obviously, we cannot expect to introduce components of physical essentialism into a digital artefact. The author, however well known, cannot print his or her mark on millions of equal digital copies. However, we can work around an entire associative universe built from the artefact, and that's exactly where digital marketing has been putting its mark. We've seen the rise of transmedia narratives (Zeiser, 2015) that guarantee greater imaginary support for products, but also the search for "virality" (Berger, 2013) and "social media" (Pulizzi, 2014) made of what most others like, which have been receiving the help of so-called "influencers" (Brown & Hayes, 2008), all to ensure through that human relationship some kind of humanness essence in the product or experience. In the past, these campaigns were organic and non-deliberate. A classic is the *Mona Lisa* which was twice stolen from the Louvre, making it gain a prominence in the collective imagination, unmatched even today by any other artwork by Da Vinci (Zug, 2011).

The familiarity concept, the fact that new experiences present some kind of connection with previous known experiences is a stimulus of interest, engagement and pleasure (Bloom, 2010). We tend to feel pleasure whenever we hear familiar melodies or chords, as if they fit into a kind of imaginary expectation that comforts us, for example, "Prenatal exposure to environmental sounds originating outside the uterus

Fig. 5.15 Bloom's "inverted U" for the level of pleasure correlated with the level of familiarity of the experience. The same graph can be used to understand MAYA by Loewenstein, putting challenge in the place of familiarity and attraction in the place of pleasure. Graph made from Bloom's description

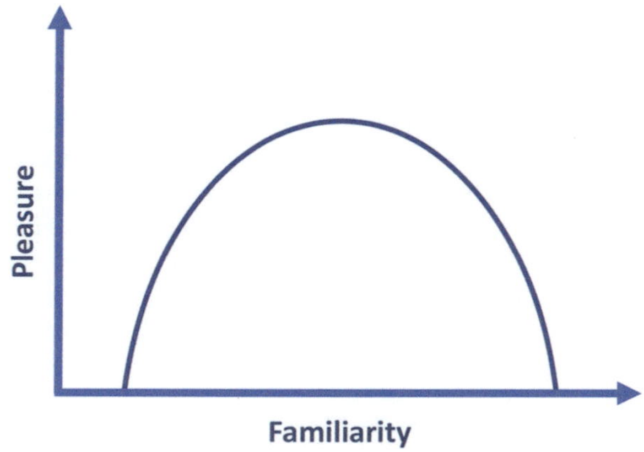

can engender subsequent listening preferences for familiar linguistic and musical stimuli" (Ullal-Gupta, Nederlanden, Tichko, Lahav, & Hannon, 2013). This process ends up explaining the genesis of aesthetic conventionalism, the creation of movements made from the stabilization of artistic patterns. When creating new works for communicative or entertaining intentions, creators follow conventions, introducing only slight variations to create a comfortable ballast and offer enough newness to appeal to receptors. Bloom (2010) speaks of an "inverted U" for pleasure, "Familiar is good. The problem, though, is that too familiar becomes cloying and unpleasant" (Bloom, 2010) (see Fig. 5.15). In exactly the same vein, Raymond Loewy, one of the most popular designers in American culture—responsible for well-known logos like Shell, BP, Greyhound Scenicruiser or Lucky Strike—developed the creative principle that he entitled MAYA: "Most Advanced, Yet Acceptable" (Thompson, 2017b). Very early in his career, he realized that people responded viscerally to challenging yet familiar products, or as Thompson puts it: "Most consumers are simultaneously neophilic, curious to discover new things, and deeply neophobic, afraid of anything that is too new. The best hit makers are gifted at creating moments of meaning by marrying new and old, anxiety and understanding. They are architects of familiar surprises" (Thompson, 2017a).

We want conventions to be followed, but we want to be surprised by the new. Hence, the complexity of works can be measured in terms of familiarity: the closer a previous work is to a previous successful work, the more easily it will be accepted, but the more quickly it will be rejected or forgotten, as is the case with traditional pop music or Hollywood cinema. That is, the absence of sound rhythms or innovative or original sequences limits the durability of our pleasure in the work. Hence, time is often equated to qualify a work as art. If a movie gives pleasure after 10 years, the issue is not that it has aged well, but rather that it continues to have something new to offer us. That is, we want conventions to be followed, but we want to be surprised. We want some challenge in decoding patterns of images, musical chords or gameplay to derive cognitive pleasure. We like our routines, and what we know, but we also reach saturation, so we want everything to keep changing. We just don't want it to change radically.

These two great concepts—essentialism and familiarity—reinforce the central idea of what this book has been working on, that the induction of pleasure and the creation of effective experiences are not only built by artefacts, but need to work through the whole communication process—people, contexts and artefacts. The formal component enhances the impressions created in our experience, but the contextual "essences" and "familiarities" of each subject condition this feeling. In this sense, some of the main design elements of the artefacts listed in each of the previously identified interaction domains—symbolic, enactive and mimetic—will now be analysed.

5.3.1 Symbolic Pleasure

In terms of the design of concrete form, the symbolic interaction component oriented to engagement can be seen from two distinct perspectives: gestalt and gamification. The gestalt case, initially conceived as a psychological tool for working with visual form, has over time been converted into many different types of forms. As we have seen in Chap. 4, the prägnanz laws—proximity, similarity, closure, symmetry, common fate, continuity, good gestalt and past experience—are key in germinating mental patterns that, in turn, support our problem-solving skills (see Fig. 5.16). In addition to prägnanz, gestalt offers us other major regulatory principles of our perception, like emergence, reification, multistability and invariance (Sternberg & Sternberg, 2012).

All of these contributions act as the basis of universal perception, being clearly at the service of the meaning-making and organization of information presented by reality that follows the organic laws of nature, which tend towards chaos. We can thus say that the way we organize ourselves in the midst of chaos is by organizing it through rules and categories and assigning values and meaning. We produce rules of generalization from the abstraction created over chaos and create notions of a whole, which is "something else than the sum of its parts" (Koffka, 1935). In this sense, we can say that symbolic interaction tends to move from unity to the whole, that there is always a stated goal, global meaning, and that its completeness is a sign of progress, advance in perception and advance in understanding experience, i.e. successful engagement.

Over the past decade, launching from game studies, we have begun talking incessantly about something that has been around for a long time, somehow emanating from that same gestalt that came to be called gamification. As currently defined, gamification corresponds to the application of game design principles to the design of non-game-related activities or gameplay (Deterding, 2012)—such as education, management, entertainment, etc.—in order to make these other activities as engaging as games. As Karl Kapp says "gamification is using game-based mechanics, aesthetics and game thinking to engage people, motivate action, promote learning and solve problems" (2012, p. 10). But these gamification activities are nothing new. They are

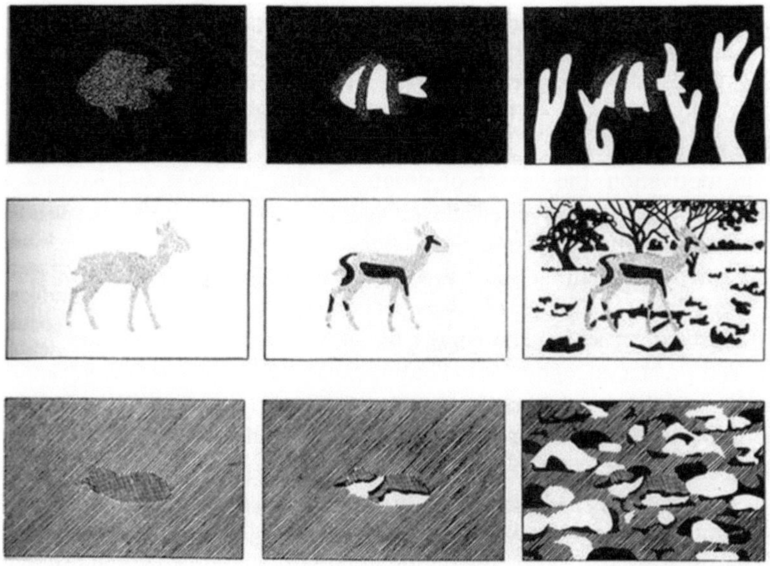

Fig. 5.16 Laws and principles of gestalt used as camouflage by nature, which creates obstacles to predators, thus working as visual puzzles, creating interactive contextual patterns of problem-solving [Picture out of copyright (https://archive.org/details/adaptivecolorati00cott) by Hugh Cott, presented in the book *Adaptive Coloration in Animals* (1940, p. 53).]

present in our ancient civilizations, they are part of the rules that structure and build our entire society, from the organization of space, territories and weddings, to the main gamifying agent of all: money.

The most commonly used gamification design process is PBL,[5] which is recognized for its swift implementation (Carvalho, Zagalo, & Araujo, 2015), due to the ease of application in symbolic and fully conventional environments. Its effects can be very quickly demonstrated by impacting relations as a motivational glue. The attribution of some value (points) to the behaviour of each individual, along with the recognition of the value attributed by comparison between individuals (leader tables), and reinforcements of this recognition (badges) is an immensely simple system of ruling and categorizing the chaos of relationships and behaviours that allow us to create in individuals the idea of meaning and reason for what they do, and the feeling of reaching their goals. PBL is also often accompanied by the idea of levels, a slightly more complex mechanic because it requires a better contextual structure and mastery of information, but allows for a better definition of progress within the task. We see it in schools, sports or airline mileage cards, but we see it today fully and instituted in evaluating the work of professors and all those working in the service industry. In schools, we have school stages and grades that can correspond to levels,

[5]Consists of inserting points, badges and leader boards (the PBL) in tasks and activities.

exam grades that can correspond to points, lists of grades that correspond to leaderboards and even honours that account for badges. The same is true of professional careers and so many other domains of adulthood, which mostly use symbolic means to secure some meaning for what per se means little to nothing.

In essence, gamification, or symbolization of work, uses a fundamental principle of human motivation, the "sense of progress", that Amabile and Kramer (2011) defined from the effect we feel whenever we reach our goals. In this sense, Amabile proposes a design strategy based on "defined goals" and "small wins", which can be found spread throughout society and well illustrated by the task of reading a book. If we reduce the number of pages per chapter, we generate more defined goals and we accelerate reaching the end of the chapters. This then creates a sense of progress and greater engagement to continue reading (e.g. the strategy used by Dan Brown). Everything that is likely to have metrics can have goals (e.g. any assessment of people) because they allow us to construct meaning from abstract tasks. Once the goal has been reached, the task, although abstract, is closed and the satisfaction of a duty accomplished is triggered in us, which, in turn, can even be amplified by attributing and displaying medals or leader boards (e.g. best employee of the month).

We can thus say that problem-solving context-oriented behaviours in symbolic interaction for abstracter's subjects tend to demarcate a path, a stream of engagement clearly oriented to progress, creating in the individual the notion of advancement to achieve goals. The experience is much broader, but engagement can be produced by the sensation of advancement, sustained by the influence of pleasure generated by progress and goal attainment.

5.3.2 Enactive Pleasure

Turning to the domain of enactive interaction, taking into account the required contexts of creativity, we can already establish that this domain, unlike the other two—symbolic and mimetic—does not follow much of the notion of familiarity, since the main motivator for interaction rests on the creation of process, based on the novelty-producing instinct that rests on the unusual, the unfamiliar. This "unusual and weird" approach is widely discussed by Godin in his book *We Are All Weird* (2011), in which he presents a comparative study of the cultural landscape of the last 60 years, showing that it is a growing trend. It seems to have shifted from the great narratives of the 1950s to the niches of the early millennium, with readers and viewers becoming creators themselves, in keeping with Lyotard's idea of "the end of metanarratives" (1979). In the case of video games, we can recall some examples that demonstrate this process of defamiliarization happening in the creation processes provided to users, two examples of which can be seen in Fig. 5.17.

The creative process exploited by games like *Spore* (Wright, 2008) or *Everything* (OReilly, 2017) develops in players the pleasure of "flow", first defined by Csikszentmihalyi as a state of "being completely involved in an activity for its own sake. The ego falls away. Time flies. Every action, movement, and thought follows inevitably

Fig. 5.17 The games *Everything* (left) and *Spore* (right) use enactive interaction to put the player in the place of a creator of worlds at different levels of abstraction. In *Everything,* animals don't walk; instead, they roll. In *Spore*, you can even create new animals from organic parts of different animals, multiplying these parts and creating this bizarre feeling of being in parallel universes

from the previous one, like playing jazz" (Csikszentmihalyi, 1996). Flow can be compared to "immersion" because the latter is "characterized by diminishing critical distance to what is shown and increasing emotional involvement in what is happening" (Grau, 2003, p. 13), but is distinguished concretely by the lack of an active component, which is missing in the immersion effect of mere "transportation into a narrative world" (Green, 2004). Csikszentmihalyi and Seligman did not understand that difference when in a 2000 article they put everything in the same bag, asking the question "Why do people choose to watch television over reading a challenging book, even when they know that their usual hedonic state during television is mild dysphoria, whereas the book can produce flow?" (Seligman & Csikszentmihalyi, 2000, p. 12), to which Hassenzahl just replied: "watching a telenovela might not lead to competence experiences but to the soothing and warm experience of security, the joys of routine and familiarity" (2010, p. 48).

And while agreeing with Hassenzahl's disagreement, we have to correct him on a point that is crucial to what is being discussed here, and also correcting Csikszentmihalyi's definition of flow, which has to do with the question of "competence". Hassenzahl points out that flow corresponds to experiences of gaining competence or mastery, and Csikszentmihalyi in his definition of flow says that this happens "when the activity one engages in contains a *clear set of goals*. These goals serve to add direction and purpose to behavior" (Csikszentmihalyi, Abuhamdeh, & Nakamura, 2005). This makes little sense to us, even being antithetical to one of the examples given by Csikszentmihalyi in his own definition (see previous paragraph), that of jazz. Jazz is defined above all by being an art of improvisation; consequently, jazz is not at all defined by clear objectives, or by concrete rules and expectations. Playing jazz, or playing *Everything*, corresponds to activities that stimulate flow, but neither are activities oriented towards the experience of gaining competences. Instead, they are oriented towards the exercise of autonomy, to the expression of self.

We consider that it is precisely through actions of self-expression that enactive interaction affords most pleasure, something Csikszentmihalyi himself agrees with when he argues about flow being autotelic, saying that "an autotelic person needs few material possessions and little entertainment, comfort, power, or fame because so much of what he or she does is already rewarding (…) They are more autonomous and independent because they cannot be as easily manipulated with threats or rewards from the outside" (Csikszentmihalyi, 1997, p. 117). That is, the flow arises through autonomy, the freedom to express oneself and to raise one's action to the level of personal fulfilment.

The essence of pleasure triggered by enactive interaction arises from the possibility of being able to act on the experience, transform it and feel the agency's exercise through constant feedback and in accordance with the needs of fulfilment and creation. Just as the artisan in full and constant contact with the production matter may or may not lead to the production of an artefact with effective value, the exercise of the creative process and its expressiveness is what is considered the true reward. In the case of HCI, the use of "computers as tools allow[s] the interactor to work with the computer as crafter" (Nitsche & Weisling, 2019), with the outcome resulting in craftworks bearing self-meaning, ready to be shared, serving the expression and communication.

5.3.3 Mimetic Pleasure

Mimetic interaction stems mainly from our ability to tell stories, being the mimetic tendency usually associated with realism (Bazin, 1958), which in turn tends to focus on drama and tragedy. This is evidenced by studies of film genre preferences in the USA (Fischoff, Antonio, & Lewis, 1998), which put the Drama genre on a prominent plane, with an interest three times that of the next genre group—Action–Adventure, Romance and Comedy—which also stand out, being twice as interesting as the rest. This preference view was also found in the UK by Redfern (2012), using data collected by the British Film Institute (Comley, Steele, Algar, Schafer-Peek, & Perkins, 2011). While not highlighting drama as much as in the US study, it still placed at the top, along with three others—Action–Adventure, Comedy and Suspense-Thriller.

To better understand these preferences, it should be added that the number of plot frameworks used by stories in literature has been identified as being no greater than six in an analysis of 50,000 novels (Jockers, 2015). The number of plots varies and Booker talks about seven (2004) regardless of the medium, but Polti, focused on theatre, concludes there are 36 (1895). In 1971, Kurt Vonnegut submitted his Master's thesis, *The Fluctuations Between Good and Evil in Simple Tasks* at the University of Chicago, which was rejected (University of Chicago, 2007), but years later he presented his research in a lecture, defining it as the "Shape of Stories" (Vonnegut, 2004). These shapes served to visualize between four and six different plot frameworks. Then, in more recent studies of literature, but now using AI algorithms to scrutinize thousands of variables, once again, only six types have been identified (Reagan, Mitchell, Kiley, Danforth, & Dodds, 2016) (see Fig. 5.18).

These small numbers of different plots can surprise us by the number of different stories presented in the millions of books and movies produced in the entire world.

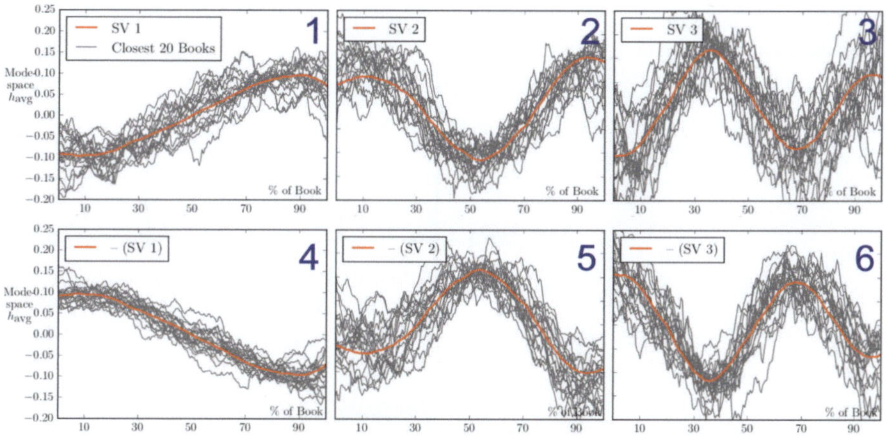

Fig. 5.18 In the figure we can see the curves for the six plots identified by (Reagan et al. 2016), labelled as follows: (1) "Rags to riches (rise)"; (2) "Man in a hole (fall-rise)"; (3) "Icarus (rise-fall)"; (4) "Tragedy (fall)"; (5) "Cinderella (rise-fall-rise)"; (6) "Oedipus (fall-rise-fall)"

However, if we bear in mind that the structures of stories can only vary in three acts—introduction, development and conclusion—and positive or negative, then the reduced variation of story shapes becomes more comprehensible. This weak variability of plot does not mean that stories are all the same, but rather serves to reinforce the main idea here that what motivates people with stories, whether in literature or cinema, is not the structure of the stories, but the individuality of the characters' behaviours and responses to the plot, which really can be infinite.

The combined genre preferences—drama, action, comedy—show an audience less focused on the tragedy plot, which determines a downward narrative structure, i.e. starting positively but never ceasing to become negative. Thus, and following the most recent study on plot preferences (Del Vecchio, Kharlamov, Parry, & Pogrebna, 2018), which confirmed again the existence of only six plots, it was also possible to identify the preferred plot: "Man in a Hole". This is the most effective for audiences, because it is adaptable to almost any narrative genre, and according to the analysis its success is less for aesthetic reasons than social impact. In other words, reviews by critics and audiences do not love movies using the "Man in a Hole" plot the most, but rather they produce a social impact, getting society to talk about them leading to more people wanting to see them.

The "Man in a Hole" (see Fig. 5.19) differs from tragedy in the way it ends, i.e. it presents happy ending. It begins positively, like tragedy, sinks into a tragedy, but it is eventually resolved, ending well (e.g. the story of the movie "Finding Nemo" (Stanton, 2003): Nemo's mother dies at the beginning of the film, and he goes through a whole host of dramas and near tragedies that make him grow as a character, finishing stronger and well). This plot can be correlated or even serve us as a summary of the plot theory presented by Joseph Campbell as "the monomyth", the unique myth Campbell believed to serve all human storytelling (Campbell, 1949). This same

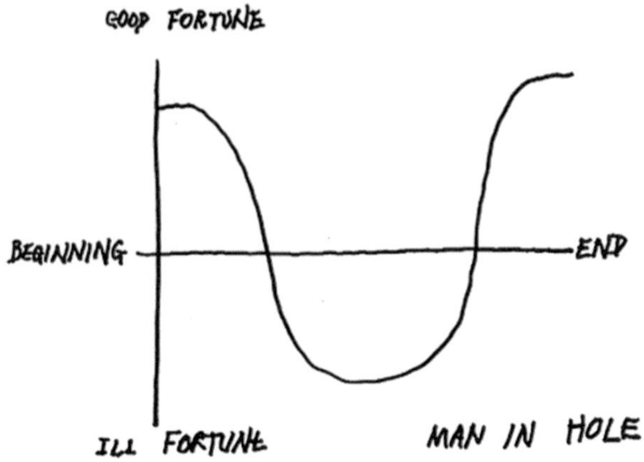

Fig. 5.19 "Man in a Hole" plot, a diagram by Vonnegut (2004)

myth was used by Lucas in the writing of "Star Wars" (1977), and since the end of the 1980s has been serving Disney scriptwriting, justifying its revival and greatest successes (Vogler, 2007). Looking at its essence, the curve of the "Man in a Hole" corresponds to the idea of equality and hope—all good people can suffer greatly in life, but there's always some way to overcome it—two fundamental values of humanity.

What disturbs us is how deep one can go in narrative dramatization, how far the suffering presented on screen or in a book goes and why we like to see or read about someone suffering. There are multiple media studies on the topic (Broderick & Traverso, 2011; Chouliaraki, 2006; Sarkar & Walker, 2009), but one of the best explanations can be found in Susan Feagin's text "The pleasures of tragedy" (1983). Feagin unfolds the pleasure of the tragic experience into two types of responses: direct and meta. In the case of the direct response, we react emotionally by crying, fear, sadness, anger, disgust, etc. But in this answer we cannot speak properly of pleasure, something that Aristotle tried to do by proposing the idea of "catharsis" (335BC). However, neither of these emotions is pleasant, or otherwise we would not qualify them as "negative" (Russell, 1980). Pleasure then arises from the meta-response, i.e. Feagin tells us that from the negative emotional reaction to what we see, we eventually realize:

> we care for, and in showing us we care for the welfare of human beings and that we deplore the immoral forces that defeat them, it reminds us of our common humanity. It reduces one's sense of aloneness in the world, and soothes, psychologically, the pain of solipsism (…) we derive pleasure from the communicability or "shareability" of a response to a work of art (Feagin, 1983)

But tragedy and drama go beyond our understanding of ourselves or hope, we rely on this idea of meta-response to derive also the idea of social comparison, or as David Herman tells us about stories serving as "technology for constructing and evaluating models of the conduct of persons" (2013, p. 294), and all that serves Bennis and Thomas's (2002) perspective on the way to learn from suffering:

> become great by finding meaning in adversity — in traumatic and unplanned crucible experiences — and then transforming those experiences into improved performance (...) being a victim of prejudice is particularly traumatic because it forces an individual to confront a distorted picture of him or herself, and it often unleashes profound feelings of anger, bewilderment, and even withdrawal. For all its trauma, however, the experience of prejudice is for some a clarifying event. Through it, they gain a clearer vision of who they are, the role they play, and their place in the world. (Bennis & Thomas, 2002)

All this brings us to the centre of what is expected in a mimetic interaction: conflict, without which there is no story and no motivation for the mimetic interaction. Accordingly, plots are based on the idea of transformation during the three acts, without which the spectators would not be interested. What engages with the artefact is the change that is caused by the conflict, and the stronger the conflict, the more the characters will be transformed. Our interaction with conflict can serve us in exploring different perspectives of the same trauma or just move from intense to less intense representations, but the objective is still mimetic: interact to mimetize, feel and consequently learn from the experience.

One of the problems with this mode of engagement is that tabloids and sensationalist media take advantage of their ability to generate attraction and interest in first-level reading, but of which nothing is left for meta-analysis and meta-response. A reported crime, without contextualization, teaches us nothing. However, our instinct to seek the suffering of others prevents us from not wanting to know what happened, and is a morbidity made of empty feelings.

This question of the instinct for morbidity and other negative sides of humanness arose in a study by Paddle Consulting (Millar, 2019b) on the content preferred by social network users. Extracted from data from over 10,000 people, the researchers felt "surprised" when the preferences of media users didn't match at all with what they expected. Company director Brian Millar says that when they started the study, they were using four major categories for the design of marketing campaigns—"funny, useful, beautiful and inspiring"—but they quickly realized that these categories concerned only what people are willing to confess as real interests, not corresponding in any way to their concrete intrinsic tastes. Millar says the collected evidence "shocked" them, presenting what they defined as a "depressing scenario" and pointing to content they didn't want to work with, as an agency. After some delay, they decided to work with the data and present the results, from which they extracted the following four categories—"sex, narcissism, sadism and hate"—which then unfold into five components each, as shown in Fig. 5.20.

We can easily recognize that what we have in this chart is nothing more than the conflicts present in most tragedies and dramas. It is possible to start from any of these elements and build fruitful stories, not only because the elements have such an arousal engagement load, but because of the potential for what one can feel and learn in such transformative situations. People enjoy conflict because conflict implies change. It is the change we look for, the change provided by the story, as well as the change we can bring about as receptors endowed with agency by the interactive artefacts.

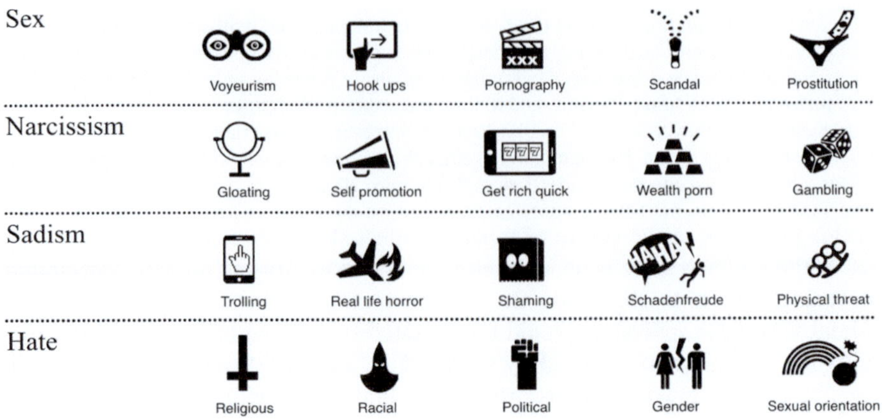

Fig. 5.20 Social users' content preferences extracted from 10,000 users by Paddle Consulting. Chart extracted from the video presentation of the results (Millar, 2019a)

This is where mimetic interaction can develop its focus on enhancing user pleasure, raising its engagement potential to the highest level, something that it has already been doing, as we can see in the video game *Life is Stranger* (2015), with a sequence in which we are invited to euthanize a friend for whom we've generated great sympathy while playing (see Fig. 5.21). The mimetic interaction goes beyond the mere telling of a story, in a book or movie, because the receptor is more like a participant in the action: we feel empathy, but we are forced to act, led to test our own beliefs, to challenge our feelings, to test our moral strength. The engagement

Fig. 5.21 The moment in *Life is Strange* (2015) when our friend asks us to disconnect the hospital machines that keeps her alive

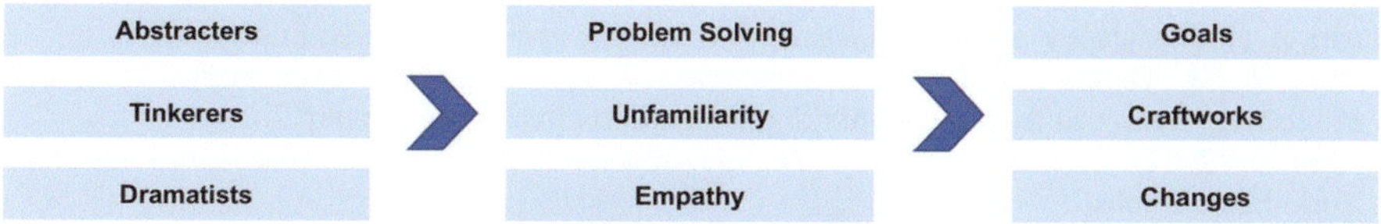

Fig. 5.22 The pragmatic correlation of engagement

stream results from human conflicts in negotiating human relationships, presenting opportunities for change and consequently the feeling of life being lived.

5.4 Pragmatic Outputs

Towards the end of the discussion of engagement artefacts, we now need to review the outputs of engagement profiles and engagement contexts, relating each element to defining the framework for our model. Thus, the following scheme has been elaborated (see Fig. 5.22) in which a pragmatic correlation has been established—subjects, contexts and artefacts—defined by the outputs of each of the studies presented throughout this and previous chapters. On the subject's side, we have abstracters, tinkerers and dramatists, framed in a relationship with context (problem-solving, unfamiliarity and empathy) and related to artefacts that have as outcomes: goals, craftworks and changes.

In the next and final chapter, this scheme will be discussed in depth in terms of the implications of these correlations, design approaches and expected outputs, presenting then the final model of engagement design.

References

Aarseth, E. (1997). *Cybertext: Perspectives on ergodic literature*. Baltimore: Johns Hopkins University Press.

Aarseth, E. (2001). Computer game studies, year one. *Game Studies*. ISSN: 1604-7982. http://gamestudies.org/0101/editorial.html.

Aarseth, E. (2004). Genre trouble: Narrativism and the art of simulation. In *First person new media as story performance and game*. https://doi.org/10.1215/00295132-1261040.

Alfonso X. (1284). *Libro de los juegos: Acedrex, dados e tablas* (R. O. Calderón, Ed.). Biblioteca Castro.

Amabile, T., & Kramer, S. (2011). *The progress principle: Using small wins to ignite joy, engagement, and creativity at work*. Cambridge, MA: Harvard University Press.

Aristotle. (335BC). *Poetics*. London: Penguin Classics.

Barthes, R. (1966). Introduction à l'analyse structurale des récits. *Communications, 8*, 1–27.

Baukal, C., Ausburn, F., & Ausburn, L. (2013). A proposed multimedia cone of abstraction: Updating a classic instructional design theory. *Journal of Educational Technology, 9*(4), 15–24. https://doi.org/10.26634/jet.9.4.2129.

Bazin, A. (1958). *Qu'est-ce que le cinéma?. 1, Ontologie et langage*. Paris: Éditions du verf.
Bennis, W., & Thomas, R. J. (2002, September). *Crucibles of leadership*. Harvard Business Publishing. Retrieved from https://hbr.org/2002/09/crucibles-of-leadership.
Bergen, B. (2012). *Louder than words: The new science of how the mind makes meaning*. New York: Basic Books.
Berger, J. (2013). *Contagious: Why things catch on*. New York: Simon & Schuster.
Black, J. B., & Bower, G. H. (1980). Story understanding as problem-solving. *Poetics, 9*(1–3), 223–250. https://doi.org/10.1016/0304-422X(80)90021-2.
Bloom, P. (2010). *How pleasure works: The new science of why we like what we like*. New York: W. W. Norton.
Bolter, J. D. (2019). *The digital plenitude. The decline of elite culture and the rise of new media*. Cambridge, MA: MIT Press.
Booker, C. (2004). *The seven basic plots: Why we tell stories*. New York: Continuum.
Bordwell, D. (1985). Narration in the fiction film. In *Narration in the fiction film*. https://doi.org/10.4324/9781315002163.
Bordwell, D. (2006). *The way Hollywood tells it: Story and style in modern movies*. Berkeley: University of California Press.
Boyd, B. (2010). *On the origin of stories*. Cambridge, MA: Harvard University Press.
Branigan, E. (1984). *Point of view in the cinema. A theory of narration and subjectivity in classical film*. Berlin: De Gruyter Mouton.
Branigan, E. (1992). *Narrative comprehension and film*. London: Routledge.
Broderick, M., & Traverso, A. (2011). *Interrogating Trauma: Collective suffering in global arts and media*. Oxon: Routledge.
Brown, D., & Hayes, N. (2008). *Influencer marketing*. https://doi.org/10.4324/9780080557700.
Brown, S. L. (2009). *Play: How it shapes the brain, opens the imagination, and invigorates the soul*. New York: Avery–Penguin Group.
Bruner, J. (1966). *Toward a theory of instruction*. Cambridge, MA: Harvard University Press.
Buckland, W. (2009). *Puzzle films: Complex storytelling in contemporary cinema*. New York: Wiley.
Cage, D. (2010). *Heavy Rain*. Quantic Dream.
Campbell, J. (1949). *The hero with a thousand faces*. New York: Pantheon.
Carvalho, A. A., Zagalo, N., & Araujo, I. (2015). From games played by secondary students to a gamification framework. In *Society for Information Technology & Teacher Education International Conference*, 737–744.
Chouliaraki, L. (2006). *The spectatorship of suffering*. London: Sage.
Comley, C., Steele, D., Algar, N., Schafer-Peek, S., & Perkins, S. (2011). *Opening our eyes. How film contributes to the culture of the UK*. London.
Conrad, J. (1910). *The Nigger of the 'Narcissus'*. New Hampshire: Heinemann.
Cortazar, J. (1963). *Rayuela*. Buenos Aires: Editorial Sudamericana.
Costikyan, G. (2000, September). Where stories end and games begin. *Game Developer*, pp. 44–53. Retrieved from http://www.costik.com/gamnstry.html.
Cott, H. (1940). *Adaptive coloration in animals*. Oxford: Oxford University Press.
Cruz, J., & Gordon, R. M. (2003). Simulation theory. In *Encyclopedia of cognitive science*. https://doi.org/10.1002/0470018860.s00123.
Csikszentmihalyi, M. (1996). Go with the flow. *Wired*. Retrieved from https://www.wired.com/1996/09/czik/.
Csikszentmihalyi, M. (1997). *Finding flow. The psychology of engagement with everyday life*. New York: Basic Books.
Csikszentmihalyi, M., Abuhamdeh, S., & Nakamura, J. (2005). Flow. *Handbook of competence and motivation* (pp. 598–608). New York, NY: Guilford Publications.
Darwin, C. (1859). *On the origin of species by means of natural selection, or the preservation of favoured races in the struggle for life*. London: John Murray.
Decety, J. (2005). Une anatomie de l'empathie. *PSN, 3*(1), 16–24. https://doi.org/10.1007/BF03006827.

Del Vecchio, M., Kharlamov, A., Parry, G., & Pogrebna, G. (2018). *The Data science of Hollywood: Using emotional arcs of movies to drive business model innovation in entertainment industries*. Retrieved from http://arxiv.org/abs/1807.02221.

Deterding, S. (2012). Gamification: Designing for motivation. *Interactions, 19*(4), 14. https://doi.org/10.1145/2212877.2212883.

Egri, L. (1946). *Art of dramatic writing: Its basis in the creative interpretation of human motives*. New York: Touchstone.

Eisner, E. W. (2002). *The arts and the creation of mind*. Yale University Press.

Ekman, P. (1997). Expression or communication about emotion. In *Uniting psychology and biology: Integrative perspectives on human development* (pp. 315–338). https://doi.org/10.1037/10242-008.

Ellmann, R. (1982). *James Joyce*. Oxford: Oxford University Press.

Elmerghany, A. H., & Paulus, G. (2017). Using minecraft as a geodesign tool for encouraging public participation in urban planning. *GI_Forum, 1*, 300–314. https://doi.org/10.1553/giscience2017_01_s300.

Elsaesser, T. (2009). *The Mind-Game Film*. (W. Buckland Ed.), Puzzle Films: Complex Storytelling in Contemporary Cinema (pp. 13–41). New York: Wiley.

Ertiö, T.-P., & Bhagwatwar, A. (2017). Citizens as planners: Harnessing information and values from the bottom-up. *International Journal of Information Management, 37*(3), 111–113. https://doi.org/10.1016/j.ijinfomgt.2017.01.001.

Eskelinen, M. (2001). The gaming situation. *Game Studies*. https://doi.org/10.1017/CBO9781107415324.004.

Everett, D. L. (2017). *How language began: The story of humanity's greatest invention*. New York: W. W. Norton.

Feagin, S. L. (1983). The pleasures of tragedy. *American Philosophical Quarterly, 20*(1), 95–104. Retrieved from https://www.jstor.org/stable/pdf/20013989.pdf.

Fisch, M. H. (1986). *Peirce, semeiotic, and pragmatism*. Bloomington: Indiana University Press.

Fischoff, S., Antonio, J., & Lewis, D. (1998). Favorite films and film genres as a function of race, age, and gender. *Journal of Media Psychology, 3*(1).

Fodor, J. A. (1975). *The language of thought*. Cambridge, MA: Harvard University Press.

García, A. M., Moguilner, S., Torquati, K., García-Marco, E., Herrera, E., Muñoz, E., Ibáñez, A. (2019). How meaning unfolds in neural time: Embodied reactivations can precede multimodal semantic effects during language processing. *NeuroImage, 197*, 439–449. https://doi.org/10.1016/j.neuroimage.2019.05.002.

Gauntlett, D. (2011). *Making is connecting: The social meaning of creativity. In Making is connecting*. Cambridge: Polity Press.

Gauntlett, D., & Thomsen, B. S. (2013). *Cultures of creativity*. Retrieved from https://www.legofoundation.com/media/1073/cultures-of-creativity-lego-fonden-2013.pdf.

Gaynor, S. (2013). *Gone Home*. Fullbright Company.

Gendler, T. S. (2008). Alief and belief. *Journal of Philosophy, 105*(10), 634–663. https://doi.org/10.5840/jphil20081051025.

Genette, G. (1966). Frontières du récit. *Communications, 8*, 152–163.

Godin, S. (2011). *We are all weird*. US: Domino Project.

Goffman, E. (1959). *The presentation of self in everyday life*. New York: Anchor Books.

Gottschall, J. (2012). *The storytelling animal: How stories make us human*. Boston, MA: Houghton Mifflin Harcourt.

Grau, O. (2003). *Virtual art: From illusion to immersion*. Cambridge, MA: MIT Press.

Green, M. C. (2004). Transportation into narrative worlds: The role of prior knowledge and perceived realism. *Discourse Processes, 38*(2), 247–266. https://doi.org/10.1207/s15326950dp3802_5.

Gunning, T. (1994). The cinema of attractions early film, its spectator and the avant-garde. In *The cinema of attractions reloaded* (pp. 381–388).

Hall, T. (1993). *Doom*. Texas: id Software.

Hassenzahl, M. (2010). Experience design: Technology for all the right reasons. *Synthesis Lectures on Human-Centered Informatics*. https://doi.org/10.2200/S00261ED1V01Y201003HCI008.
Hemingway, E. (1929). *A farewell to arms*. New York: Scribner.
Herman, D. (2002). *Story logic: Problems and possibilities of narrative*. London: University of Nebraska Press.
Herman, D. (2013). *Storytelling and the sciences of mind*. Cambridge, MA: MIT Press.
Hudson, C. (2007). *Mass Effect*. Bioware.
Huizinga, J. (1938). *Homo Ludens: The study of play-element in culture*. London: Routledge.
Israel, P. (2016). The invention factory. In *Thomas A. Edison papers*. http://edison.rutgers.edu/inventionfactory.htm.
Iwatani, T. (1980). *Pac-Man*. Namco.
Jockers, M. L. (2015). Revealing sentiment and plot arcs with the syuzhet package. Retrieved August 8, 2019, from MatthewJockers.com website: http://www.matthewjockers.net/2015/02/02/syuzhet/.
Johnson, E. (2019, June 26). The problem with tech people who want to solve problems. *Recode*. Retrieved from https://www.vox.com/recode/2019/6/26/18758776/joi-ito-mit-media-lab-resisting-reduction-exorcist-kara-swisher-recode-decode-podcast-interview.
Joyce, J. (1922). *Ulysses*. Relógio D'Agua.
Juul, J. (2001). Games telling stories. *Game Studies*. ISSN:1604-7982. http://gamestudies.org/0101/juul-gts/.
Kapp, K. (2012). *The gamification of learning and instruction: Game-based methods and strategies for training and education*. Hoboken, NJ: Wiley.
Koffka, K. (1935). *Principles of Gestalt psychology*. Oxford: Harcourt Inc.
Kress, G. (2009). *Multimodality: A social semiotic approach to contemporary communication*. https://doi.org/10.4324/9780203970034.
Kuhn, T. S. (1962). *The structure of scientific revolutions*. Chicago: University of Chicago Press.
Kushner, D. (2003). *Masters of Doom: How two guys created an empire and transformed pop culture*. Random House.
Lane, H. C., & Yi, S. (2017). Playing with virtual blocks: Minecraft as a learning environment for practice and research. In *Cognitive development in digital contexts* (pp. 145–166). https://doi.org/10.1016/B978-0-12-809481-5.00007-9.
Lopes, C. (2004). *Ludicidade Humana. Contributos para a busca dos sentidos do Humano*. Aveiro: Universidade de Aveiro.
Lucas, G. (1977). *Star Wars*. US: Lucasfilm Ltd.
Lyotard, J.-F. (1979). *La Condition postmoderne*. Paris: Les Editions de Minuit.
Mateas, M., & Stern, A. (2005). *Façade*. Atlanta: Self published.
McCarthy, J. F., & Rose, D. (1991). *Joyce's Dublin: A walking guide to Ulysses*. London: St Martins Press.
Metz, C. (1966). La grande syntagmatique du film narratif. *Communications, 8,* 120–124.
Millar, B. (2019a). *How dark content hacks our subconscious and what we can do about it*. Retrieved from https://vimeo.com/330119765.
Millar, B. (2019b, May). We studied what 10,000 people love online. The results would make Freud blush. *Fast Company*. Retrieved from https://www.fastcompany.com/90343372/we-studied-what-10000-people-love-online-the-results-would-make-freud-blush.
Miyamoto, S. (1985). *Super Mario Bros*. Nintendo.
Muncy, J. (2019, July). The "Super Mario maker 2" community is a Haven of player creativity. *Wired*. Retrieved from https://www.wired.com/story/super-mario-maker-2-community/.
Nabokov, V. (1973). *Strong opinions*. New York: Vintage.
Nebel, S., Schneider, S., & Rey, G. D. (2016). Mining learning and crafting scientific experiments: A literature review on the use of Minecraft in education and research. *Educational Technology and Society*.

Nitsche, M., & Weisling, A. (2019). When is it not craft? In *Proceedings of the Thirteenth International Conference on Tangible, Embedded, and Embodied Interaction—TEI '19*, 683–689. https://doi.org/10.1145/3294109.3295651.
Nolan, C. (2000). *Memento*.
OReilly, D. (2017). *Everything*. San Francisco: Double Fine Productions.
Oshino, Y. (2015). *Super Mario maker*. Tokyo: Nintendo.
Oshino, Y. (2019). *Super Mario maker 2*. Tokyo: Nintendo.
Pajitnov, A. (1984). *Tetris*. Moscow: Academy of Science of the Soviet Union.
Peirce, C. (2000). *Semiótica*. São Paulo: Perspectiva.
Perec, G. (1978). *La Vie Mode d'Emploi*. Paris: Hachette Littératures.
Persson, M. (2009). *Minecraft*. Mojang.
Pinchbeck, D. (2012). *Dear Esther*. Chinese Room.
Pinker, S. (1997). *How the mind works*. New York: W. W. Norton.
Polti, G. (1895). *Les Trente-Six situations dramatiques*. Paris: Édition du Mercure de France.
Pratt, A. E. (1949). *Cluedo*. Leeds: Waddingtons.
Pulizzi, J. (2014). *Epic content marketing: How to tell a different story, break through the clutter, and win more customers by marketing less*. New York: McGraw-Hill.
Reagan, A. J., Mitchell, L., Kiley, D., Danforth, C. M., & Dodds, P. S. (2016). The emotional arcs of stories are dominated by six basic shapes. *EPJ Data Science, 5*(1), 31. https://doi.org/10.1140/epjds/s13688-016-0093-1.
Redfern, N. (2012). Correspondence analysis of genre preferences in UK film audiences. *Participations: Journal of Audience and Reception Studies, 9*(2), 45–55.
Rexhepi, A., Filiposka, S., & Trajkovik, V. (2018). Youth e-participation as a pillar of sustainable societies. *Journal of Cleaner Production, 174,* 114–122. https://doi.org/10.1016/j.jclepro.2017.10.327.
Russell, J. A. (1980). A circumplex model of affect. *Journal of Personality and Social Psychology, 39*(6), 1161–1178. https://doi.org/10.1037/h0077714.
Ryan, M. (2001). *Narrative as virtual reality*. Baltimore: Johns Hopkins University Press. https://doi.org/10.1017/CBO9781107415324.004.
Salen, K., & Zimmerman, E. (2003). *Rules of play: Game design fundamentals*. Cambridge, MA: MIT Press.
Sarkar, B., & Walker, J. (2009). *Documentary testimonies. Global archives of suffering*. New York: Routledge.
Schell, J. (2008). *The art of game design: A book of lenses*. Morgan Kaufmann.
Seligman, M. E. P., & Csikszentmihalyi, M. (2000). Positive psychology: An introduction. *American Psychologist, 55*(1), 5–14. https://doi.org/10.1037/0003-066X.55.1.5.
Short, E. (2000). *Galatea*. Self published.
Stanton, A. (2003). *Finding Nemo*. Emeryville: Pixar Animation Studios.
Sternberg, R., & Sternberg, K. (2012). *Cognitive psychology*. Belmont: Wadsworth.
Stevens, T. (2009). Character-driven/plot-driven. Retrieved August 16, 2019, from EditTorrent website: http://edittorrent.blogspot.com/2009/10/character-drivenplot-driven.html.
Straubel, L. H. (2006). Character and plot nodes: Writing fiction with concept maps. In *Second International Conference on Concept Mapping* (pp. 63–70). Retrieved from http://eprint.ihmc.us/140/.
Sutton-Smith, B. (1978). The dialectics of play. In F. Landry & W. A. R. Oban (Eds.), *Physical activity and human well-being* (pp. 759–768).
Sutton-Smith, B. (2005). Play and ambiguity. In *The game design reader: A rules of play anthology.*
Thompson, D. (2017a). *Hit makers: The science of popularity in an age of distraction*. New York: Penguin Books.
Thompson, D. (2017b). The four-letter code to selling just about anything. What makes things cool? *The Atlantic*. Retrieved from https://www.theatlantic.com/magazine/archive/2017/01/what-makes-things-cool/508772/.

UChicago. (2007). Part of Vonnegut's legacy, cat's cradle, also earned him master's. Retrieved August 8, 2019, from The University of Chicago Chronicle website: http://chronicle.uchicago.edu/070510/vonnegut.shtml.

Ullal-Gupta, S., Nederlanden, C. M. V. B. der Tichko, P., Lahav, A., & Hannon, E. E. (2013). Linking prenatal experience to the emerging musical mind. *Frontiers in Systems Neuroscience, 7*. https://doi.org/10.3389/fnsys.2013.00048.

Vanaman, S. (2012). *The walking dead*. California: Telltale Games.

Varotsis, G. (2018). The plot-algorithm for problem-solving in narrative and dramatic writing. *New Writing, 15*(3), 333–347. https://doi.org/10.1080/14790726.2017.1374414.

Vogler, C. (2007). *The writer's journey: Mythic structure for writers*. San Francisco: Michael Wiese Productions.

Vonnegut, K. (2004). *Kurt Vonnegut lecture*. Retrieved from https://www.youtube.com/watch?v=4_RUgnC1lm8.

Wallenstein, G. (2008). *The pleasure instinct*. Hoboken, NJ: Wiley.

West, R. E. (2017). *Foundations of learning and instructional design technology*. Retrieved from https://lidtfoundations.pressbooks.com/.

Wiltermuth, S. S., & Heath, C. (2009). Synchrony and cooperation. *Psychological Science, 20*(1), 1–5. https://doi.org/10.1111/j.1467-9280.2008.02253.x.

Wright, W. (2008). *Spore*. Redwood: Electronic Arts.

Zagalo, N. (2013). *Videojogos em Portugal: História, Tecnologia e Arte* (FCA Editora, Ed.). Lisboa.

Zeiser, A. (2015). *Transmedia marketing*. https://doi.org/10.4324/9781315880112.

Zug, J. (2011, June). Stolen: How the Mona Lisa became the world's most famous painting. *Smithsonian Mag*. Retrieved from https://www.smithsonianmag.com/arts-culture/stolen-how-the-mona-lisa-became-the-worlds-most-famous-painting-16406234/.

Chapter 6
The Engagement Design Model and Applied Cases

Abstract In this final chapter, we present the full engagement design model, introducing the whole analysis model developed to work on the research carried out in both the literature and the empirical data supporting the model. Each of the three streams is then presented in contrast to different applications that make use of their principles, from which we launch the analysis of various applied cases in order to understand the model's dimensionality and discreetness. A problem with the crossing between two streams—Relation and Progression—is identified and some explanations supported by cognitive traits are offered.

Throughout this book several elements related to the components of human interaction in their specificity and design potential have been presented in depth. The approach followed was based on pragmatics as a communication model, as discussed in Chap. 2, corresponding to the communication relationship between the elements: subjects, contexts and artefacts. The foundation on pragmatics as a conceptualization of experience had as its object to reach the meaning created from the engagement between agents. On the other hand, the interaction between the agents was defined by interaction design theory, which grounds the process in three elements—know, do, feel. Thus, the whole engagement model developed here is focused on the search for a meaning developed at the pragmatic and interactive level, reaching the essence of the user's interests. This modelling shows a clear move from "meaningful engagement" (McCarthy & Wright, 2004), the subjective understanding of the experience, to the idea of streams of engagement. These streams are made up of universal concepts moulded by cognitive contextual needs, subject profiles and artefact representations that serve the design of flow paths through the expected user's experience. The goal is to create comfortable flows and streams of engagement, supported by the user's motivations and profiles, leaving the content of meaning to each user.

The question that arises is: how do interaction functions relate to pragmatics, and produce meaning capable of maintaining active engagement? To understand this process, we need to resort to the neurosciences and how they help us shape human consciousness in its interaction with the real. To this end, Verplank's interaction model fits perfectly with neuroscientific models such as that of Pereira Jr. (2018) (see Fig. 6.1). However, in both models, we can see that both cycles—"know/knowing"

N. Zagalo, *Engagement Design*, Human–Computer Interaction Series,
https://doi.org/10.1007/978-3-030-37085-5_6

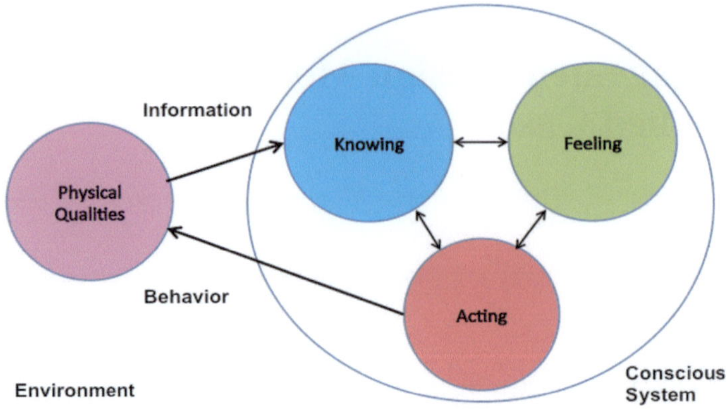

Fig. 6.1 Conscious person interacting with the environment. In the model we are purposing, we defend that different personalities give preference to interact through one of these three dimensions—Knowing, Acting or Feeling (reproduced from Pereira Jr., 2018)

and "feel/feeling"—are formed and then react via only one cycle—"do/acting". But in the model developed here, an engagement model is presented that subdivides engagement as reacting through only one of these functions—know, do, feel. The reason this was done was based on user profiling. That is, study based on the findings of players' motivations concluded that there are very marked profiles of relationship with interaction, which tend to privilege one of the functions—know, do, feel—over the other two. Groups of interactors were found that privilege the cognitive and logical components, neglecting or not allowing great permeation of feeling, or feeling over cognition, or action and doing at the expense of thinking and feeling. With this approach, it is not assumed that human beings do not follow the full cycle of awareness, but only that they privilege one of the elements of the system more, and thus engagement focuses more on that one element. As A. N. Whitehead said about the "three cultures", "there must be a dominant emphasis" (1917, p. 24).

6.1 Model Presentation

Before presenting the design model, a complete analysis model will be presented to ensure a more comprehensive conceptual understanding, while providing more detailed information about the entire model that can serve those interested in refining it. Analysis models are usually built to analyse a problem or a situation, but in this case we used it to analyse the modes and matters we have to comprehend user engagement. In Table 6.1, we can see all the paths followed to respond to pragmatic needs, all the concepts and each dimension, which were thoroughly studied and discussed in the previous chapters. It was then from these dimensions—namely, through their components and indicators—that the grounds for our design model

Table 6.1 The full analytical model, with all the concepts as discussed throughout the previous chapters

Concepts	Dimensions	Components	Indicators
Subjects	**Meaning through interaction** (grounded in I×D theory and empirical game preferred activities)	Get to know	Collect Information Mastery
		Get to do	Explore Worlds Creativity
		Get to feel	Comprehend People Affinity
	Personality (personality and vocational psychological theories)	Conscientiousness	Rigour Organization Efficient Goal-driven Hardworking
		Open to experience	Independent Curious Discovery Imagination Action
		Agreeableness/neuroticism	Persuade Cooperative Friendly Sensitive Compassionate
	Users (construct from the motives and personality)	Abstracters	Abstract and create rules Generalization
		Tinkerers	Associative thinking Experimentation
		Dramatizers	Emotional and social Concrete and human
Contexts	**Curiosity** (grounded in epistemic, perceptual and social curiosity theories)	Uncertainty	Need to fill in information gaps
		Novelty	Sensation seeking and quick saturation
		Comparability	Gossip, self-esteem and learning
	Motivation (self-determination theory)	Competence	Achievement and skill
		Autonomy	Independency and liberty
		Related	Socialization and connectedness

(continued)

Table 6.1 (continued)

Concepts	Dimensions	Components	Indicators
	Patterns (construct from the Curiosity and Motivation)	Problem-solving	Logic and causation
		Unfamiliar	Functional and mechanics
		Empathizing	Understanding others' emotions
Artefacts	**Representation** (grounded in cognitive and aesthetics theories)	Symbolic	Conventional, abstract and pre-learned
		Enactive	Expressive, indexed and functional
		Iconic	Mimetic, body and face
	Design (grounded in game design, play theory and narrative studies)	Puzzle	Goals and obstacles
		Play	Building and simulations
		Characters	Choices and bonds
	Outcomes (construct from the representation and design)	Goals	Advancing knowledge
		Craftworks	Self-realization and self-expression
		Changes	Conflicts and relation interpretation

have been extracted. Also, for each dimension, we present concepts—users, patterns and outcomes—, which correspond to an effective result of the analysis of correlation between the pragmatic communication component and the needs of interaction design, thus consisting in essential dimensions of the production of engagement streams.

Having presented the analysis model, the engagement streams in their relationship to the experience should now be introduced. In Fig. 6.2, we can see the streams as flow channels serving the catalysation of the experience. This means that we are not considering the streams as full attention grabbers, simply because outside of the streams we still have the content of what is being conveyed and all the associative thinking and feeling being produced by the user while fully experiencing the moment by moment. Looking back to the conscious system (see Fig. 6.1), we know that even if the user privileges one of the conscious modes—know, do, feel—and consequently gives preference to one of the streams, it's not possible to halt all that's happening throughout the rest of the conscious system, the unstoppable experiencing of meaning-making.

In this modelling, an approach based on three potential interaction streams of the experience according to user preferences has been followed. These streams were

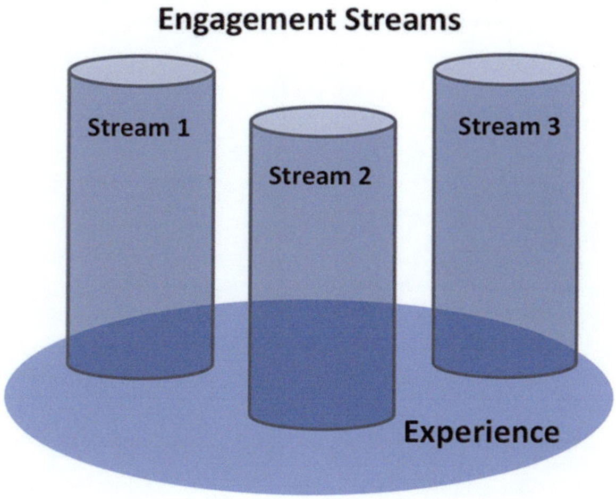

Fig. 6.2 The triadic engagement design model is applied directly to the user experience

named from the correlations established above, between pragmatic communication and interaction, which provided empirical data for the personality profiles—Abstracters, Tinkerers, Dramatists. In turn, the relationship between motivation and curiosity provided contextual patterns—Problem-Solving, Unfamiliar, Empathizing. And finally, the correlation between representation and design needs eventually gave the expected results for each stream—Goals, Craftworks, Changes. From the relationship between the three constructs through a correlation of needs, the following three streams have been identified: Progression, which stands for a stream that makes the user go through a succession of resolutions, progressing towards the desired goals; Expression, which opens spaces for the creation of different world perspectives, resulting in expressive original artefacts and Relation, which pushes the user to interpret people (see Fig. 6.3).

For the final design model, we chose a six-level categorization (see Fig. 6.4). However, as seen in Fig. 6.3, there were three essential ones per stream, because they follow the dimensions considered to be the basis for producing the engagement in the analysis model. These three have been considered, but for the actual work of design creation and production, it was considered that it would be a less clear

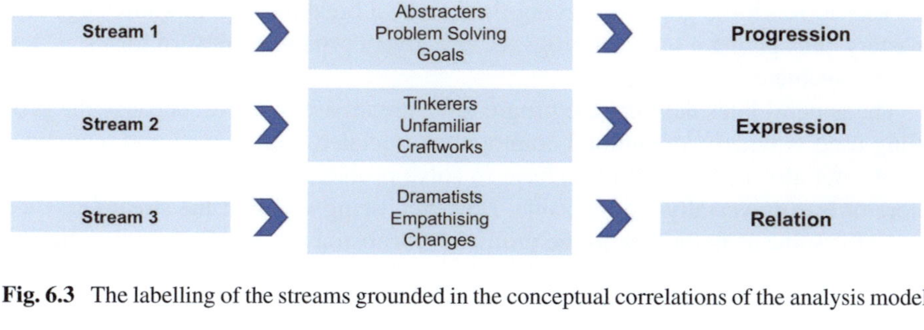

Fig. 6.3 The labelling of the streams grounded in the conceptual correlations of the analysis model

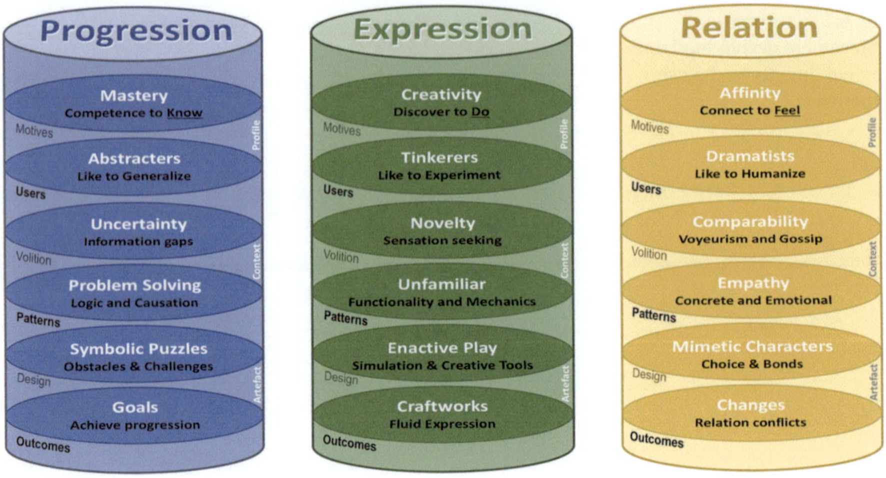

Fig. 6.4 The engagement design model

model, so it was decided to substantiate each dimension with another of support and explanation. The goal is to ensure that the model is as self-sufficient as possible, requiring no explanations.

6.1.1 Progression

Progression modelling is based on abstracters' profiles, motivated by intentions of mastery and interaction searching for skills and knowledge improvement. Users are focused on formal knowledge and its usefulness in a specific domain, seeking to understand the organization of knowledge and its structure and applicability outside the strict framework presented. For this purpose, the production of interactive media content needs to be developed based on problem-solving patterns, offering elements and stimuli that allow deduction processes, based on responding to information or solution uncertainties. In terms of effective design, the optimal mechanisms for the effect are based on the puzzle, that is, on the construction of obstacles that challenge the user to reach the goal. Achieving the goal is a breakthrough in knowledge and mastery, thus giving a sense of progress, effectively producing reward for users, i.e. full engagement.

The general lines defining the progression stream are intuitive, because the profiling used is widely known and commonly associated with logical and analytical minds, but also because all of us have to solve problems daily, making the stream more or less universally recognizable. However, being aware of the stream essence is not the same as belonging to the profile of the abstracter. The Progression stream is projected for the passionate of problem-solving, intending to create ecosystems for those getting real pleasure from the reasoning about and struggling for solutions.

The simplest, non-digital examples of progression engagement design can be seen in crossword puzzles and sliding puzzles (see Fig. 6.5), two examples that also serve to categorize two major puzzle modes in video games: analytics and mastery. On the analytic side, we have games that require deductive reasoning efforts to come up with solutions, while on the mastery side we have puzzles that require dexterity, meaning dedication and repetition efforts to reach resolution. So for the former, we can look at puzzle games—e.g. *Portal* (Swift, 2007), *The Room* (Dodd & Hamilton, 2012), *Monument Valley* (McFarland, 2014) (see Fig. 6.6)—or strategy games—e.g. *Civilization* (1991) (see Fig. 6.6), *Europa Universalis* (Andersson, Berndal, Strandberg, & Thibaut, 2000), *FTL: Faster Than Light* (Ma & Davis, 2012)—in which interaction takes place largely by reasoning about the elements presented by the game, their mental decomposition and consequent interactive transformation to reach solutions. For mastery games, we have different action game subgenres like platforms—*Super Mario Bros.* (Miyamoto, 1985), *Super Meat Boy* (McMillen

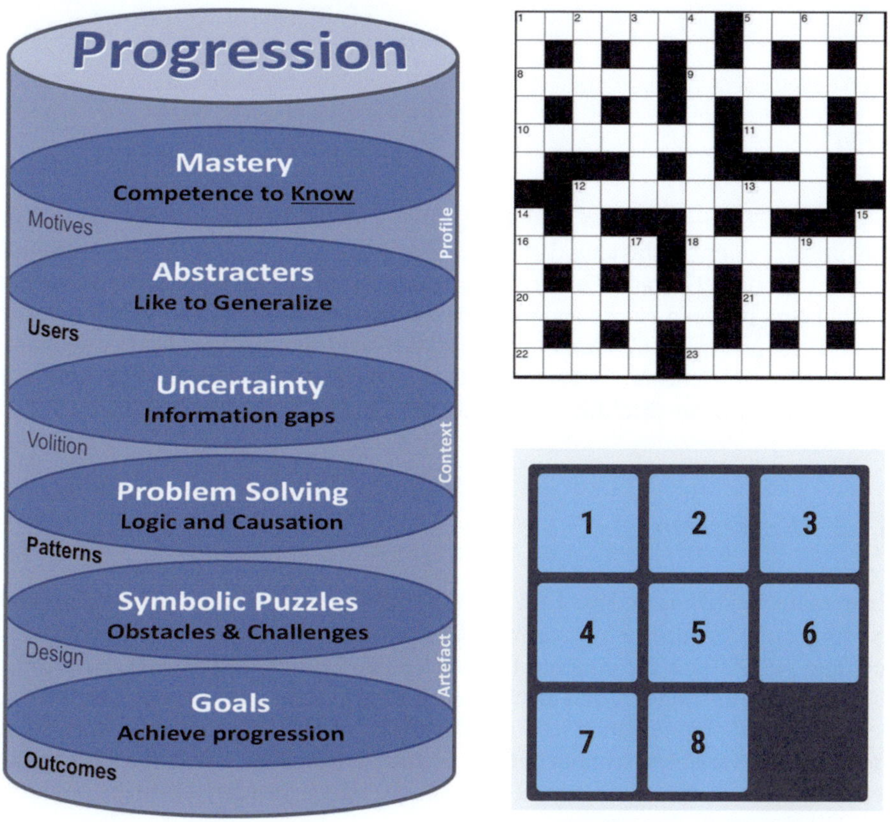

Fig. 6.5 The Progression stream and two simple types of puzzles: crosswords and sliding tiles

Fig. 6.6 Some of the examples mentioned, showing the symbolic representation and interaction of the Progression stream: *Monument Valley* (2014), *Civilization* (1991), *Street Fighter* (1987), *Diablo* (1996)

& Refenes, 2010)—beat 'em up and fighting—*Double Dragon* (Kishimoto, 1987) and *Street Fighter* (Nishiyama, 1987) (see Fig. 6.6)—or sports—*FIFA International Soccer* (Sports, 1993) and *The Need for Speed* (Lemke, 1994). We can also have a combination between puzzle and mastery, with, for example, shooters/FPS—*Doom* (Hall, 1993) and *Halo: Combat Evolved* (2001)—and dungeon crawlers/roguelike—*Diablo* (Brevik, Schaefer, Schaefer, Sexton, & Williams, 1996) (see Fig. 6.6) and *The Binding of Isaac* (McMillen & Himsl, 2011).

6.1.2 Expression

Expression modelling is based on the Tinkerers profile, motivated by doing and experimenting and driven by creativity. Content standards present a need to provide multiple possibilities for creating the unfamiliar, the new and unseen, by experimenting with functionality and mechanics, aiming to satisfy new sensations. In turn, design is based on production in simulated environments, that is, free for recreation and play with variables, without defined or closed objectives, where the tools themselves are part of the experience. The results of interaction are self-made products filled by the expressive features of the users.

Of the three streams, this one is the least easily identifiable, not least because of its novelty. Nonetheless, only in the twenty-first century have we begun to give it due value. Chris Anderson has devoted an entire book to the tinkerer ecosystem, *Makers. The New Industrial Revolution* (2012) in which he realizes the endless possibilities for new business creation (following the DIY—Do It Yourself approaches) and the new professions of the makers (going from hobbyists to professionals). Anderson also talks about crowdsourcing networks (e.g. Kickstarter) and digital distribution, all linked with the "long tail" phenomenon (Anderson, 2006). Schneiderman has worked on the idea of developing "interactive tools" to "enable more people to be more creative" (Shneiderman, 2002, 2007). In 2011, the documentary "PressPause-Play" (Dworsky & Köhler, 2011) was released with dozens of interviews with artists about the state of creativity and its relationship to new digital tools and distribution technologies. Zagalo and Branco edited the book *The Creativity in the Digital Age* (2015) aiming at defining these so-called new "creative technologies" (e.g. 3D printing, visual coding, microcontroller boards, sensors, tangibles) that colleagues on the "Creative Technologies" degree at Auckland University of Technology, defined as:

> a multiplicity of design, communication, computing, engineering, entertainment and manufacturing media, employed to produce ideas, intellectual property and artefacts that characterise the outputs of emerging occupations and professions operating across a wide range of entrepreneurial creative industries contexts. (Connor, Marks, & Walker, 2015)

All these advances account for a fundamental movement involving tinkerers and their transformative capacity with respect to society. This stream is not aiming at any cultural revolution; instead, it is just following the motivations to interaction of users, as unveiled in the research performed throughout the previous chapters, mainly the preference for activities privileging autonomous behaviours, which have been copiously enhanced by recent artefacts, as will now be explained.

To support the Expression stream, we already have the classic kits for creating and experimenting, like the Arduino kits or the more recent kits that permit the production of experimental flavours or beverages (see Fig. 6.7), following in the steps of LEGO-type kit systems. In turn, these same sets can come in two distinct formats: guided, with recipes or building instructions and open, giving complete freedom to the creativity and inspiration of the creators. Thus, in the field of guided digital kits, we can find some creation-based artefacts like *Super Mario Maker* (Oshino, 2015) or *Nintendo Labo* (Kawamoto, Sakaguchi, & Ogasawara, 2018) or simulators such as *Planet Coaster* (Dixon, 2016) (see Fig. 6.8) or *Farming Simulator 17* (Frey, 2017) that present concrete and delimited development scenarios (the recipes) that enhance an already framed creation. In the most open artefacts, we have the digital sandboxes—*Minecraft* (Persson, 2009) or *Spore* (Wright, 2008) or virtual worlds such as *Second Life* (Rosedale, 2003) (see Fig. 6.8) or *Active Worlds* (Britvich, 1995).

In the expression domain, complete freedom is offered to players, which may entail additional reasoning, such as learning programming languages in order to master some applications to effectively earn the full offered experience—e.g. the sandbox creator "Roblox" (Baszucki & Cassel, 2006) (see Fig. 6.8) or the authoring

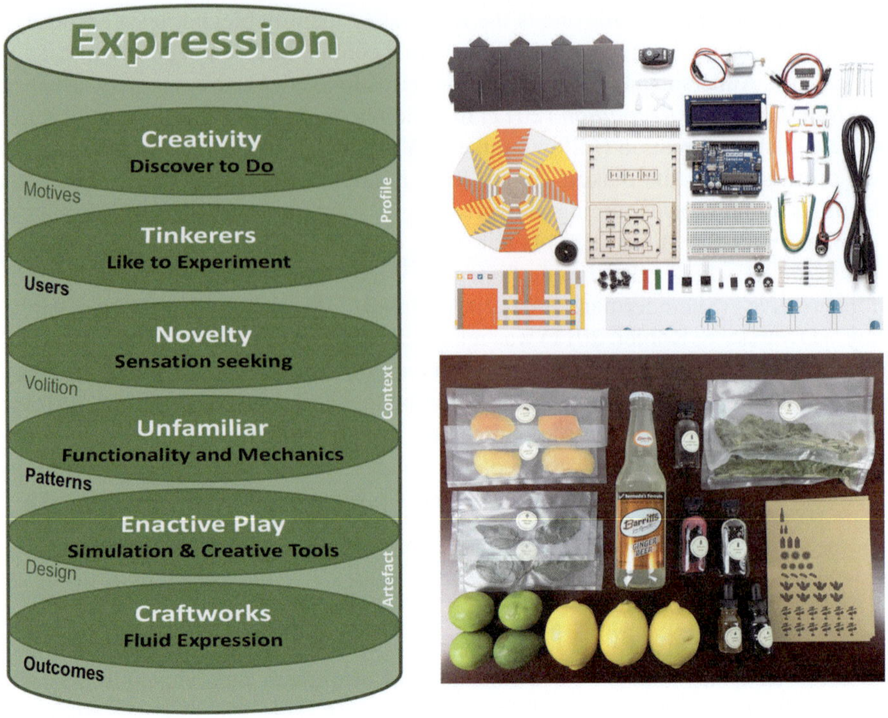

Fig. 6.7 The Expression stream and two simple types of creative kits: electronics and coding (Picture of the content of a Genuino Kit. Reproduced from the Arduino webpage at https://blog.arduino.cc/2016/07/08/starter-kits-now-available-in-spanish-and-german/); alcoholic beverages (Picture of the content of a Shaker & Spoon box. Reproduced from the Hello Subscription webpage at https://hellosubscription.com/2015/11/shaker-spoon-subscription-box-review-coupon-november-2015/)

tool "Scratch" (Resnick, Silverman, & Bonta, 2007) (see Fig. 6.8). However, the reasoning needed rarely outdoes the creative investment, as would happen in the Progression stream. As an example, for someone doing creative work, the use of game engines like Unreal or Unity 3D is preferably done through visual scripting plug-ins—e.g. Playmaker (Chouls & Ko, 2010), Bolt,[1] Node Canvas[2] or Blueprints.[3] All of these systems are based on DIY logic and can be more or less confined and more or less regulated, though allowing free creation.

---

[1]Information about Bolt can be read online at https://ludiq.io/bolt.

[2]Information about Node Canvas can be reached at https://nodecanvas.paradoxnotion.com/.

[3]Blueprints are part of the Unreal software, all the information about the module can be seen online at: https://docs.unrealengine.com/en-US/Engine/Blueprints/index.html.

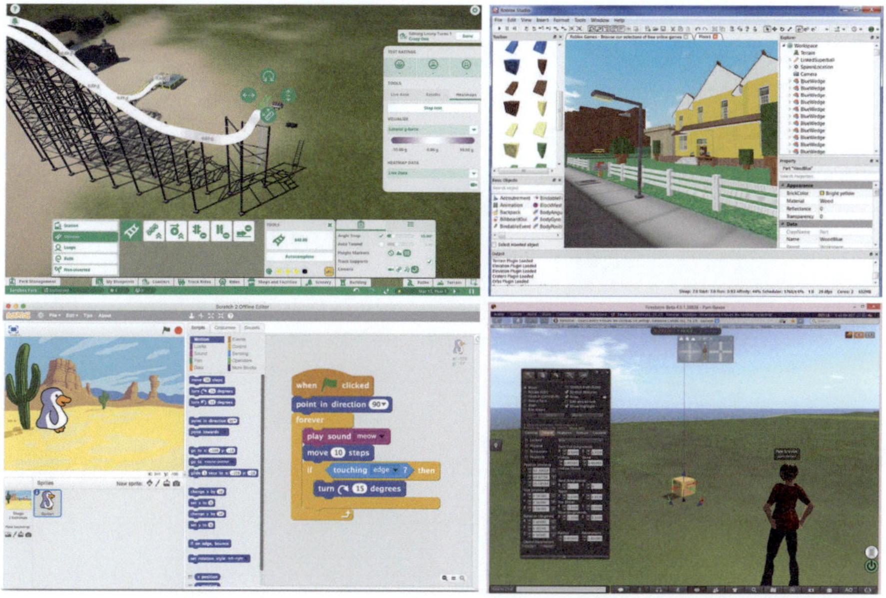

Fig. 6.8 Some of the examples mentioned, showing the autonomy, exploration and building approaches of the Expression stream. Pictures reproduced from the following applications: *Planet Coaster*, *Roblox*, *Scratch* and *Second Life*

6.1.3 Relation

For relation modelling, users get defined as dramatists, being motivated by the connection with other humans, and thus by the desire to humanize everything to which they relate. Patterns result from people's interrelations allowing the particularization of feelings, enhancing empathy. Situations permit comparability between oneself, one's mental models and others, implicitly through gossiping and voyeurism. Design is based on the performing of human conflicts that can provide the analysis and experimentation of changes, presenting choices and decisions about relationships, following processes of behavioural mimicry.

As with Progression, the Relation stream feels like a classic type of approach to the world. All of us love to see a good movie or read or hear a good story, about people with affinities with us, similar professions or families, or just the way of life, be it about a footballer, a professor, a preacher or just about the people in the city we were born. We like to see through the keyhole and get to feel the sameness or the superiority of our lives. But this stream is not about a mere "peeping Tom"; the focus is on the constellations of social relations, their dependencies, submissions and dominions, seeing the world as made of social bonds. It is about putting humans above numbers and statistics, believing in individuality and at the same time demanding collective effort, accepting that the masses exist but that they are made up of individual subjects,

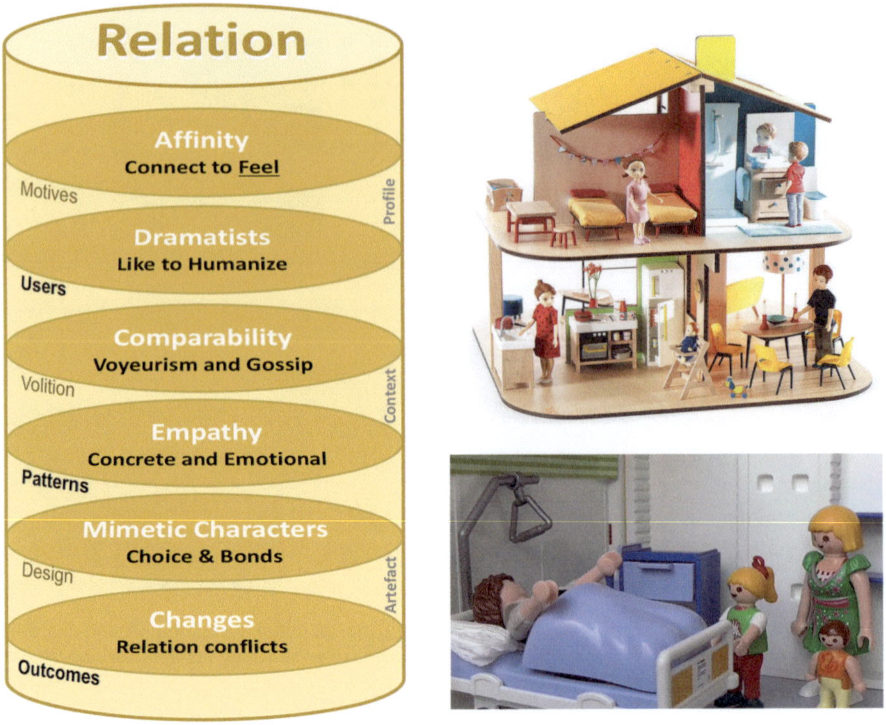

Fig. 6.9 The Relation stream and two simple types of situation: a doll's house (The doll's house is made by Djeco and is reproduced from http://www.djeco.com/en/games-toys/dolls-house.) and a Playmobil family [The Playmobil family is reproduced from (Hauser, 2018).]

all different from any other. Each person is an entire world and deserves our time and effort in trying to comprehend him or her, and each part is more than the whole.

The archetype of this domain is undoubtedly the doll's house (see Fig. 6.9), with the home spaces serving in the identification of human traits and behaviours. In turn, these spaces can be populated with characters, to which the Playmobil (see Fig. 6.9) toy line actively contributes. These two physical approaches highlight two distinct modes: the linear, marked by the spaces and hierarchy of the doll's house, and that of choices, enhanced by the freedom of the Playmobil dolls. Thus, and looking now to digital artefacts, in the linear field, we can identify games like *Gone Home* (Gaynor, 2013) or *Florence* (Wong, 2018), while for choice we have *Episode* (Gems, 2014) or *The Walking Dead* (Vanaman, 2012). In the former, the story recounts the conflicts the characters have gone through, so we can know what happened, but even following the story moment by moment we cannot change anything, as if the walls of the doll's house were glued together, and it was not possible to move them. In choice-based games, the conflicts that arise are likely to be dealt with, reflected and changed by us, the players. Both narrative structures may also vary by story genre: crime—*Her Story* (Barlow, 2015) or *Return of the Obra Dinn* (Pope, 2018), thriller—*The Last of Us*

Fig. 6.10 Some of the examples mentioned above, showing the effect and relevance of the human relationships as the foundation of the Relation stream. Pictures reproduced from the video games: *Heavy Rain*, *Florence*, *The Walking Dead* and *Brothers: A Tale of Two Sons*

(Straley & Druckmann, 2013), sci-fi—*Mass Effect* (Hudson, 2007), fantasy—*The Witcher 3: The Wild Hunt* (Tomaszkiewicz, Kanik, & Stępień, 2015) or drama—*Heavy Rain* (Cage, 2010), *Brothers: A Tale of Two Sons* (Fares, 2013) and *Firewatch* (Moss & Vanaman, 2016).

There is always an attempt to explain the whys of what we do, and on the evolutionary side more even to arrive at a utilitarian explanation. Hence, social comparison and human improvement through social interaction can explain the need for others and the pleasure produced by watching and following others, but on the other hand, as we can see in the pictures in Fig. 6.10, the foundation of the Relation stream is the interaction motive to feel. We cannot escape the search for knowing, but there is no progression, no struggle to attain goals. The feeling for these others makes dramatists interact, not the conscious idea of comparison with these others. Dramatists privilege the human, their feelings, instead of the abstract reasoning of the Progression stream, as we will see in the next section.

6.1.4 Streams Interrelated

From the presentation of each stream, and from the analysis of contexts, profiles and artefacts, we can now extract an axis that seems fundamental to us in determining the properties of design using the streams of engagement. This has to do with the content interest of the users, which varies from the rationalization of the abstract, non-concrete and non-human, to the emotionalization of everything that concerns the particular and the human, namely, their behavioural traits. This could already be seen in personality traits (see Chap. 3), with "agreeableness" pointing to the human side, varying in inverse relation to "conscientiousness", which points towards ideas, in an opposition classified by McCrae and John as "'strong-willed' versus 'weak-willed'" (1992). To this axis, we can add the concrete world and its objects to respond to the

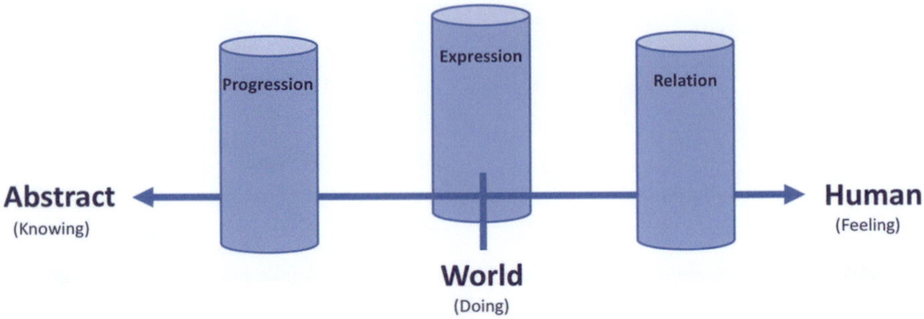

Fig. 6.11 The axis of engagement interest presents on opposite sides the abstraction and human, and at the centre the things of the world. The streams following each of these interests become aligned in a dimensionality that helps us to understand their possible interrelations

tinkerers' interests—defined by the "openness" personality traits—which may then lean towards a more human focus or, in turn, to the abstraction side (see Fig. 6.11).

This axis of engagement interest is reinforced when analysing the structures and mechanics of artefacts in the representation form—symbol, enactive, mimetic—as in the way content gets operated—ranging from the most abstract to the most human and concrete, passing through the world of things, following the logics evidenced by the "Ladder of Abstraction" (Hart, 2007) (see Chap. 4). Thus, the tripartite engagement model can be seen through a dimensional axis, having as extremes the Progression and Relation, with the Expression at the centre, creating bridges with each of the extremes. To make this design variability clearer, let's look at a case study of a game that uses all of the three streams simultaneously.

6.2 Applied Case: The Multi-engagement of *Assassin's Creed*

Assassin's Creed (Désilets, Raymond, & May, 2007) (AC) is one of the most successful and prolific video game series, with more than 20 titles—among major games and cross-platform spin-offs—released over a decade. Thematically, the series began by focusing on the struggle between two factions, the Assassins and the Templars, who could travel back in time to find the best killers and thus eliminate competition. Over the years the series has evolved the theme, or rather refined it as it completely transformed the gameplay, from Action–Adventure to RPG with very particular attributes added to DLC components that extended the gameplay simulation and creativity. In this sense, we are interested in analysing this series because we consider that having started mainly focused on the design of one single engagement stream—Progression—over time it would eventually seek to respond to all design streams—adding Expression and Relation. Through this analysis we intend to see the streams working discretely and dimensionally to understand what kind of problems can arise when streams get mixed.

Despite the amount of games and impact of the series, and despite all the interest expressed by the academy in the study of video games, it is strange that a review article by Joly-Lavoie (2017) about the series has only found 22 papers discussing the games, of which only 13 are in journals. Stranger still is the fact that all these texts frame exclusively aspects of critical analysis—"historical agency, consumption, culture, collective memory, narratology, past representation, school use, and transmedia" (Joly-Lavoie, 2017)—leaving the design only laterally discussed via narratology and transmedia. Thus, what we will discuss here concerns only the design of the series, which will be viewed in a macro way, i.e. focused on transformations and transitions through the years. In this sense, we have divided the main games into three chronological periods. The first to fourth main games, 2007–2013 (*Assassin's Creed* (Désilets et al., 2007), *Assassin's Creed II* (Désilets, 2009), *Assassin's Creed III* (Hutchinson, 2012), *Assassin's Creed IV: Black Flag* (Guesdon, Ismail, & Kieken, 2013)), framed as the early action and adventure phase. Then the fifth and sixth main games, 2014–2015 (*Assassin's Creed Unity* (Amancio & Albinet, 2014) and *Assassin's Creed Syndicate* (Côté, Phillips, & Pincombe, 2015)) form the middle stage, where the design becomes more elaborated with the appearance of RPG elements and greater dedication to narrative. And finally, in the seventh and eight main games, 2017–2018 (*Assassin's Creed Origins* (Guesdon & Ismail, 2017) and *Assassin's Creed Odyssey* (Dumont & Phillips, 2018)), the dramatic layer gains prominence, as the simulation becomes evident and game creation opportunities are finally offered.

So, in the initial phase, 2007–2013, we have video games focused on the wide, labyrinthine and gamified space. We play with a time-travelling character who is more observer than agent of the narratives presented. The focus is all on solving obstacles and finding areas and items, all requiring the player's planning and strategy. There is some historical lore mixed with the fiction, with the action taking place first in the Middle East, then Italy, followed by the USA and the Atlantic, but the lore is never deep enough to define itself as a major narrative object of the games. In addition to the confusion arising between the relation of past and present, provided by the VR time machine, the Animus (Kuchera, 2018), the player always seems to be positioned as an outside observer of historical events, stepping in and out and failing to create an effective relationship with the characters. In this sense, the game tasks the main character just to enter the system and discover an alleged "Apple of Eden", for which the player must focus on a map, explore each space and follow the clues. The design is made of puzzles inside puzzles, rewarding the player for problem-solving and moving forward (see Fig. 6.12).

Putting us inside a virtual environment with audiovisual properties centred upon a historical theme, the places, objects and some of the characters are not mere abstractions. They have direct connotations with historical reality, thus enhancing the engagement with the nostalgia of the places. However, these elements are mere window-dressing surrounding interactive properties, with the player being mostly responsible for solving problems, developing the necessary game skills, mastering

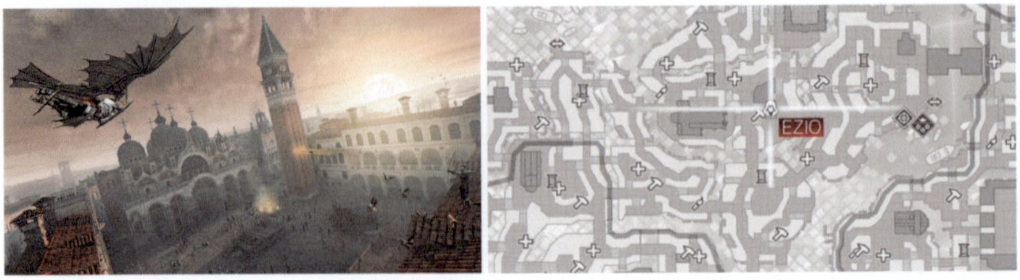

Fig. 6.12 Despite the beautiful audiovisual component, the focus is on the game, the resolution of puzzles, as can be seen in the different representations in these two pictures. One is the 3D perspective of the world and the second the topographic dimension, which ensures the player the means to solve problems. Pictures reproduced from *Assassin's Creed II* (Désilets, 2009)

them and getting the task done. It is true what Doug Church says about action–adventure games, "the story has been written in advance by designers", but this does not fail to make these stories merely an "abstract tool", in the sense that they are still viewed by game designers as pathways to create gaming conditions—"Because of X, Y has happened" (Church, 1999, p. 5)—guaranteeing identifiable props for problem-solving.

In the intermediate phase, 2014–2015, Ubisoft introduced a major design change—Experience Points (XP)—a change that would drive the series to become more like a traditional role-playing game. However, even if the RPG label seems to identify more with narrative and drama, the mechanics per se say something different, as we will see. The goal of defining XP in a game is to parameterize the progression of characters, that is, to create player-adjustable metrics—through what is conventionally known as "skill trees" (see Fig. 6.13)—to guide characters as they see fit in the game. The focus is not the story, but the game, and this can easily be confirmed by the weight of the different areas in the creation of these games by analysing the game credits. In *AC Syndicate*, when the credits open, the General Team responsible for the game has no narrative or story-related role. The Narrative Director, Corey May, appears only within the Quebec-specific team, and yet practically at the bottom of the various directors' list, something that is then changed in the following phase.

Fig. 6.13 Skill trees quantification defines the progress of the character and the game. On the right we can see the main characters, siblings, disagreeing and creating more connection with the story and drama than any RPG metric

The real focus of the design is on the quantification and abstraction of characters and their external actions on the quantifiable world, and not on the psychology that underpins relationships and conflicts. Recently, the historian Matt Barton has explained in detail how cognitive role-playing systems work, which elucidates why adding RPG to Assassin's Creed didn't add story value per se:

> It's not so much that you learn valuable content from playing these games, but you do learn habits of thinking. So really it comes down to the scientific method, learning about statistical reasoning. If you really are good at these games and you play them enough, you'll start to pick up on things like, 'I should use this weapon rather than that weapon' or 'Here's a different kind of creature, they have these resistances.' It's those kinds of observations, and then you try something, you measure the results, you modify your tactics along the way. And even though these are fights with rats or skeletons or zombies—or whatever the case may be—you're training your mind to approach problems in a certain way that's really just straight out of a science textbook. (Barton, 2019)

Despite this development towards deepening problem-solving patterns, *AC Syndicate* introduces a novelty, which is a playable duo, based on two twins, a man and a woman, a clear response from Ubisoft to the sexism it has been accused of (Dockterman, 2014). But in doing so, it created a set of relationships between the two characters that began to broaden the series also in the sense of narrative and drama. Since *AC Unity* we had already noticed the detachment from the history component in the present, keeping the focus on the past, but in *AC Syndicate*, there was already an effort to feed the characterization of the characters, their personalities and behaviours. In this case, Evie and Jacobson, although twins, have opposite temperaments (see Fig. 6.13), which serves the dramatic expansion of the plot, even if yet with no possibility of intervention by the player.

However, in the last phase, 2017–2018, not only are all the game elements discussed above immensely deepened, with the application of XP becoming more pervasive throughout the game, with more complex skill trees, but simultaneously a huge investment in the dramatic component has been made (e.g. in *AC Origins* the main character sets out on the adventure to avenge his son's death). The narrative component is not left to mere exposition, with *AC Origins* presenting some narrative choices, which were then consolidated in *AC Odyssey*, offering effective agency on the relations and conflicts (see Fig. 6.14). Unlike what happened in the credits of the previous phase, in *AC Origins* we can see in the first part of the General Team a whole team responsible only for Story. The series moved towards creating concrete bridges between the Progression and Relation engagement audiences, offering increasingly robust, analytical and abstract problem-solving systems while feeding the characters' psychological nature, motivations and needs. Critic Axon even states that "For the first time in more than a decade with the franchise, I can actually recount the entire story to you in detail, because giving me a voice in its outcome made me care" (2019).

AC is an open-world game, and throughout each phase it has continued to enlarge the virtual world, giving more and more interactive opportunities to players, offering lots of autonomy throughout the vastness of the virtual territories. This means that the Expression engagement audiences have not been forgotten and have always received

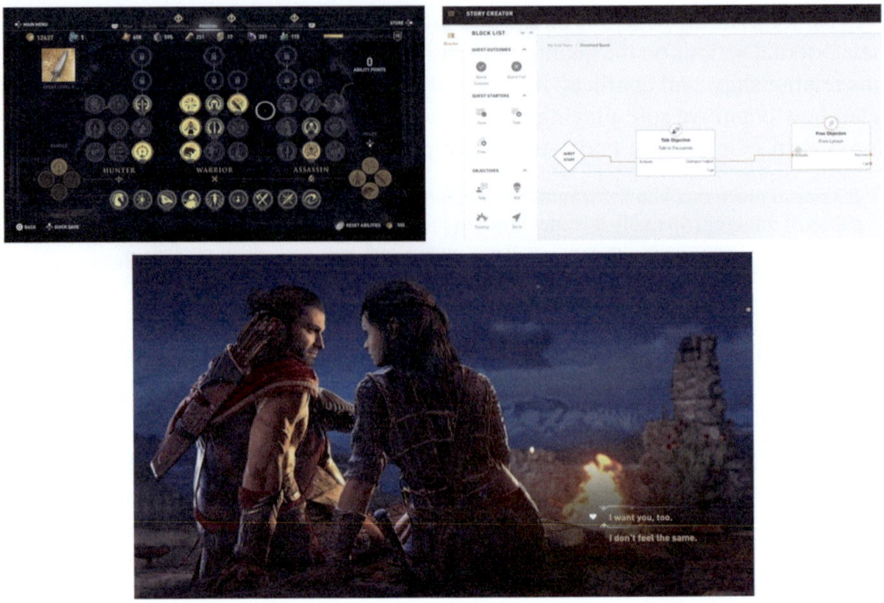

Fig. 6.14 Assassin's Creed series and the three different gameplays—XP and Skill trees, the Story Creator Mode and the drama choices—demonstrating how AC brings together the three different engagement streams: **Progression**, **Expression** and **Relation**

attention from the designers. We could even say that the Expression open world has been used by the designers as a bridge between Progression and Relation, not only as a playground allowing each audience to serve themselves whatever they prefer at their own pace, but also mixing the Progression (its problem-solving and item collecting) with the world simulation, and mixing the Relation (using geographic and historical attributes and behaviours for characters) with time-period simulation.

However, Ubisoft seems to have understood that something related to the Expression stream was still missing. The simulation could be more realistic, and the creative aspects could be greatly improved, so they offered two free DLC: *Discovery Tour Mode* for *AC Origins* and *Story Mode Creator* for *AC Odyssey*. In the *Discovery Tour,* the series uses all the knowledge and information gathered from historical reality and makes it accessible through simulation, allowing players to explore the Egyptian architecture in depth (namely, the interior of the pyramids) as well as Egyptian customs, drawing them in via their perceptual curiosity and thirst for novelty, never before experienced and unknown to players. In the second DLC, the *Story Mode Creator* (see Fig. 6.14), the series goes further than ever, for the first time, after more than 12 years, putting in the hands of players the possibility of creating their own adventures, drawing and making their creative desires real, and exploring the side of doing, of creating and sharing, giving full sway to the Expression stream.

We can say then that the Assassin's Creed series completes the full cycle of engagement, producing a final game capable of offering content and interaction that touches all different audiences, lovers of Progression, Expression and Relation. While this convergence of engagement streams seems ideal, it has ultimately contributed to a less than perfect gaming experience, reported by critics and online gamers as "bloated", with "too many different" approaches, "too many systems" running concurrently and "lacking focus". In the reports by players we can see how overwhelmed players feel by the amount of options, but also with the different directions that the game seems to want or to force in terms of design, although this is not felt in the same way by everyone, and not even everyone feels this excess. To have a better understanding of the user experience, we qualitatively analysed a discussion between players (with 147 comments[4]) about the last two games—2017 and 2018—focusing on the gameplay, its weaknesses and strengths, dividing the users, through their arguments, into our profiles and engagement streams, as follows:

RELATION (Dramatists)

- The size of the map. It needs to be vastly reduced. I want to be familiar with my environment (…) I'd like to see the amount of missions and systems vastly reduced in favor of deeper experiences (…) I'd like to develop relationships with NPCs that tell deeper stories (…) I'd also scrap a lot of Assassin tree skills.
- I don't absorb any of it because there's too much and it's often unmemorable.
- 'Working' through Odyssey… It's a game, it shouldn't be work.
- They should make future AC games a little smaller/shorter (…) have much more depth when it comes to story missions (…) with more dialogue options, consequences and deeper characters act.

PROGRESSION (Abstracters)

- I want what AC 1 was going for. Smaller map, but with new tech. Focused (…) the highlights being how to effectively assassinate a big target.
- I was just completely overwhelmed. There was way too much to do and I had a hard time telling if anything was much of actual progression.
- More unique loot from different sources (…) more robust reputation system (…) more enemy variety.
- I recently platinumed Origins and I really think this is the way the game has to be played. I do agree that the game need to go back to its assassination roots (…) give us a target per area and let us come up with different methods of assassinating the target.
- It is too overwhelming (…) I didn't feel to make any progress.

[4]The entire discussion can be read in the following Resetera forum: https://www.resetera.com/threads/assassins-creed-origins-odyssey-their-bloat-problem-what-to-do-moving-forward.74513/.

EXPRESSION (Tinkerers)

- "I want Assassins Next map to be even bigger. Exploring is what I like most"
- "No, they don't need to reduce the size of the map!"
- "The more bloat the better I say, doesn't mean you have to do every single little bit of side content/distraction, it's just there to keep the world feeling engaging."
- "It's an open world RPG. Every game in that genre has an expectation that you aren't only there for the story (…) If you want to just drive through the 'story' (…) this isn't the game for you."
- "Completely disagree with the idea that we need smaller maps. Part of the appeal with these kinds of games is exploring and getting lost in these huge real like maps."

As we can see, both the dramatists and the abstracters complain about the excess of possibilities and choices that seem to hinder their access to what interests them most in the game. On the dramatists' side, the story (its depth of meaning) and the mimetic interactions (the relationships). On the side of the abstracters, we have the focus on problem-solving (the murders) and symbolic interaction (understanding progress). Note that there are still players in this stream that do complete all the tasks, following the "collecting" trait. On the other side, the tinkerers (even without any creative possibility like the Story Mode Creator; it was released only in January 2019) feel particularly content with the almost infinite variety of possibilities presented by the open-world simulation, which responds to the exploration's personality trait. The miscellaneous simulation, bloated for the Progression and Relation streams, seems to contribute to the enactive interaction (autonomous experimentation) of the Expression stream.

From this analysis, we can conclude that it is possible to work the streams separately and together, showing that they are not impermeable. We realize, however, and now reflecting on the axis of engagement interest, that the extremes of this axis—Progression and Relation—have greater difficulty in bringing together users. That is, players at each end seem to be loyal to their interests, not expressing interest in the representations of the other end. In order to deepen our knowledge about the mix of streams, we will carry out another case analysis, now using explicitly only two streams, ensuring coverage of three pairs—Progression and Expression, Relation and Expression, Progression and Relation—in order to understand if we really have a problem with the extremes.

6.3 Applied Cases: Dual Engagement

For each pair, we chose one widely popular game, having analysed the design domains in which it specifically responds to the streams being analysed, and then looked at the game critiques and forums for users' reported reactions.

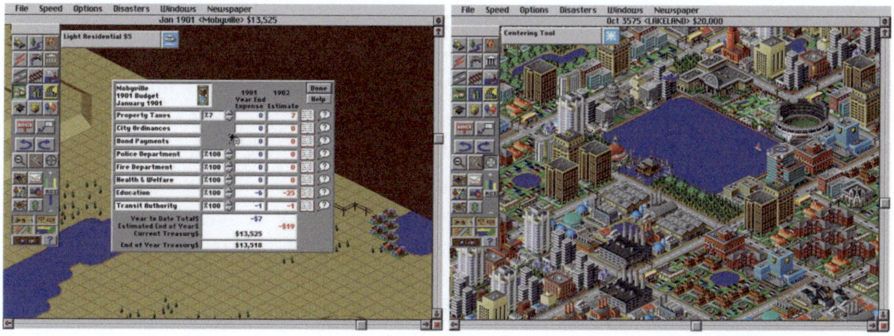

Fig. 6.15 The parameters and indicators and the world simulation in *SimCity 2000* (Wright, 1993)

6.3.1 Progression and Expression

For the analysis of the relationship between Progression and Expression streams, we chose *SimCity* (Wright, 1989) (and its more complete successor, *SimCity 2000* (Wright, 1993)), a game that not only succeeded in creating a whole franchise, but also created a whole wave of copycats, applied to the most varied domains, having been chosen as one of the first 10 video games to be preserved by the US Library of Congress in 2007.[5] The game has won many awards, and just looking at the award titles[6]—e.g. Best Simulation and Best Computer Strategy—gives the notion of a gameplay duality, because SimCity "offers a choice between two types of play: building a system from scratch or solving the problems in a specific scenario" (Starr, 1994). The game appeals to the mastery of strategy, focused on the Progression stream, as well as to the exploration of simulation, belonging to the Expression stream. The reason for this duality lies in the objectives set for the game, which calls for the construction of a simulated city, but following the vision of a mayor who is looking for the best strategy, finding how to make progress indicators such as allocating budget for services and building infrastructure; managing the city divided into three branches—residential, industrial and commercial; setting tax rates and allocating the budgets of different city bodies—police, firemen and public transportation (Fig. 6.15).

In this mode of city governance, gameplay is entirely defined by strategy, following problem-solving modes. Although the possibility to build a city is offered, if the basic ideology of the game is not followed, it can make the game almost unplayable. In fact, this has been the biggest discussion around the use of *SimCity* as an educational city simulator (Friedman, 1999), as it accepts only one mode of well-being and progress, i.e. it contains an implicit ideology in the system (Adams, 1998;

---

[5]The Game Canon was started by Henry Lowood, curator of the History of Science and Technology Collections at Stanford University. More information is available at https://en.wikipedia.org/wiki/Game_canon.

[6]The full list of awards can be checked online at Wikipedia https://en.wikipedia.org/wiki/SimCity_(1989_video_game).

Starr, 1994). However, as with *Assassin's Creed*, the fact that it presents a whole explorable map, and a whole set of elements to make up a city, ends up offering an unabridged space of freedom, guaranteeing players autonomy to just follow their own wishes, setting up the city of their dreams, or one that no one has ever seen, thus "encourag[ing] tinkering and experimentation" (Loguidice & Barton, 2009, p. 207).

Will Wright defended *SimCity* as having departed from the toy, citing as a root of his motivation the pleasure of discovery and creativity he learned at Montessori School (Gingold, 2016, p. 230), to which he would add "goals" to build the game (Hopkins, 2018). That is, we have, on the one hand, the engagement of Expression in the form of creative freedom, and on the other hand, the Progression to encourage the player to improve the city by following the rules and achieve the maximum reward. This same approach can be seen in other games, such as *Microsoft Flight Simulator* (Artwick, 1982), which Wright also refers to as an influence, with the difference that instead of the players trying to solve a problem, they are trying to master aircraft flight. But in *Microsoft Flight Simulator* we also have space for discovery and freedom of flight by providing the simulation with different airplanes, places and air traffic routes, creating a sort of personal "micro-world" as Wright said, "the idea that you could build your own little micro-world inside the computer intrigued me" (Richard, 2005, p. 409).

Overall, and aside from the ideological issues, these games have been well received by the community, although they generate some strangeness, as Keighley says "Who would have imagined that building roads and power lines and zoning land for residential or commercial use would be considered a recreational activity, much less fun?" (Keighley, 1999). Thus, and since there is no negative reaction to the duality of engagement in design, not only the existence of streams crossing but also their ability to generate relevant results is demonstrated.

6.3.2 Relation and Expression

To analyse the relationship between the Progression and Expression streams, we chose the game *The Sims* (Wright, 2000), which, like *SimCity*, uses simulation and play processes, but instead of a city, of humans and their behaviour, social relationships and places. No wonder the codename for *The Sims*, before the release was *Dollhouse* (Hopkins, 2018). Wright thus moved from the abstractions that build the problem of managing a city to the particularity of what makes us human: social relations. So, in *The Sims* the big immediate goals disappear, if *SimCity* looked like a toy, *The Sims* is a toy, that is, it is a mediator of human play. *The Sims* opens a direct door to the mental simulation we carry out when watching a movie or reading a novel, and transports us to the Playmobil play phase and the invention of character conflicts, but with one difference that of "free will". *The Sims*, unlike Playmobil, not only do what we want, they have a kind of will of their own that feeds their actions and makes the game more unpredictable and more autonomous and feels more like a vivid simulation.

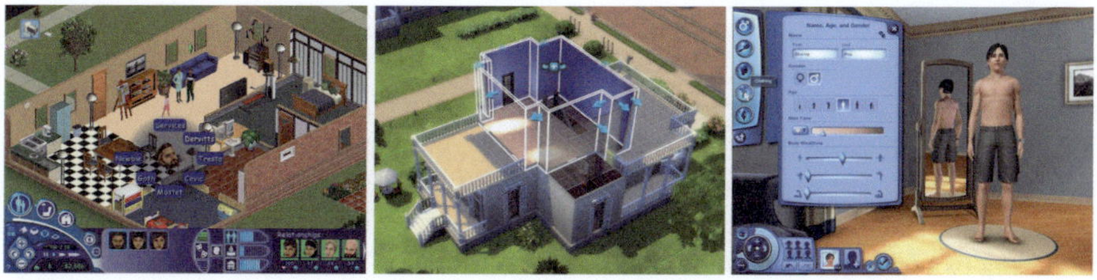

Fig. 6.16 In the pictures we can see the space inside the house, where relations occur, and in the two other pictures the building of houses and the customization of characters. Picture reproduced from *The Sims* (2000), *Sims 3* and *Sims 4*

The duality of engagement did not affect the success of *The Sims*, making it, in 2000, the best-selling game ever, and also the first game to have more female than male players, "a key demographic that many game developers have failed to interest or simply ignored entirely" (Loguidice & Barton, 2009), or as it was said on CNET when the online version was released, "'The Sims' has drawn one of the most diverse audiences in gaming—more than 50% female, and broadly distributed across age groups—with a unique style of game play that emphasizes creativity and self-made narratives" (Becker, 2003). In that same article, an analyst from an investment group even stated that "I think it's a good test to see if online gaming can stretch past the hard-core fantasy gamers online. With games like 'EverQuest' and 'Ultima Online,' you're dealing with a fairly targeted audience. 'The Sims' is a test to see if we can get a broader population interested in online gaming" (Becker, 2003). This comment is central because it reveals a clear knowledge of player profiles. Even discounting the female–male note, it explains the difference between players who strongly value Progression and what *The Sims* brought that was new, Relation, but this opposition will be returned to in the next point.

Thus, we have the Relation stream projected across the range of actions that support the sims in the game, producing relationships between them as well as developing their careers, and in turn the Expression stream, through the way we can play with sims, to which is added all the architectural construction of houses and spaces (see Fig. 6.16). We can say that the dual aspect of engagement works, even more than in *Simcity*, in favour of broadening player demographics, highlighting the ability to operate both streams simultaneously without problems.

6.3.3 Progression and Relation

For the third duality another game has been considered, *Myst* (Miller & Miller, 1993), which was hugely successful at its release, although more motivated by the innovation effect (Rothstein, 1994) than by the relationship between its design and the engagement streams, as we'll see. *Myst* was met with immense satisfaction by different groups of players, both those linked to Progression and those related to

Relation. On the one hand, we had a narrative based on a fantastic story between a father and two children trapped inside books. On the other hand, the game required the resolution of highly complex puzzles to overcome the obstacles presented, which fascinated Progression fans. But much of the fascination and success came from the high-quality 3D scenarios for the time, with point-and-click allowed the presentation of much higher quality pre-rendered scenarios than we were used to with real-time rendering of games such as *Doom* (Hall, 1993).

In the narrative domain, *Myst* was recognized by the academy for its innovation in non-linear storytelling (Jones, 1997; Miles, 1996), by presenting a space in which navigation between islands could follow any order desired by the user, accessing the story of what happened in a non-linear way, followed by an ending choice that allowed each player to reach their own ending, depending on their choices (Zagalo, 2009). The story engaged players through the relationships between father and sons, and between siblings, as well as the discovery of the conflict that involved them. All the enthusiasm for narrative innovation was further enveloped by the mysterious graphical and audio presentation, which created in players an immersive sensation with the artefact. To tell their story and to generate non-linear access, Myst's creators designed an imaginary place made up of islands, where they hid the clues that made it possible to interpret the story, but to access it users had to solve complex puzzles that required effort of abstraction, deduction and memory. The information needed to solve the puzzles was scattered in various texts in several books on the various islands, and for many of them, even with all the information, it was still necessary to use logical reasoning to get the answers. Sengstack refers to the paradoxical effect *Myst* ends up producing, "Some puzzles are very challenging, even obtuse, creating an odd paradox: many buy Myst, but few complete it" (Sengstack, 1996). Many reviews of recent years report these same problems with the puzzles, defining them as "arbitrary puzzle-filled" (DeVries, 2012) or that they "serve no real in-universe purpose beyond being arbitrary roadblocks" (Carter, 2015), referring to the lack of "coherency or cohesiveness to the environmental designs that just isn't present in *Myst*" (Dingman, 2014). A simple Google search for the question "Has anyone ever beaten Myst?" returns dozens of results from discussion forums and web texts about the immense difficulty, or no engagement with the puzzle solving, from its launch to the present day.[7] This is not to say that the game does not continue to generate interest, mainly for the players in the Progression stream, for whom *Myst* is synonymous with puzzles (Barr, 2016; Weir, 2009).

For this purpose, see the short qualitative analysis revealed in an online forum (with 56 comments) on the puzzles in *Myst*:

[7] 56 answers at NeoGaf, 2009, https://www.neogaf.com/threads/has-anyone-ever-actually-finished-a-myst-game-without-a-walkthrough.367854/; 42 answers Reddit, 2017 https://www.reddit.com/r/myst/comments/4tui84/ok_be_ honest_no_seriously_seriously/; 4 answers Escapist, 2012 https://www.escapistmagazine.com/forums/read/9.339523-Has-anyone-ever-actually-beaten-Myst-Riven-without-walkthrough-assistance; 7 answers Reddit 2016, https://www.reddit.com/r/gaming/comments/3gslpq/riven_the_sequel_to_myst_how_in_the_heck_would/.

RELATION (Dramatists)

- Of course I had to use walkthroughs from time to time because some of the puzzles were just too complex for me to figure out. Basically, if I wasn't able to solve one just with the things that were presented in front of me, I wasn't able to think outside the box enough to do it. With these games though, I find that most of your experience comes from enjoying being in the beautiful worlds, listening to the gorgeous music, and soaking in every bit of the story you can read/hear. Who cares if you need to check a walkthrough for a minute, to avoid getting frustrated at the game and thus losing out on some of the magic that's to be had.
- I couldn't really figure out what to do.
- Myst and Riven were always pretty incomprehensible to me.
- I used a strategy guide for every single puzzle in the original MYST.

PROGRESSION (Abstracters)

- "I was pretty hardcore, I had a fat big notebook where I wrote down all the clues, sketched stuff etc. When I was stuck for some time I just took a 1–2 weeks break, after which I once again reviewed the clues and tried again."
- "I thought Myst was pretty simple."
- "I beat it the day I bought it with no help. It was this weird thing where I just knew exactly what the designers were going for."
- "I still consider it the very best puzzle ever created for a videogame. And the sense of accomplishment I got when I figured it out was amazing. To this day I still can use the whole D'ni numerical system easily".

The great problem evidenced by *Myst* rests on the high abstraction required by puzzles, which requires a whole mental predisposition (reasoning), vastly different from that which a story requires (interpretation). Note that to understand the story we also had to read the texts in the books, and from these texts we could reach the resolution of the puzzles. However, the puzzles were not limited to answers related to the story. The game puzzles were not narrative puzzles, as when we read Virginia Woolf's *Mrs Dalloway* (1925) and we are trying to understand who the character is talking to, and who, about what and where she is at each moment. In *Myst*, the puzzles only concern obstacles that prevent us from advancing in the story, and they are not elements related to the knowledge of the story characters or world but only the possibility of moving from one space to another to get to the next bits of story (see Fig. 6.17). It is as if to turn a page in *Mrs Dalloway* you had to enter information or code on the page, with little to no relation to what you were reading.

We can see how *Myst* highlighted the problems of the dual design of Progression and Relation, which became conventionally known as the irreconciliation between game and story (Aarseth, 1997; Juul, 2001), which ultimately gave rise to the great discussion of ludology versus narratology. It is, however, very interesting to see how the debate calmed and practically disappeared in the late 2000s. What happened

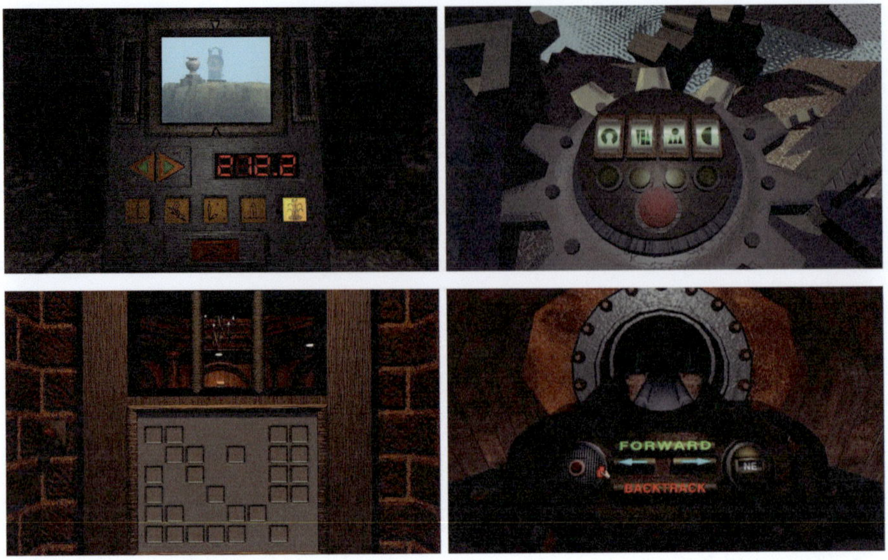

Fig. 6.17 The abstract puzzles of *Myst* (1993)

was that in the dual Progression/Relation design of action–adventure games, Progression was being given less and less weight. The puzzles and dexterity in games like *Tomb Raider* (Hughes, Chayer, & Neuburger, 2013), *Prince of Persia* (Guyot, 2008) or *Uncharted 2: Among Thieves* (Straley & Hennig, 2009) became simpler, allowing players to move forward and focus more on character relationships and story interpretation. In the early 2010s, we even saw the emergence of the Walking Simulator genre, in which Progression was simply removed from the design. If we compare *Dear Esther* (Pinchbeck, 2012) with *Myst*, we have very close universes, yet Progression is almost absent.

With this, we are not saying that we have given up on creating artefacts that draw on this duality of engagement, yet recently Jonathan Blow presented us with a full tribute, in the form of *The Witness* (2016), going far beyond *Myst* in the component of Progression, with even more abstract puzzles (see Fig. 6.18). Despite some success, just a quick search through the online forums, revealing impressions of the game and users' experiences, highlights the same engagement problems we discussed about *Myst*. Even more recently, we have *Puzzle Tales* (Tidhar & Olefsky, 2019a), a kind of new interactive fiction that mixes abstract puzzles—like crosswords, sudoku or cryptograms—with text stories. However, the authors seem to be aware of the problems arising from the mixing of the streams, evidenced by the message on their website: "If you get stuck, don't worry. This website can provide you with as many hints as you need to get past any roadblock (…) if you get truly stuck on something, try a hint and let us know. We're here to help you complete the experience" (Tidhar & Olefsky, 2019b).

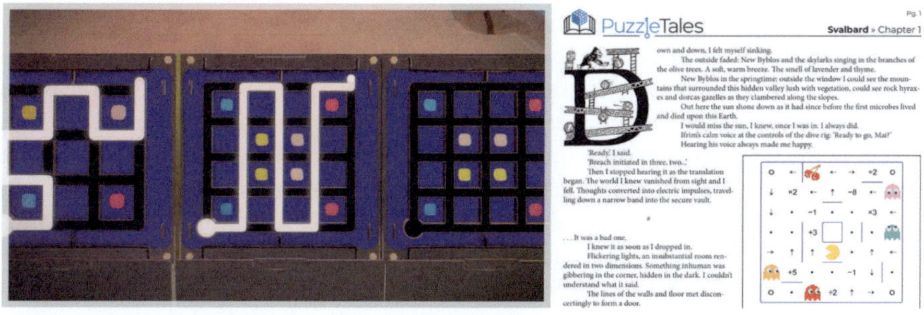

Fig. 6.18 The abstract puzzles of *The Witness* (2016) and *Puzzle Tales* (2019a, 2019b)

6.4 Multiple Stream Usage Analysis

As we can see, in both dual and multi-engagement, the engagement relationships making use of the Expression stream work perfectly. We found problems with the relation between Progression and Relation (see Fig. 6.19), which indicates problems related to the type of cognitive traits expected for interaction. Logical thinking and deductive reasoning seem to conflict with holistic thinking and inductive reasoning. On the one hand, there is a need for multiple clues linked by abstract conventions that guarantee their causality and generalization, while on the other hand, particular events are related to each subject making them particular, gaining more interpretative value as they become more singular.

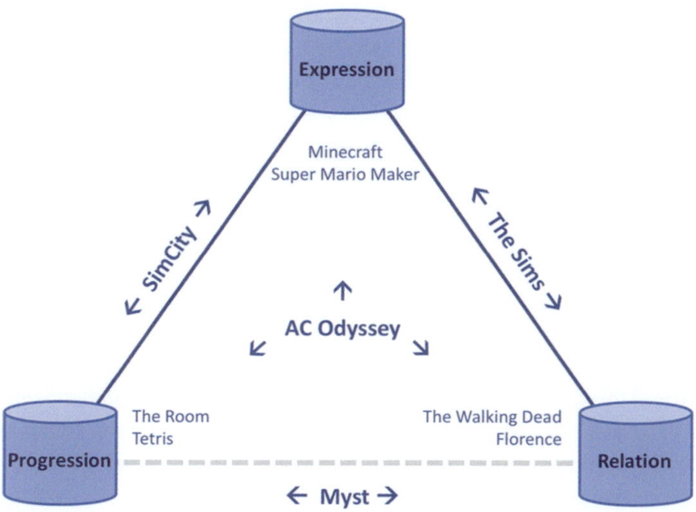

Fig. 6.19 The streams with their specific artefacts, the artefacts at the crossing of streams and the crossover between Progression and Relation in the broken line

This is in line with a design approach regarding the design to physiologically inactive emotions, such as melancholy and sadness, for which "passive interaction" design was recommended (Zagalo, Torres, & Branco, 2006), clearly followed in *Heavy Rain* (2010) interaction design (Zagalo, 2017). In that case, concern was related to the need to lower the levels of interaction in order to allow players space and time to reach specific emotions. In the case above, of the crossover between Progression and Relation, the issue is broader, as it has to do with building relationships across the full emotional range, but when we look at the kind of interaction that takes place at the level of any Walking Simulator game, we realize that probably what is at stake is the cognitive burden expended on the interaction. Let's look then at cognitive processes in more detail.

6.4.1 Cognitive Load: Critical Thinking Versus Problem-Solving

The issue of the effort spent on interaction can be analysed from the differentiation of critical thinking and problem-solving processes. If critical thinking corresponds to "active, persistent and careful consideration of any belief or supposed form of knowledge in the light of the grounds that support it, and the further conclusions to which it tends" (Dewey, 1910, p. 6), it involves problem-solving, since going beyond the analysis and reflection on the whole surrounding of the issue requires the taking of a position, that is, a decision on what to believe or not, hence the problem-solving. On the other hand, problem-solving concerns only the concrete situation and its immediate resolution, while critical thinking encompasses all possibilities and different ways of looking at the problem, including questioning its own existence, or belief in its existence. Critical thinking seeks to understand the problem and its surroundings, as well as the potential effects of its resolution, while problem-solving focuses exclusively on finding the best resolution process.

When applying problem-solving to puzzle solving, for example, in *Myst*, and critical thinking to understanding what happened on the islands of Myst and interpreting what each character represents, a clash between cognitive needs occurs. The player is not led to reflect on the characters, the critical analysis of their multiple facets, contexts and behaviours. The game does not lead the player to focus on beliefs and question them for the simple reason that it keeps demanding effort in solving problems that only concern the overcoming of obstacles. Problem-solving runs in parallel with the critical thinking, to which is added the lack of correlation between the needs of the problem-solving and the needs of critical thinking. In summary, we have a problem of cognitive overload, not so much from too much information, but from too much processing. No wonder the solution found by the industry was the creation of difficulty regulators in video games.

6.4.2 Difficulty or Engagement Regulation?

The industry response first began by facilitating game logic in modern games (Iannone, 2018), something that has been widely criticized (Fitchett, 2017; Herndon, 2015), clearly supported by players of the Progression profile (see Fig. 6.20). On the other hand, larger budget games, which need to reach wider audiences, are increasingly developing better and more effective regulators of the so-called "difficulty level". The regulators can, in some sense, be seen as engagement stream regulators, with "hard" and "easy" varying in the number of challenges or enemies, requiring more or less mastery to overcome obstacles and progress in the game, thus varying between Progression and Relation. In the recent *Shadow of the Tomb Raider* (Chayer, 2018), developers presented the players with a difficulty adjustment made of three regulators—for Combat, Exploration and Puzzle (see Fig. 6.21)—going deeper in the approach to function as engagement stream regulators.

Analysing these Tomb Raider difficulty adjustment screens more in depth, starting with Exploration, Expression players are offered the ability to increase their autonomy, the effect of discovery and sensation seeking, by reducing guides (space markings or highlights) and aids to navigation and controlling the world (something *Assassin's Creed Odyssey* (2018) also featured (see Fig. 6.22). Given that the Expression stream works well with any of the other streams, this setting will directly serve Expression profile players looking to increase their involvement with the game. It can still serve Progression by increasing navigation difficulty or Relation by reducing effort invested in understanding and solving the space/world.

Regarding Progression, Tomb Raider explicitly presents two modes: "Combat", which affects the mastery and achievement dimensions and "Puzzle", which affects the problem-solving. In the first, the mastery of the player is amplified or reduced by the performance optimization (the health of Lara and enemies). In the second,

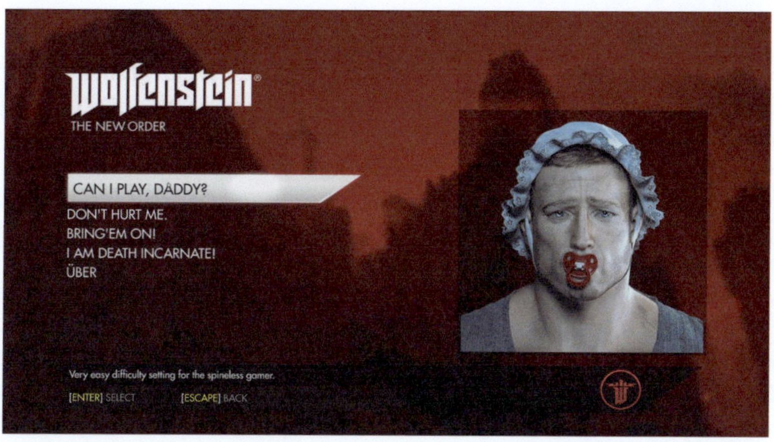

Fig. 6.20 The critique of gameplay easing used as satire in the difficulty adjustment screen of *Wolfenstein II: The New Colossus* (Matthies, 2017), a clear nod to the Progression players

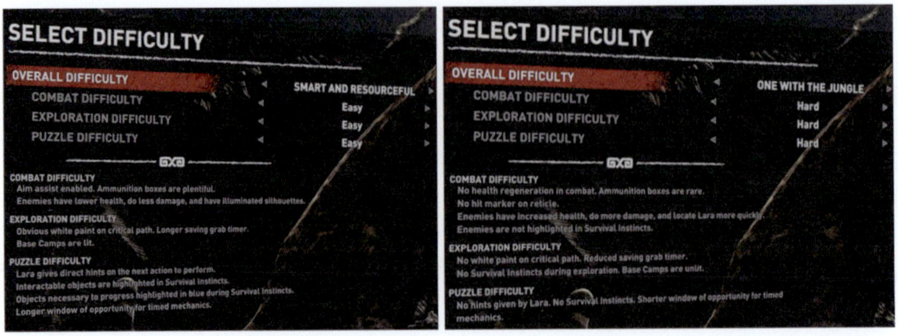

Fig. 6.21 In *Shadow of the Tomb Raider*, the difficulty adjustment can be set for Combat, Exploration and Puzzle. These adjustments can hardly be just seen as related to difficulty: they are really serving the engagement adjustment of the different types of players

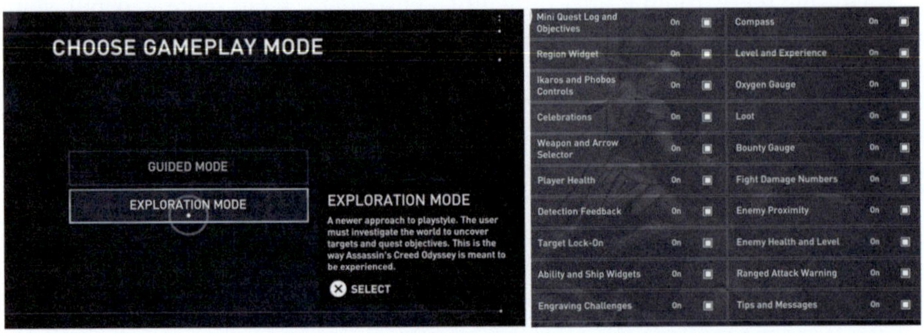

Fig. 6.22 AC Odyssey allows us to choose, apart from "difficulty" and "enemy levelling", between Guided or Exploration game mode, which increases or decreases the information present on the screen to aid navigation and understanding activities. This game mode can be further enhanced by disabling information in the HUD

the level of information offered to solve the different puzzles, requiring more or less reasoning, is altered. Thus, these two adjusters, when pulled to the easy side, guarantee an artefact with diminished game components, allowing the player a greater focus on the story. See, for example, how *God of War* (Barlog, 2018) (see Fig. 6.23) presents the difficulty regulators, relating them to a "story" versus "game" relation.

That is, the difficulty regulators of today's video games seem to indicate that they are actually systems of mixing the conditions of engagement streams, so that the same games can appeal to players with very different engagement profiles. Deepening the question, does it really make sense to talk about difficulty regulators? Would we put these labels in a movie or book: "reducing or increasing levels of dialogue complexity"? We don't make James Bond more or less erudite, and we don't do it in a game either; what we do is adjust the interaction conditions. Relation players don't play worse than Progression players, they just play differently, because their engagement interest is different.

Fig. 6.23 *God of War* (2018) difficulty adjustment screens. Left: "Story" selection; right: God-like selection for the levels of reflexes and strategy demanded

6.5 Future of Streams

As we saw in the previous section, *Assassin's Creed Odyssey* comes with a set of regulators that allow you to optimize each player's experience based on their engagement preferences, but as we have seen in the analysis of discussion forums, players continue to complain about problems related to engagement, which suggests that many players simply choose to play in the default, or so-called Normal, modes. This raises a number of problems. On the one hand, an investment in optimizing an experience that seems to be wasted on players, while, on the other hand, there are complaints about and negative reactions to something that the game has predicted and has solutions for. It seems that we will have to tend towards a different type of engagement stream regulation, so-called "dynamic difficulty adjustments" (DADs). DADs have been around for a few years (Hunicke & Chapman, 2004; Yu et al., 2010), but in more recent years, with the increase of AI, we have seen more and more proposals appearing (Xue, Wu, Kolen, Aghdaie, & Zaman, 2017), including Electronic Arts patenting a DAD application method (Patent No. US10286323B2, 2019). These systems, as we have already seen in the discussion above, do not have to do with difficulty but with engagement and, above all, with customizing that engagement. Even considering the profiles presented in this model for engagement design, we know that humans have tremendous variability, so problem-solving processing tolerance varies from player to player, as does the interest in focusing on critical thinking processes. In this sense, it seems to us that the future will hardly escape more in-depth DAD systems.

Alternatively, we can think of Warren Spector's proposals to get immersive sims to live up to their initial promise—"If I play a shooter or a stealth game and I'm not good enough, all I can do is stop playing. Same if I'm playing a puzzle game and I'm not clever enough. In the immersive simulation, if the combat or stealth is too hard you try something else" (Spector, 2019). The underlining is ours and serves to account for the mistake of looking at engagement as a player problem, when the problem is in the design, which did not account for player engagement differences. Game design must tend to be rich enough in possibilities and interaction alternatives to give each player complete freedom to decide how they want to relate to the game world, whether wanting to invest in combat, puzzles, thorough exploration, construction or just talking to the characters.

6.6 Final Notes and Limitations

Throughout the book, but especially in this chapter, the focus of discussion has been objects created by the video game industry, rather than more general artefacts from the large domain of interactive media. However, as mentioned before, this happens because the game industry has been increasingly advancing with respect to engagement profiles. This should not, however, lead us to think that this model applies exclusively to the medium of video games.

The model is designed to be applied in any scenario that uses interaction processes. There are clear limitations to its application in environments where content is defined at the outset, as in educational or training games. In such cases, the content will condition the form, i.e. interactivity, so that the model can only serve to improve the techniques defined according to the target audience chosen for the content. This is not to say that you cannot work mixes of streams, to ensure greater interest, as in the cases of multi- and double engagement presented above that serve in helping in the design of these stream crossings.

References

Aarseth, E. (1997). *Cybertext: Perspectives on ergodic literature*. Baltimore: Johns Hopkins University Press.

Adams, P. C. (1998). Teaching and learning with Simcity 2000. *Journal of Geography, 97*(2), 47–55. https://doi.org/10.1080/00221349808978827.

Aghdaie, N., & et al. (2019). *Patent No. US10286323B2*. https://patents.google.com/patent/US10286323B2/en.

Amancio, A., & Albinet, M. (2014). *Assassin's Creed unity*. Montreal: Ubisoft.

Anderson, C. (2006). *The long tail: Why the future of business is selling less of more*. New York: Hyperion.

Anderson, C. (2012). *Makers: The new industrial revolution*. New York: Crown Business.

Andersson, J., Berndal, K., Strandberg, H., & Thibaut, P. (2000). *Europa Universalis*. Stockholm: Paradox Development Studio.

Artwick, B. (1982). *Microsoft Flight Simulator*. Redmond: Microsoft.

Axon, S. (2019, March). I played 11 Assassin's Creed games in 11 years, and Odyssey made them all worth it. *Ars Technica*.

Barlog, C. (2018). *God of War*. Santa Monica: SIE Santa Monica Studio.

Barlow, S. (2015). *Her Story*. London: Sam Barlow.

Barr, N. (2016). The problem with The Witness. Retrieved July 19, 2019, from Medium website: https://medium.com/@nsbarr/the-problem-with-the-witness-c00861a13de6.

Barton, M. (2019). The YouTuber on a mission to save the classic RPG. *Wired*. Retrieved from https://www.wired.com/2019/06/youtuber-quest-save-rpg/.

Baszucki, D., & Cassel, E. (2006). *Roblox*. San Mateo, CA: Roblox Corporation.
Becker, D. (2003). Will "Sims Online" alter gaming world? Retrieved July 19, 2019, from CNET website: https://www.cnet.com/news/will-sims-online-alter-gaming-world/.
Blow, J. (2016). *The Witness*. San Francisco: Thekla Inc.
Brevik, D., Schaefer, E., Schaefer, M., Sexton, E., & Williams, K. (1996). *Diablo*. California: Blizzard North.
Britvich, R. (1995). *Active Worlds*. Massachusetts: ActiveWorlds Inc.
Cage, D. (2010). *Heavy Rain*. Quantic Dream.
Carter, G. (2015). Myst—Mystery Man. Retrieved July 9, 2019, from The Escapist website: http://www.escapistmagazine.com/articles/view/video-games/goodoldreviews/15030-Good-Old-Reviews-Myst.
Chayer, D. (2018). *Shadow of the Tomb Raider*. Montreal: Eidos Interactive.
Chouls, A., & Ko, E. (2010). *Playmaker*. Hutong: Hutong Games.
Church, D. (1999, July). Formal abstract design tools. *Gamsutra*, 7.
Connor, A. M., Marks, S., & Walker, C. (2015). Creating creative technologists: Playing with(in) education. In *Creativity in the digital age* (pp. 35–56). https://doi.org/10.1007/978-1-4471-6681-8_3.
Côté, M.-A., Phillips, S., & Pincombe, W. (2015). *Assassin's Creed Syndicate*. Quebec: Ubisoft.
Désilets, P. (2009). *Assassin's Creed II*. Montreal: Ubisoft.
Désilets, P., Raymond, J., & May, C. (2007). *Assassin's Creed*. Montreal: Ubisoft.
DeVries, J. (2012). Myst review. Retrieved July 19, 2019, from IGN website: https://www.ign.com/articles/2008/05/16/myst-review-2.
Dewey, J. (1910). *How we think*. New York: Dover Publications.
Dingman, H. (2014). The same Myst you know and love, but prettier. Retrieved July 19, 2019, from PC World website: https://www.pcworld.com/article/2109283/realmyst-masterpiece-edition-review-the-same-myst-you-know-and-love-but-prettier.html.
Dixon, J. (2016). *Planet Coaster*. Cambridge: Frontier Developments.
Dockterman, E. (2014, June). Why Assassin's Creed killed off all its women. *Time*.
Dodd, R., & Hamilton, M. (2012). *The Room*. Fireproof Games.
Dumont, J., & Phillips, S. (2018). *Assassin's Creed Odyssey*. Quebec: Ubisoft.
Dworsky, D., & Köhler, V. (2011). *PressPausePlay* (p. 80m). Sweden: House of Radon.
Fares, J. (2013). *Brothers: A Tale of Two Sons*. Stockholm: 505 Games.
Fitchett, D. (2017). Mainstream video games have become too easy.
Frey, T. (2017). *Farming Simulator*. Schlieren: Giants Software.
Friedman, T. (1999). The semiotics of SimCity. *First Monday*. https://doi.org/10.5210/fm.v4i4.660.
Gaynor, S. (2013). *Gone Home*. Fullbright Company.
Gems, P. (2014). *Episode*. San Francisco: Pocket Gems.
Gingold, C. O. (2016). *Play design* (UC Santa Cruz). Retrieved from https://escholarship.org/uc/item/8qr533m2.
Guesdon, J., & Ismail, A. (2017). *Assassin's Creed Origins*. Montreal: Ubisoft.
Guesdon, J., Ismail, A., & Kieken, D. (2013). *Assassin's Creed IV: Black Flag*. Montreal, Milan, Kiev: Ubisoft.
Guyot, J.-C. (2008). *Prince of Persia*. Montreal: Ubisoft.
Hall, T. (1993). *Doom*. Texas: id Software.
Hart, J. (2007). *A writer's coach: The complete guide to writing strategies that work*. New York: Pantheon.
Hauser, F. (2018). *Hospital stories with the Hauser family*. Retrieved from https://www.youtube.com/watch?v=Pw8am2CI6tg.
Herndon, N. (2015). 1999 mode: Are modern games too easy? Retrieved July 20, 2019, from Forbes website: https://www.forbes.com/sites/archenemy/2015/09/24/1999-mode-are-modern-games-too-easy/.

Hopkins, D. (2018). Will Wright on designing user interfaces to simulation games (1996). Retrieved from Medium website: https://medium.com/@donhopkins/designing-user-interfaces-to-simulation-games-bd7a9d81e62d.
Hudson, C. (2007). *Mass Effect*. Bioware.
Hughes, N., Chayer, D., & Neuburger, D. (2013). *Tomb Raider*. Redwood: Crystal Dynamics.
Hunicke, R., & Chapman, V. (2004). AI for dynamic difficulty adjustment in games. In *Challenges in game artificial intelligence AAAI*. https://doi.org/10.1145/1178477.1178573.
Hutchinson, A. (2012). *Assassin's Creed III*. Montreal: Ubisoft.
Iannone, J. (2018). The real reasons video games are easier today. Retrieved September 20, 2019, from SVG website: https://www.svg.com/103112/real-reasons-video-games-easier-today/.
Joly-Lavoie, A. (2017). Assassin's Creed: Synthèse des écrits et implications pour L'enseignement de l'histoire. *McGill Journal of Education, 52*(2), 455–470.
Jones, S. (1997). The book of Myst in the late age of print. *Postmodern Culture*. https://doi.org/10.1353/pmc.1997.0003.
Juul, J. (2001). Games telling stories. *Game Studies*.
Kawamoto, K., Sakaguchi, T., & Ogasawara, Y. (2018). *Nintendo Labo*. Tokyo: Nintendo.
Keighley, G. (1999). Simply divine: The story of maxis. *Gamespot*, 14. Retrieved from https://web.archive.org/web/20100110051049/http://www.gamespot.com/features/maxis/index.html.
Kishimoto, Y. (1987). *Double Dragon*. Tokyo: Taito.
Kuchera, B. (2018, October). It's time to take the Animus out of Assassin's Creed. *Polygon*.
Lemke, H. (1994). *The Need for Speed*. Redwood: Electronic Arts.
Loguidice, B., & Barton, M. (2009). *Vintage games: An insider look at the history of grand theft auto, Super Mario, and the most influential games of all time*. Burlington: Focal Press.
Ma, J., & Davis, M. (2012). *FTL: Faster than light*. Subset Games.
Matthies, J. (2017). *Wolfenstein II: The New Colossus*. Maryland: Bethesda Softworks.
McCarthy, J., & Wright, P. (2004). *Technology as experience*. Cambridge, MA: MIT Press.
McCrae, R. R., & John, O. P. (1992). An introduction to the five-factor model and its applications. *Journal of Personality, 60*(2), 175–215. https://doi.org/10.1111/j.1467-6494.1992.tb00970.x.
McFarland, N. (2014). *Monument Valley*. Ustwo Games.
McMillen, E., & Himsl, F. (2011). *The Binding of Isaac*. Santa Cruz: Edmund McMillen.
McMillen, E., & Refenes, T. (2010). *Super Meat Boy*. Santa Cruz: Team Meat.
Miles, D. (1996). The CD-ROM novel Myst and McLuhan's fourth law of media: Myst and its "retrievals". *Journal of Communication*. https://doi.org/10.1111/j.1460-2466.1996.tb01471.x.
Miller, R., & Miller, R. (1993). *Myst*. Cyan.
Miyamoto, S. (1985). *Super Mario Bros*. Nintendo.
Moss, O., & Vanaman, S. (2016). *Firewatch*. San Francisco: Campo Santo.
Nishiyama, T. (1987). *Street Fighter*. Osaka: Capcom.
Oshino, Y. (2015). *Super Mario Maker*. Tokyo: Nintendo.
Pereira Jr., A. (2018). The projective theory of consciousness: From neuroscience to philosophical psychology. *Trans/Form/Ação, 41*(spe), 199–232. https://doi.org/10.1590/0101-3173.2018.v41esp.11.p199.
Persson, M. (2009). *Minecraft*. Mojang.
Pinchbeck, D. (2012). *Dear Esther*. Chinese Room.
Pope, L. (2018). *Return of the Work Dinn*. Japan: 3909 LLC.
Resnick, M., Silverman, B., & Bonta, P. (2007). *Scratch*. Cambridge, MA: MIT Media Lab.
Richard, R. (2005). Game design : Theory and practice. In *Design*. Sudbury, MA: Jones & Bartlett.
Rosedale, P. (2003). *Second Life*. San Francisco: Linden Lab.
Rothstein, E. (1994, December 4). A new art form may arise from the "Myst." *New York Times*. Retrieved from https://www.nytimes.com/1994/12/04/arts/a-new-art-form-may-arise-from-the-myst.html.
Sengstack, J. (1996). Myst review. Retrieved July 19, 2019, from Gamespot website: https://www.gamespot.com/reviews/myst-review/1900-2542724/.

Shneiderman, B. (2002). Creativity support tools. *Communications of the ACM, 45*(10). https://doi.org/10.1145/570907.570945.

Shneiderman, B. (2007). Creativity support tools: Accelerating discovery and innovation. *Communications of the ACM, 50*(12), 20–32. https://doi.org/10.1145/1323688.1323689.

Spector, W. (2019). Warren spector: "If immersive sims disappear, I disappear." Retrieved from GamesIndustry.biz website: https://www.gamesindustry.biz/articles/2019-04-23-warren-spector-if-immersive-sims-disappear-i-disappear.

Sports, E. (1993). *FIFA International Soccer*. Redwood: Extended Play Productions.

Starr, P. (1994). Seductions of sim. *The American Prospect*. Retrieved from https://www.princeton.edu/~starr/17star.html.

Straley, B., & Druckmann, N. (2013). *The Last of Us*. Naughty Dog.

Straley, B., & Hennig, A. (2009). *Uncharted 2: Among Thieves*. Santa Monica: Naughty Dog.

Swift, K. (2007). *Portal*. Valve Corporation.

Tidhar, L., & Olefsky, J. (2019a). *Puzzle Tales*. USA: Braingle.com.

Tidhar, L., & Olefsky, J. (2019b). *Puzzle Tales webpage*. Retrieved August 14, 2019, from https://www.puzzletales.com/.

Tomaszkiewicz, K., Kanik, M., & Stępień, S. (2015). *The Witcher 3: Wild Hunt*. CD Projekt Red.

Vanaman, S. (2012). *The walking dead*. California: Telltale Games.

Weir, G. (2009). Analysis: Puzzle design in the Myst series.

Whitehead, A. N. (1917). Presidential address: Technical education and its relation to science and literature. *The Mathematical Gazette, 9*(128), 20. https://doi.org/10.2307/3605222.

Wong, K. (2018). *Florence*. California: Mountains, Annapurna Interactive.

Woolf, V. (1925). *Mrs Dalloway*. London: Hogarth Press.

Wright, W. (1989). *SimCity*. Redwood: Maxis.

Wright, W. (1993). *SimCity 2000*. Redwood: Maxis.

Wright, W. (2000). *The Sims*. Maxis.

Wright, W. (2008). *Spore*. Redwood: Electronic Arts.

Xue, S., Wu, M., Kolen, J., Aghdaie, N., & Zaman, K. A. (2017). Dynamic difficulty adjustment for maximized engagement in digital games. *International World Wide Web Conference Committee*. https://doi.org/10.1145/3041021.3054170.

Yu, X., He, S., Gao, Y., Yang, J., Sha, L., Zhang, Y., & Ai, Z. (2010). Dynamic difficulty adjustment of game AI for video game dead-end. In *The 3rd International Conference on Information Sciences and Interaction Sciences*, 583–587. https://doi.org/10.1109/ICICIS.2010.5534761.

Zagalo, N. (2009). *Emoções Interactivas, do Cinema para os Videojogos* (*Interactive emotions, from film to videogames*). Retrieved from http://repositorium.sdum.uminho.pt/handle/1822/27674?locale=en.

Zagalo, N. (2017). Narrative design of sadness in Heavy Rain. *Journal of Science and Technology of the Arts, 9*(2 Special Issue). https://doi.org/10.7559/citarj.v9i2.246.

Zagalo, N., & Branco, P. (2015). *Creativity in the digital age*. https://doi.org/10.1007/978-1-4471-6681-8.

Zagalo, N., Torres, A., & Branco, V. (2006). Passive interactivity, an answer to interactive emotion. In R. Harper, M. Rauterberg, & M. Combetto (Eds.), *Entertainment computing—ICEC 2006* (pp. 43–52). https://doi.org/10.1007/11872320.

Index

N. Zagalo, *Engagement Design*, Human–Computer Interaction Series,
https://doi.org/10.1007/978-3-030-37085-5

MIX
Papier aus verantwortungsvollen Quellen
Paper from responsible sources
FSC® C105338

If you have any concerns about our products,
you can contact us on
ProductSafety@springernature.com

In case Publisher is established outside the EU,
the EU authorized representative is:
Springer Nature Customer Service Center GmbH
Europaplatz 3, 69115 Heidelberg, Germany

Printed by Libri Plureos GmbH
in Hamburg, Germany